Architecture of Fear

For Theodora with love
May your heart, courage, and inspiration
tame the lions, tigers, and bears
who cross your yellow brick road.
—N. E.

Published by
Princeton Architectural Press, Inc.
37 East 7th Street
New York, New York 10003
212.995.9620

For a free catalog of books, call 1.800.722.6657
or visit our Website at www.papress.com

Editing and design: Clare Jacobson
Special thanks to: Caroline Green, Therese Kelly, Mark Lamster,
Anne Nitschke, and Sara Stemen of Princeton Architectural Press
—Kevin C. Lippert, publisher

On the cover
Cayewah Easley, from the series *Body/Brick*, 1995

Photo credits
Christine Amado and Martha Conway: 87; Edward J. Blakely:
91b; John Chase: 161–79; Michael Dear: 192t, 192c, 195t;
Cayewah Easley: cover, 132–141; Nan Ellin: 29, 51br; Steven
Flusty: 51tl, 51tr, 51bl; Jane Harrison: 75, 77–83; Richard
Ingersoll: 257; Charles Jencks: 222tl, 222tr, 222br; Lucas
Jordogne: 231; Craig Kim: 76; Robert Lerner: 222bl; Julius
Shulman: 116–131; Mary Gail Snyder: 91t, 91c; courtesy Sharon
E. Sutton: 243; Lois Takahashi: 208; Anne Troutman: 144–54;
Urban Redevelopment Authority: 230; Jonathan Weatherill: 74;
Wolch/Dear: 192b, 195b; Jody Zellen: 260–77

Library of Congress Cataloging-in-Publication Data
Architecture of fear / Nan Ellin, editor.
    p. cm.
    Includes bibliographical references.
    ISBN 1-56898-082-5 (alk. paper)
    1. Architecture—Psychological aspects. 2. Architecture and
society. 3. Fear I. Ellin, Nan.
NA2542.4.A735 1997
720'.1'104—dc21   96-37635
                                                  CIP

Architecture of Fear

Nan Ellin, editor

Princeton Architectural Press, New York

Acknowledgments

My interest in the relationship between fear and urban design was sparked while doing dissertation fieldwork in the French new town of Jouy-le-Moutier in 1985. Taking an ethnographic approach to the study of urban design, I lived there and visited many of its inhabitants, inquiring about their likes and dislikes regarding the town. Invariably, the subject of fear (*l'insécurité*) arose despite the minuscule crime rate in the area. I initially paid little heed and simply waited for the conversation to turn back to the subject of my thesis, an evaluation of neotraditional urban design principles. But I soon realized how integral the concern about insecurity was to both the nostalgia for the past that incited neotraditional urbanism and to my evaluation of its realization in Jouy-le-Moutier. I wish to thank all those "Jocassiens" who shared their hospitality and points of view with me. I am also indebted to Françoise Choay who—on Thanksgiving Day 1985—encouraged me to further pursue this line of inquiry.

After returning from the immaculate French new town, I saw New York City with different eyes. Amid abandoned buildings, crack houses, fortified housing projects, and scores of homeless people in my East Harlem neighborhood, I began reflecting not only on the motivations for defensive urbanism but also on possibilities for diminishing fear through design. I am grateful to the members of the Committee on Theory and Culture at New York University, particularly Dorothy Nelkin, Jerrold Seigel, Juan Corradi, and Richard Sennett, for providing a first opportunity to present my ideas on "Reconceiving Space, Time, and Fear" in 1989. I also wish to thank those who offered constructive commentary on the paper I delivered at the American Studies Association Meeting in San Diego in 1994, which had as its theme "Cities on the Edge." By this time, there was a groundswell of interest on the topic, epitomized by Mike Davis's work, which has informed and provoked me and many other contributors to this book. I wish to thank him and the rest of my colleagues at the Southern California Institute of Architecture—an almost unimaginably rich center of creativity, learning, sharing, and fun—especially Margaret Crawford, Elyse Grinstein, and Michael Rotondi for their ongoing support. I also want to thank my many wonderful students at SCI-Arc as well as at the University of Southern California, New York University, and the University of Cincinnati for not allowing me to stray from the big questions and for their persistent idealism and will to betterment against all odds. For a gracious welcome to the College of Design, Architecture, Art, and Planning at the University of Cincinnati, I wish to express my utmost appreciation to Brenda Scheer, Charles Ellison, and Jay Chaterjee.

As *Architecture of Fear* is a book about place, it is only befitting to acknowledge the inspiration and setting for many of the pieces in this book and my home for four and one-half years, the City of Angels. Los Angeles is a city for which one pays to enjoy its sunshine, beaches, and palm trees at the rate of smog, traffic, an occasional civil uprising, and the chronic threat of fire, flood, and earthquake. The toll may be high, but then so are the dividends, a dynamism and audacity that has given rise over the last decade to various peculiarly L.A. "schools" of thought. I love L.A. despite its fault lines, and, though I now bid farewell, it will always occupy a special place in my heart. For reliably intoxicating Friday night conversation, I thank L.A. architects and dear friends Raun Thorp, Brian Tichenor, Jamie Schwentker, Harvey Watts, and Kevin Oreck, as well as travel consultant John Bernatz. I also thank Caroline and Garreth Stover who were always there with remarkable pasta as well as nourishment for the soul. Along this entire path and onward, I am ever grateful to be accompanied by anthropologist, muse, and soul mate Tad Ballew.

At Princeton Architectural Press, Kevin Lippert helped ignite the excitement that propelled this project forward and Clare Jacobson flawlessly shepherded the book to production. I wish to salute all the contributors whose passion and enthusiasm for this undertaking are evident in the pages ahead.

N.E.

Preface

Nan Ellin

All mammals share three neurophysiological responses to fear and anxiety: freeze, flight, and fight. While the first two involve disengagement and distancing from the source of fear or anxiety, the third involves direct engagement with it, but in a might-equals-right kind of way. Humans, however, are equipped with several attributes that allow us to transcend these primal responses to fear and anxiety. One of these attributes is reason, whose vulnerability to fear is captured in the popular 1952 movie *The Day the Earth Stood Still* when the beneficent space man who lands on the Washington Mall announces to earthlings, "I only fear that fear has replaced reason." Another is creativity, the ability to combine things in novel ways to produce novel results. And there is the human spirit, which prizes togetherness, connectedness, and sanctity over separateness and the profane. This drive—to literally and figuratively procreate—leads us to improve upon our world for future generations with the faith that things can and will get better. Rather than crush this human spirit and the desire for connectedness, we must nourish them through our words and our works.

This collaborative project is a step in that direction. Accordingly, its "architecture" is decidedly not one of fear. The book begins by laying a foundation, proceeds to construct personal and collective spaces of expression, and concludes by situating these within the outside world and the future. The compelling pieces collected here aspire to go beyond defensive urbanism to generate what might be called offensive urbanism, or living—as opposed to moribund—architecture. The resultant collection represents a fairly wide spectrum of intellectual traditions and professional activities as well as viewpoints. Contributors include architects, planners, urban critics/theorists, educators, geographers, writers, artists, photographers, a television news producer, a choreographer, a sociologist, and a physicist, most of them a combination of two or more of these pursuits. Their pieces describe a variety of efforts to reinvigorate (or generate) a meaningful public realm in order to diminish fear, from physically demarcating community boundaries, to applying rhetorical devices, creating fictional kin, organizing communities, or establishing networks of computer users.

The emphasis in the first section, Fear Manifest, is on the range of ways in which fear is physically expressed. My introduction, "Shelter from the Storm or Form Follows Fear and Vice Versa," offers a historical and theoretical excursion upon the relationship between fear and city building. In "Building Paranoia," Steven Flusty develops a typology of defensive architecture and urbanism, using Los Angeles as a case study. Richard Sennett describes the new kind of city that must emerge given contemporary insecurities in "The Search for a Place in the World." In "Multiplication + Subdivision," Jane Harrison examines the fictions of safety applied in the transition from farmland to suburb along Interstate 29 in Virginia. "Divided We Fall" by Edward J. Blakely and Mary Gail Snyder presents a history, typology, and critique of gated communities in the United States. Peter Marcuse describes the variety of walls applied to city and community building in "Walls of Fear and Walls of Support." In "Mirrors," Kevin Sites reflects upon the way in which enclosed space can either offer security or threaten it, depending upon the context. Julius Shulman muses upon fears generated by and expressed through building in "The Fear of Architecture: A Photo Essay."

The second section, Personal Manifestations/Solutions, contains testimonies about how buildings and cities instill fear and are sought as refuges from it. In "Abject Terror: A Story of Fear, Sex, and Architecture," Dora Epstein asks how our individual "cartographies" of fear and avoidance develop and how gender influences this development. "Inside Fear: Secret Places and Hidden Spaces in Dwellings" by Anne Troutman explores house interiors from a personal as well as a literary angle, focusing on peripheral spaces. In "My Urban History: Paranoia Informing Place Making," John Chase chronicles his own search for a home and a "family" in several Los Angeles neighborhoods

The third section, Collective Manifestations/Solutions, looks at how various groups of people are affected by and react to fear in their environments. Michael Dear and Jurgen von Mahs describe a "dome village" in downtown Los Angeles that provides transitional housing in "Housing for the Homeless, by the Homeless, and of the Homeless." Lois M. Takahashi's "Addressing Fear through Community Empowerment" examines efforts to diminish fear in some poor neighborhoods through congregational organizing. In "Hetero-Architecture for the Heteropolis: The Los Angeles School," Charles Jencks describes an attempt within the architectural profession to design for a changing world. David Turnbull reports on the politics of safety in Singapore, as expressed through recent urban design and other means, in "Soc. Culture; Singapore:" Through speaking with children from a variety of backgrounds, Sharon E. Sutton asks what a landscape of safety might look like and how it might function in "Creating Landscapes of

Safety." Richard Ingersoll reflects upon the creation of landscapes as scapegoats, or ritual territories for deliverance from fear, in "Landscapegoat."

The final section, From Suburbia to Cyburbia, explores the impact of the revolution in electronic media on our contemporary sense of self, community, and place. Continuing the discussion of Louis Wirth in "Urbanism as a Way of Life" (1938) and Herbert Gans in "Urbanism and Suburbanism as Ways of Life" (1962), Fred Dewey offers "Cyburbanism as a Way of Life," in which he bemoans the replacement of face-to-face with facade-to-facade and proposes a return to self-governing townships. Elaborating upon and extending J. B. Jackson's story of the "Westward-moving House" (1953), Udo Greinacher introduces three more American experiences in "Fear and Dreaming in the American City: From Open Space to Cyberspace." Margaret Wertheim's "The Pearly Gates of Cyberspace" concludes this collection by highlighting the similarities between contemporary hopes pinned on cyberspace and the medieval notion of heaven.

While wide-ranging in scope, *Architecture of Fear* is not intended as a comprehensive survey of work on fear and urban design, but as a sampling, and the emphases are on what these particular writers know best, which happens to be the Western world, especially the United States. Nor is this anthology intended as the last word. It is merely a pause prior to embarking upon the third millennium to critically assess our landscape in a holistic fashion with an eye towards detecting less than optimal design trends and suggesting viable alternatives.

Shelter from the Storm
or
Form Follows Fear and Vice Versa

Nan Ellin

Fear has never been absent from the human experience, and town building has always contended with the need for protection from danger. Protection from invaders was in fact a principal incentive for building cities, many of whose borders were defined by vast walls, from antiquity through the Renaissance. The city was a relatively safe space. Since then, however, the city has become associated more with danger than with safety. This is because the cannon and then atomic arms rendered city walls feeble protection and because dangers such as civil unrest, crime, and contaminated air and water are usually intensified by the density of cities. Other dangers, such as natural disasters, illness, domestic violence, and poverty, strike everywhere equally, without sparing areas of concentration. We persevere in seeking shelter from these dangers lurking in our midst through a range of architectural and planning solutions, which are described in this collection of essays. To contextualize these essays, I provide here some broad historical strokes that convey the evolving nature of fear in the Western world along with corresponding changes in urban design.

Modern Fear and Modern Urbanism, 1789–1900

A logical starting point for this history of fear is the French Revolution (1789), which marked the emergence of not only new social and power structures, but also new ways of perceiving the world, and, along with these, new sources of fear. Along with the ascendance of a bourgeoisie, time[1] and space were reconceived as being more dynamic and malleable. The new conception of time was expressed in the substitution of a revolutionary calendar for the Christian one in 1793 (though it was abandoned in 1805). The new conception of space was expressed in the adoption of the metric system, new political administrative units (departments replacing provinces), and new street and place names.

While these changes permitted a certain freedom and control over one's life that did not previously exist, they also created a new kind of insecurity because they introduced the notion of change itself—or our contemporary notion of history—as inevitable. As Alberto Movaria explains,

> In history, as is well known, nothing endures or remains fixed or stable; everything is in continuous movement, in a continuous state of development. Everything is subject to aging, to obsolescence, to de-fashionization. Everything transforms itself from the tragic into the comic, from the real into the unreal, from the true into the false, from the adequate into the inadequate, from the current into the obsolete.... If nothing stands still, then everything—opinions, styles, information, fortunes, success, groups, society—falls victim to continuous change. Snobbery comes to stand as the fickle and arbitrary surrogate of good taste, which is based no longer on the canon of the beautiful but on that of fashion, of whatever is in vogue.[2]

Reactions among the bourgeoisie to these rapid changes, and to the notion of the inevitability of change itself, included infatuations with primitivism (as discerned through archaeological remains) and exoticism.

The transition from feudalism to capitalism and the attendant rise of a middle class occasioned versions of these changes throughout the Western world. The Swedish sociologists Jonas Frykman and Orvar Lofgren have described this transition in their country, explaining that the ambivalent—if not contested—relationship of the bourgeoisie to the aristocracy, peasantry, and emerging working class impelled the bourgeoisie to establish a clear identity for itself, to secure its ascendant social position by claiming superiority rather than simply difference, and to ultimately become a "colonizing culture."[3] It did this through a strict compartmentalization of the world, often into "hierarchical polarities,"[4] and an obsession with control, discipline, and rationality.

Members of the bourgeoisie viewed time as "evolutive,"[5] aiming to scale the career and/or social ladder at a faster pace than others. Time became "geared to the future, obsessed with development, and the goal [was] to gain control over it."[6] The middle class began measuring time by using their personal calendars and wristwatches, both mass produced in the bourgeois-owned factories, rather than by tracking the movement of the sun and the seasons or by checking the village clock mounted on the church steeple, whose bells announced the important moments of the day, week, and year. For the middle class, time was no longer in the hands of God. It was in their own hands or, at least, on their wrists.

The middle class interpreted events as cultural or willed, rather than as natural,[7] such that competence became the core of their "new charter of legitimacy."[8] With regard to time, for instance, the "new message [was that time] is in short supply and must be properly managed [and] that people create their own futures."[9] Whereas the answers to "Who are you?" and "Where are you from?"

were the major identity markers for the aristocracy and the peasantry, it was the answer to "What do you do?" that assigned identity and status for the middle class. This led to an unprecedented social and geographic mobility as well as a shift in emphasis from the church to the individual or household. The middle class derided "the peasant world [that was] peopled with supernatural beings, dreadful ghosts, and spirits"[10] and based its own knowledge of the world on so-called "scientific" or "rational" evidence. Accompanying this shift from a religious/divine view of the world to a secular/rational one was a value shift from an emphasis on the collective, what many historians describe as "civic society," to a striving for independence and self-determination, variously referred to as "familism," "privatism," or the "disciplinary society."

At the same time, "greater moral demands came to be made on parents," so the privacy of the home "was penetrated by admonitions and counseling."[11] The bourgeoisie criticized the peasantry and the working class for being "unable to bring up their children in a spirit of discipline"[12] as well as for lacking control of bodily functions.[13] And they were horrified by the lower classes' ignorance of the rules of privacy, which, for the bourgeoisie, included separate rooms replete with closing doors for specific individuals and activities. In contrast to the aristocracy and the peasantry who "had a more pragmatic view of marriage and a freer attitude to sexuality,"[14] the emergent middle class was victim to repressed sexuality that they disguised "in a cloak of gallantry,"[15] rendering sexuality "both a mystery and a problem as never before."[16] The bourgeois woman's dress concealed her body from herself as well as from others for "she had consented to regard herself from a man's viewpoint," which saw the female body as "shameful."[17] When it came to sex, "The women had to learn that male sexuality was animal, something natural to which they were forced to be subordinate. The Victorian woman's given role was to 'close her eyes and think of the Empire.'"[18] While men were free to roam the public sphere of Oscarian society, women were largely confined to the domestic sphere.

Like the emergent French middle class, the Swedish one checked and balanced its leap into the future with a nostalgia for the past—often mythologized and reified into ancestor cults and family altars—and a fascination with the other, as demonstrated by the popularity and prestige of history and ethnology as scholarly "disciplines." This attitude toward time and fate distinguished the bourgeoisie from the peasants who did not reify nature and the past and who viewed life in a more cyclical and collective fashion with established and predictable rights of passage that were communally celebrated.

But this proliferation of sanctions and prohibitions exacted costs, as manifest in the many physical and emotional ailments experienced by bourgeoisie of all ages. As Lofgren maintains, the "need for absolute self-control combined with uncertainty about the reactions of others created a seedbed for many mental disturbances and illnesses, from everyday neurotic meditation about the self to hysteria and other common Oscarian complaints."[19] In response, new kinds of specialists emerged to offer advice for handling these ailments. They produced an outpouring of guidebooks and manuals on etiquette, homemaking and interior decorating, and sexual relations.

As by-products of industrial capitalism, the new bourgeoisie was bounded by the very logic of the industrial mode of production, which propelled capitalists around the globe in search of markets. They set off a chain effect wherever they went, much like that in the children's story about the goose who laid golden eggs. A man stole this coveted goose, but to his great dismay found that he could not release it. Having discovered the thief, a policeman grabbed him but found that he too became stuck. The wife of the policeman tried to extricate him from the thief but also became glued and this process continued until a long human chain had formed, each link bound to those on either side. The treadmill metaphor is also appropriate for conveying the plight of the capitalist who must keep running just to stand still, who must run faster than others to get ahead, and who slows down or stops at the risk of oblivion.

The insecurities incited by the transition from feudalism to capitalism led to new proposals for building. In the same year that the French Revolution began, the English philosopher Jeremy Bentham conceived the Panopticon (Greek for everything, place of sight, or all-seeing), a circular building for containing criminals or workers with cells radially disposed around the perimeter and a circular guardhouse in the center for the inspector. Bentham's proposal allowed the inspector to see the criminals or workers but not vice versa through incorporating very narrow black galleries and strategically placed blinds. This building was conceived explicitly to carry out the task of enlightenment. As Bentham explained, "Morals reformed—health preserved—industry invigorated—instruction diffused—public burdens lightened—economy seated, as it were, upon a rock...all by a simple idea in Architecture."[20]

In this way, Anthony Vidler maintains, Bentham "turned utopia inside out" by translating city form into building form so that "the radial lines, which in the ideal [eighteenth-century] city were streets converging on the center, were now the partition walls of the cells; the center was no longer the common public place but the exclusive domain of the all-powerful inspector."[21] Vidler contends that with this development, "the great age of confinement had begun," from the hospital to the prison, insane asylum, old-age home, day-care center, and school.

The predominant metaphors for cities in the late-eighteenth century as organic and/or machinelike guided urban designs, which were conceived in the spirit of performing surgical operations or repairing broken parts.

From that moment on, "a problem had only to be identified as socially irritant and situated within a group or classified according to a class for a building to be built as the institutional solution to that problem."[22]

This marked a shift from the Enlightenment language of natural reason to technical reason.[23] While early- to mid-eighteenth-century Enlightenment city plans relied upon classical geometry and proportional harmony to express man's triumph over nature through the faculty of natural reason, late-eighteenth-century and early-nineteenth-century plans drew from technical reason[24] to design cities as agents of progress by applying science and technology to bring about social reform, especially by instilling morals and the work ethic. The opening of communication networks and decentralization were recurrent themes. These concerns led to the 1794 establishment of the École Polytechnique in Paris during the revolutionary period to train an elite corps of engineers for the French army (and the École de Chirugie shortly thereafter). The predominant metaphors for cities at this time as organic and/or machinelike guided these urban designs, which were conceived in the spirit of performing surgical operations or repairing broken parts.[25] Countering the rationalist tendency of post-Enlightenment city planning, these plans also began to incorporate elements of romanticism and the picturesque.

Examples include Claude-Nicolas Ledoux's Salines-de-Chaux (1774–1804), Robert Owen's Parallelogram plan (1820), Claude-Henri St. Simon's New Christianity (1825—St. Simon, who was deeply influenced by Bentham, used to host dinners to which he invited the leading professors of the École Polytechnique to discuss social engineering, and hundreds of St. Simonians were at the school),[26] Charles Fourier's Phalanstery concept (1829), Etienne Cabet's plan for Icaria (1840s), James Silk Buckingham's Plan of Victoria (1849), and Louis Napoléon's Cité Napoléon in Paris (1849), among others. In the United States a number of attempts at realizing these plans were undertaken, such as Cabet's Icaria in Texas and Illinois, Owen's New Harmony in Illinois, Fourier's Phalanstery at Brook Farm, Massachusetts (1841), and dozens more.

On a larger scale, European capitals were redeveloped during the latter half of the nineteenth century in a variety of ways to accommodate modern life. The most famous instance is the redesign of Paris from 1853–72 overseen by Baron Haussmann and the Emperor Napoleon III, who was closely affiliated with St. Simon in his youth. Haussmann described his interventions in the urban fabric of Paris as "constructive destruction."[27] He conceived of the city as an organism and himself as a surgeon cutting out the sick parts and opening clogged arteries in the urban circulatory system. He sought to "clear" slums (*îlots insalubres*, unhealthy islands) and open up "breathing space" (*nettoyage par le vide*). These medical metaphors were used in part to suggest a key motive for the redevelopment, that of preventing further cholera epidemics by reducing overcrowding and improving the water system.

A principal theme of this redevelopment of Paris was *régularisation* or standardization. Haussmann sought to standardize housing, the distance between trees, and much more, to give the city a sense of order. The most important feature of this intervention was the cutting of straight wide boulevards through the medieval urban fabric of Paris. Haussmann "envisioned the new roads as arteries in an urban circulatory system,"[28] an image that was revolutionary at the time because the problem of vehicular traffic was new. Streets had been for walking to work or shops and for socializing. Now they were primarily for movement. The goal was to link, to put into communication, and to get rid of sinuosity.[29] The boulevards were also intended to quicken the pace of commerce and to stimulate local business by uniting previously isolated sectors of the city and thereby defraying building expenses through an increase in tax money.

There was also a social function for these boulevards. The inherent adversarial relationship between the emergent working class and the propertied class led to considerable uprisings as well as vandalism of property. The propertied class commonly referred to the working class as the "dangerous class," the crowd, or the mob (*la foule*). The construction of these straight, wide boulevards would contend with this danger by employing tens of thousands (at times as much as one quarter of the city's labor force) on public works, which in turn enhanced profit making and provided jobs in the private sector; by razing working-class districts and thereby dispersing established communities, diffusing their power to stage uprisings and perhaps their anger; by creating long broad corridors in which troops and artillery could move effectively against barricades and popular insurrections; and by providing short, direct routes from military barracks to the working-class districts. Finally, there was a representational goal. The redevelopment of Paris would assert state power and prestige through monumental architecture and urban design, with strategically placed monuments at the ends of vistas. The plan would celebrate the values of the new bourgeoisie by prominently housing this class along the boulevards.

Individual building design was similarly reconceived on the basis of social patterns and the new bourgeoisie's ideas about order. This was particularly apparent in the cultural institutions sponsored by the bourgeoisie, as epitomized in the Barcelona Opera (1837–44)[30] and the Paris Opera (1861–75). In housing design, Napoleon III called for uniform facades, apartment buildings (as opposed to townhouses), and separate districts for the middle class to protect them from the threat posed by the working class.[31]

Transformations in interior design occurred alongside those in building and city design. As architecture and planning were growing more rational and functional over the course of the nineteenth century, so were the floor plans of bourgeois homes in their clear division between public and private spaces as well as clearly designated purposes for all spaces, including separate rooms for each child (replacing the nursery for all children) and separate spaces for women's and men's activities. In contrast to this rationalizing and compartmentalizing of space, the decor of these interiors grew more romantic. As Lofgren recounts of the new Swedish middle class, rooms that had previously been austere and simple but multipurpose became opulently and theatrically appointed according to the single function they were to serve.[32] These decors connoted "romance, sentimentality, and fantasy"[33] and included generously scattered mirrors so people could observe and appropriately modify their appearance and behavior.[34] This elaborate decoration could be interpreted as a compensation for the growing rationality of life or as a reflection of inner fantasies and fears generated by such rationalization. Not incidentally, it was also a means of keeping the bourgeois women busy and thereby diverted from participating in public life.

Modern Fear and Modern Urbanism, 1900–1960s

The nature of fear continued to change during the early part of the twentieth century because of the vast changes wrought by industrialization and urbanization. In order to accommodate factory work, the day took on new rhythms, as did the week, month, and year. There were also changes in gender and family relations and in the relationship between public and domestic spheres. The landscape evolved in order to accommodate the railroads, factories, warehouses, skyscrapers, working-class districts, middle-class suburbs, cars, and highways of the modern industrial city. In addition, the movement of populations and capital around the globe accelerated and the global class and power structure enlarged its scope.

The new constellation of fear accompanying modern industrialization derived from this accelerated change as well as from the unreliable and often substandard working conditions of the new wage-earning class, the inherent antagonism between it and the small class of owners, increased geographic mobility due to the unrelenting search by people for better wages and by workplaces for greater profits, and the constant change in consumer tastes upon which mass production relied. In the United States, the vast cultural diversity resulting from European and Asian migration and from the urban migration of African-Americans also contributed greatly to a sense of insecurity for people of all ethnicities given the concentrated panoply of languages and customs. Insecurity was thus an integral component of industrial capitalism, both within the factory and outside of it.

The means for coping with this new constellation of fear also evolved. Appropriated by the socioindustrial machine, time and space were more precisely measured and divided into units that could be allocated for specific purposes. This allowed for accurate predictions of labor output as well as worker and consumer behavior. Within the factory, time was used as a mechanism for control over others. For instance, some companies did not allow workers to wear watches, so they would not know how long they were working.[35] Frederick Winslow Taylor's scientific management, introduced in 1911, refined the process of inscribing work patterns into units of time, and Henry Ford's moving assembly line incorporated space into the process in 1913. The architect Albert Kahn assisted Ford in 1910 by providing a functional shell of steel, concrete, and glass for his plant, a formula for industrial plants that he and others reproduced all over the world. Control over time and space thus joined control over labor power as all were harnessed in the interests of mass production.

Outside the factory, the rationalization and commodification of space was facilitated by various impositions of the grid for urban development and speculation from the early New York City Commissioner's Map of 1811 and the division of central and western United States into one-mile squares to the early twentieth-century city-functional plans, numbering in the hundreds. Beginning around 1900 in Germany and in the 1910s in the United States, zoning marked a further rationalization of space by determining the nature of built form (height, windows, solids and voids) as well as which activities (commercial, residential, business, recreational) should take place in which spaces. As all of this was occurring, the nature of public space altered. Rather than combine production, consumption, movement through the city, and social interaction, public spaces grew more singular in their function. The social and productive aspects of the street and marketplace particularly were suppressed in favor of movement and consumption respectively. And as public space was transforming, so was private space and the relationship between the two.

As change came to be regarded as inevitable, time became a commodity of which there never seemed to be enough, inciting expressions such as "to spend time," "time is money," "how time flies," "*pas de temps de vivre*," and "*metro, bulot, dodo*." The new conception of time led to a valorization of "leisure" time and an anticipation of a future moment when time would be less tyrannical—retirement—along with a continued fascination for the past (primitivism) and the other (exoticism). The attempt to harness time led to efforts to go beyond the precise measurement and allocation of time in the present to predict the future. This was manifest in efforts to "forecast" weather, in demographic and environmental trends, and in the exchange of stocks, bonds, and, indeed, futures. Space and time lost their anchoring and securing attributes as they appeared to grow increasingly scarce and tyrannical in the single-minded pursuit of greater productivity. It was within this climate that Albert Einstein developed the theory of relativity (1911) and that abstract art flourished, both of which emphasized multiple perspectives as opposed to a single one. This shift—which modern architecture shared (see below)—might be understood as a reflection of rapid change, as a means of acknowledging cultural diversity, or as an expression of rapid movement in a train or car.

The vast and rapid transformations occurring since the late nineteenth century have led observers to remark that the only secure thing about modernity is insecurity.[36] Charles Pierre Baudelaire, a participant/observer of late-nineteenth-century Paris, wrote in "The Painter of Modern Life" (1863), "Modernity is the transient, the fleeting, the contingent; it is the one half of art, the other being the eternal and the immutable."[37] Invoking Karl Marx, Marshall Berman described modernity one century hence as

> a unity of disunity; it pours us all into a maelstrom of perpetual disintegration and renewal, of struggle and contradiction, of ambiguity and anguish. To be modern is to be part of a universe in which, as Marx said, all that is solid melts into air.[38]

What has been described as an institutional revolution occurred over the course of the nineteenth century, featuring not only the separation and formalization of different aspects of life—work, home, leisure, shopping, recreation—but also that of knowledge into the academic "disciplines," and the professionalization of many activities and areas of knowledge. By the early part of the twentieth century, there was a shift from merely organizing the masses of people, knowledge, and objects (in prisons, libraries, museums, maps) to a more concerted effort to understand and control them. These efforts included the emergence of the social sciences as

The modernist opening up of interior space reflected a desire to be released from traditional societal morays and barriers among social classes, ethnic groups, generations, and genders.

academic disciplines, of urban planning as a profession, and of modern architecture and planning theory.

Since the rapid changes in the physical fabric of the industrial city were unlike the incremental piecemeal interventions into the preindustrial city, new kinds of specialists were needed to decipher the changes and to effectively guide them. To fulfill this need, social reformers refashioned themselves into social scientists and urban planners who attempted, in the words of Paul Rabinow, to "link norms and forms."[39] What distinguished modern urban planning from that which preceded it was its scale and its effort to contend with industrialization, in part by "normalizing" the population.[40] In the United States, these efforts were apparent in the City Efficient plans devised by the newly formed city planning commissions around the country; in France, in the plans of the Musée Social, Le Corbusier, Tony Garnier, and Henri Sellier; and in England, in the efforts to realize Ebenezer Howard's Garden City concept.

Modern architecture and planning theory was codified in the Athens Charter (written by Le Corbusier based on discussions at the CIAM—International Congress of Modern Architecture—convened in 1933) to include the separation and organization of functions (habitation, work, recreation, circulation) through zoning regulations, a regional plan, and measurements derived from the human body. Modern architecture and planning theory generally reconceived the "relationship between residence, work, and commerce, and between market and marketplace"[41] recommending, for instance, that sports replace the public activity of streets and that collective services replace private ones.

This undertaking was to be carried out by experts with the assistance of modern technologies in an effort "to transform society by forging new forms of collective associations and personal habits, and by precluding those considered undesirable."[42] The appropriate role of the architect followed from these intentions. The modern era, says Jean Guiheux, saw

> the emergence of an Architect with the desire to take in hand the salvation of
> humanity, a radically new role with the stated aim of transforming the conditions of

life emanating from the apparently anarchic and cancerous development of towns from the industrial revolution. . . . Neither Vitruvius, Alberti, nor Perrault had envisaged for an instant that their science would extend beyond its limits.[43]

For modern architects of the early twentieth century, however, "The project was total: art, politics, housing, the territorial and social aspects of life, everything in fact." For them,

> The supposed model inhabitant was particularly basic: his needs were evidently primary. Above all he had no desires and certainly no fantasies. Transparent, he was also universal, whatever his culture, age, sex, or profession. His size, his gestures in the kitchen were coded. Art was transformed into an anthropometric laboratory.

Architects were designing for an ideal man rather than for real people and were seeking to discover universal solutions. They aspired toward the architectural object, a building that stands alone and does not refer to its particular setting either physically or socially. Although this concept was not new—Leone Battista Alberti, Andrea Palladio, and others also designed architectural objects—the assertion that all building types should exist as isolated objects was new.[44]

Meanwhile, city designers such as Ebenezer Howard, Tony Garnier, and Le Corbusier proposed "ideal types" that could be applied anywhere rather than specific plans appropriate for specific sites. The French architect Bernard Huet explains that the "functional" city was conceived as a

> space of Euclidean abstraction regulated by quantity and industrial repetition, a space whose three fundamental characteristics are homogeneity, isotropy, and fragmentation, and which presents itself as the absolute antithesis of the space of the "historic" city. The model of the "functional" city is the most accomplished expression of a "scientific" urbanism which progressively detached itself from the practices of urban art at the beginning of the twentieth century and whose exclusive object is the rational administration of housing the masses in industrial society.[45]

Modern housing was to consist of "buildings sited in the middle of continuous open spaces, transparent glass facades, [and] gardens on rooftops"[46] situated among avenues without intersection. Modern interior design supplanted the central hallway and multiple, small, single-function rooms of the Victorian house with "open plans," "flowing space," and fewer but more capacious rooms. The modernist opening up of interior space, made possible by steel frames eliminating the need for structural walls, reflected a desire to be released from traditional societal morays and barriers among social classes, ethnic groups, generations, and genders. It corresponded to the mass ownership of cars in the United States along with massive road building and, as Vincent Scully suggests, reflected the American love of movement.[47] Subsequent to the Second World War, it corresponded to a period of affluence that allowed more people than ever before to own their homes and to enjoy larger living spaces. These conditions encouraged the pursuit of opened, undefined, flowing interior space in the modern house by architects and nonarchitects alike. Modern decor sought to simplify that of the late nineteenth century in order to save on the costs of decorating and the housework it required, to express a more egalitarian as opposed to hierarchical spirit, and to reflect the new aesthetic of minimalism, or "less is more."

Regarding the academic eclecticism of the Beaux-Arts tradition as no longer evocative or symbolic of its time, modernism employed imagery related to machinery, reflecting a faith in technology and a desire to create a technocratic utopia. The machine provided a suitable organizing metaphor in the quest to contend with the disruptions and apparent disorder of industrialism. Anthony Vidler suggests that this metaphor grew out of the need to confront mass production, especially the mass production of machines by machines. Tracing the evolution of modernist thought, Vidler writes

> The natural analogy of the Enlightenment, originally brought forward to control the messy reality of the city, was now extended to refer to the control of entire nature....A vision of Taylorized production, of a world ruled by the iron law of Ford supplanted the spuriously golden dream of neo-classicism.[48]

With the growth of corporate capitalism after the Second World War, the international power system grew relatively stable and so did beliefs in linear progress, absolute truths, and rational planning. The eighth CIAM (held in London in 1945) took the Athens Charter to its logical extreme in declaring that industrialization had rendered social categories irrelevant. Participants in this conference, organized by Josep Lluís Sert with the theme "The Heart of the City," declared that the industrial mode of production had reduced everyone to *homo economicus*, yielding a monolithic mass society with widely shared aspirations and tastes. This conception of society at "degree zero" (from Roland Barthes) further justified a design mentality that aspired to be pure, sterile, avant-garde, elitist, and esoteric. Manfredo Tafuri points out that this period—often described as universal or high modernism—was characterized by a desire to control the future and thereby eliminate the risk that comes with it, not unlike the contemporaneous Keynesian economics.[49]

An unintended side effect of this mentality, however, was the unprecedented influence it allowed the market in shaping cultural forms of expression, including urban design. Frederic Jameson contends, "The new utopianism of high modernism unwittingly and against the very spirit of its revolutionary and utopian affirmations prepared the terrain for the omnipotence of the fully 'rationalized' technocratic plan, for the universal planification of what was to become the total system of multinational capital."[50] This period of modernism, he says, "ended up rationalizing the object world more extensively and ferociously than anything Ford or Taylor might have done on his own momentum."[51] More than ever before, form was following finance.

The co-option of urban design by the growing reach and power of the market was epitomized in the United States by the Housing Acts of 1949 and 1954 and the Highway Act of 1954. Lobbied for by real-estate, building, and automotive interests, these acts allowed for massive suburbanization along vehicular patterns and the appropriation of urban design by developers. A symposium held at the Museum of Modern Art in 1947 called "What Is Happening to Modern Architecture?" also revealed the technocratic bias of high modernism. Ridiculing recent regionalist design in the Bay Area, participants in this symposium called for returning to essentialist modernism with Le Corbusier's Radiant City as the universal model.[52]

As a result, much of what was built after the war in the United States—as well as western Europe—consisted of isolated towers and slabs as well as unending blocks of mass-produced individual houses. Informed by market dictates as well as by modern architecture and urban planning theory, this massive amount of postwar building has been widely accused of destroying much of western urban heritage, disrupting communities and displacing people from their homes and businesses, increasing social segregation on a regional scale, accentuating gender role distinctions and disfavoring that of women, diminishing the public realm, being insensitive to the environment, and generating aesthetic monotony. Although modern urbanism may have been elegant and socially responsible in the abstract, its realization, as Edward T. Relph contends, "turned out to be repressive, ugly, sterile, antisocial, and generally disliked."[53]

By the late 1950s and early 1960s, the critique of modern urbanism began to mount. In its dogmatic insistence on purity, critics proclaimed, modernism bespoke its own death. The various expressions of discontent with architectural and planning training and practice registered during the 1960s attested to the severity of the crisis.[54]

Postmodern Fear and Postmodern Urbanism

The more recent wave of confusion and uncertainty beginning in the late 1960s may be attributed to yet another acceleration in the rate of change as globalization, specialization, and geographic mobility have continued apace. Other contributors to the peculiarly postmodern sense of insecurity include the virtual eclipse of the public realm, the growing encroachment of the marketplace and the state into the private realm, the shift to flexible accumulation, the growing gap between rich and poor, increased access to information technologies and influence of intelligent machines, the consequent obscuring of power, and the resultant challenge to the dominance of the modern world view.[55] The fear factor has certainly grown, as indicated by the growth in locked car and house doors and security systems, the popularity of "gated" or "secure" communities for all age and income groups, and the increasing surveillance of public spaces (see below), not to mention the unending reports of danger emitted by the mass media.

Whereas modern fear and the positivistic climate in which it occurred led to efforts to detect causes and effects—to rationally understand the present in an effort to guide the future—postmodern fear amid the reigning anti-technocratic climate has incited a series of closely related and overlapping responses including retribalization, nostalgia, escapism, and spiritual (re)turn.

The search for "roots" and the assertion of cultural distinctions have been predominant responses to postmodern insecurity. As Marshall McLuhan correctly foresaw in the 1960s, the world village engendered by the widespread use of electronic media has diminished actual diversity while also provoking a distrust of distant authority and a desire for "in-depth" participation, along with regionalist, separatist, fundamentalist, and reactionary sentiments. Parallel to a growing cosmopolitanism, this desire to preserve (or invent) differences—or "retribalization"—has been assisted by transnational culture flows of products, capital, people, and ideas, as well as media. In urban design, the retribalization reflex is manifest in attempts to design in the growth of retirement communities as well as other de facto segregated communities (by ethnicity or social class).

A second response to the accelerated change of the contemporary period has been nostalgia, a desire to return to an apocryphal rosy past in reaction to high modernism's clean break from the past. An obsession with the past is interpreted psychologically as a desire to return to the womb, to the mother, to nature, to archetypes, to some paradise or state of bliss that has been lost. In its collective manifestation, the nostalgic impulse might be understood as a response to the rapid change that occurred during the industrial/modern era. In the transition to a postindustrial society, the sense of insecurity grew along with the nostalgic impulse.[56] This late-twentieth-century version added an infatuation with mass culture and its imagery in yet another effort to find meaning and security in a world that appeared increasingly meaningless and scary.[57] The massive appropriation and recombining of already existing ideas or images may suggest a depletion of creative energies or a fear of being original.

Joining retribalization, then, another response to the growing encroachment of the marketplace and the state into our private domain has been the return to "traditional" values and institutions, a return that was appropriated and assisted by the advertising industry, which dubbed it "neotraditionalism." A full-page advertisement placed in the *New York Times* for the magazine *Good Housekeeping* in 1989 explained that neotraditionalism was "now being recognized as the most powerful social movement since the sixties." The new traditionalist, this ad implied, is a housewife and mother, perhaps with a career, who believes in "timeless quality" and "commitment" and who is "simple, honest, real, unpretentious, and genuine." A similar advertisement explains that the new traditionalist

> started a revolution—with some not-so revolutionary ideals. She was searching for
> something to believe in—and look what she found. Her husband, her children, her
> home, herself. She's the contemporary woman who has made a new commitment to
> the traditional values that some people thought were "old-fashioned." She wasn't fol-
> lowing a trend. She made her own choices. But when she looked over the fence she
> found that she wasn't alone.[58]

In other realms, the desire for familiarity—recalling one's own childhood or even someone else's—and the exhaustion of creative energies are evident in the popularity of Nickelodeon cable network's "Nick at Nite," which rebroadcasts 1960s and 1970s sitcoms for the twenty- and thirty-something crowds; feature films based on popular television programs; movie remakes and sequels; new covers of old songs; advertising that attempts to make products seem old or established; "classic rock" stations; lounge music and old nightclubs; retro-clothing and retro-furniture; diners; and much more. These allusions can reassure continuity, can be a homage, or can be a high-camp parody.

The nostalgic impulse has been evident in music as well, as jazz began a hard-bop revival and rock and folk referred back to their earlier incarnations. Perhaps most significantly, country music, that quintessentially American musical genre, has made a major comeback. As this rural nation became a suburban one, country music also suburbanized, so to speak. Subsequent to the de-twanging of country music in the 1970s, which record producers called "countrypolitan," there was an effort to "sound old-fashioned" in the 1980s, which producers described as "neotraditionalist." Played with guitars and fiddles, this neotraditionalist country music recalls a time "when life was simple and roles and choices were clear." Its lyrics, distinct from traditional country lyrics that console their listener in hard times, look "to the past through rose-colored binoculars," using this idealized past as just one more comfy stage set. In fact, two of these neotraditionalist songs are entitled "Home" (by Alan Jackson and by Joe Diffie).[59]

Enhanced access to material goods through increasingly sophisticated means of production and distribution (particularly home shopping via catalogues and television) has put a premium on having something before anyone else has it. Being able to purchase an item that is fashionable no longer carries the cache that having already had it before it was fashionable does. Retailers have accommodated this fascination for the old by resurrecting past styles and by "wearing out" new goods in a mass-produced fashion through, for instance, multiple washings of clothes or special finishes on furniture or picture frames. To give new things the aged look, a salesperson explained, their "paint finishes intentionally show signs of wear and aging."[60] Explaining this sensibility, a shopowner asserted that these items represent "nostalgia for the simple life," and another maintained, "I feel that esthetic is more important than authentic."[61]

This infatuation with the past has made renovation of old houses a popular pastime. It has also translated into a nostalgia towards both city and country life and an aversion to suburban life. Although the actual number of people renovating old houses is small, their impact has been significant in gentrifying both urban areas and rural communities. The retrofitting of vacated factories and warehouses for housing has also contributed to this gentrification. Such "loft living" is another example of valorizing the past, but this time it is the industrial past. And it represents nostalgia not only for an old building but also an old way of life, that of combining home and workplace in one space. Although architects such as Frank Lloyd Wright, Walter Gropius, and Le Corbusier were greatly inspired by industrial design, they adapted it for residential buildings by prettifying it (with their female clientele in mind) and adjusting its scale appropriately. It was not until the 1970s that industrial design began to appear in nonindustrial markets in a less-disguised fashion, suggesting a changed aesthetic that reflected a quest for authenticity, efficiency, and beauty without artifice. The search for a more human habitat, Sharon Zukin deftly observed, turned to factories.[62] Ever solicitous to consumer desires, some developers began offering new constructions that resemble old industrial buildings and merchandising them as "new lofts."

As the housing stock was being gentrified, so was the retail sector, either in a piecemeal fashion or through larger-scale interventions. James Rouse, the developer of the 1960s new town of Columbia, Maryland, was most influential in this "adaptive reuse" of abandoned downtown districts. In the late 1970s he oversaw the conversion of Boston's Faneuil Hall Market Place (originally built in 1742) and its adjacent Quincy Market (built in 1826) into a new kind of urban shopping mall combining shops, restaurants, small-cart boutiques, and performance spaces. Rouse thus introduced the new typology of the "festival marketplace," which, in

Disneyland
Anaheim, California

CityWalk at Universal Studios
Los Angeles, California

Two Rodeo Drive
Beverly Hills, California
Kaplan McLaughlin Diaz Architects/Planners

Two Rodeo Drive

Gatehouse of a gated community
Boca Raton, Florida

Grand entryway of house
Cincinnati, Ohio

the words of Benjamin Thompson, the architect for several of these, were to be "settings for festive human interaction, made of food and clothes as well as buildings."[63] Quincy Market was followed by various implementations of the same formula including Lawrence Halprin's conversion of a former chocolate factory into Ghirardelli Square in San Francisco (1964), and Benjamin Thompson's building (from scratch) of Harborplace in Baltimore (1980) and the South Street Seaport in New York City (1983–85). This so-called "urban revitalization" usually entails a partnership between the public and private sectors. The goal is to generate new economic base and to generate a renewed sense of pride in downtowns, but the actual results are uneven.

On the scale of the city, the nostalgic impulse is revealed by numerous efforts since the 1970s to recreate preindustrial townscapes and to plan settings that appear to have evolved spontaneously and that encourage inhabitant appropriation. It was the "illegible" quality of post-WWII urban development and the fear this generated that incited efforts to create more familiar "legible" landscapes.[64] Usually, these design strategies involved combining the human scale of traditional townscapes with the benefits of contemporary technologies.[65]

Nostalgic urban design has been most evident in neotraditional urbanism, more recently christened the "new urbanism." Dissatisfied with the conventional post-WWII suburban tract development as well as the master-planned and gated communities that succeeded them, neotraditional urbanism draws inspiration from townscapes of the past in an effort to engage the surroundings rather than retreat from them. In order to achieve this, neotraditional urbanism seeks to provide quality public spaces that are semienclosed and legible, and that connect places that people use, in contrast to the amorphous, illegible, isolated, and largely unused public spaces of the master-planned community. It is hoped that these measures, rather than increase the fortress mentality and fear, will alleviate the sources of insecurity themselves. The central motivation behind these efforts is to avoid modern urbanism's excessive separation of functions along with the social and environmental harm that accompanies it. Though inspired by preindustrial environments, these urban designs seek to acknowledge current needs and tastes—including the preference for the individual house—and to take full advantage of new technologies for achieving these ends. Efforts along these lines have been undertaken in Europe beneath the rubric of the movement for the reconstruction of the European city[66] and in the United States under the titles of "traditional neighborhood development" or "district" (introduced and diffused foremost by Elisabeth Plater-Zyberk and Andres Duany) and "pedestrian pocket" or "transit-oriented development" (as promulgated primarily by Peter Calthorpe).[67]

Paralleling the urbanistic trend to create enclosed "roomlike" public spaces, postmodern interior design has marked a return to separate rooms with specific purposes.[68] The perennial search to expand markets by diversifying products offers one explanation for this shift, but there are more substantial reasons as well. During the 1970s post-WWII baby boomers were reaching childbearing age at the same time that a fiscal crisis restricted new construction, thus producing cramped living spaces, the partitioning of spaces, and the need for greater privacy. In addition, new home technologies (particularly the VCR and computer) and growing privatism have conspired with a diminished public realm to make people stay home more. With increased time at home, and the need to engage in a greater number of activities there, we have returned to nineteenth-century uni-functional rooms. This time, however, the production rooms (for canning, sewing, woodworking) are supplanted by rooms for consumption, leisure, and recreation, such as the media room, the exercise room, room-size closets, and large master bedroom suites to incorporate features such as Jacuzzis and saunas. On a more abstract level, this return to the room can be attributed to a loss of faith in progress (expressed symbolically in the modernist open plan) and to the sense that we lack an overarching organizing myth (or *grand récit*), both of which in turn incite a nostalgia for more traditional living spaces.

Despite the new technologies integral to contemporary homes, postmodern house forms and decor draw from the past, both an urban leisured past and rural past of "abundant simplicity." In contrast to the starkness of modern home design, certain postmodern homes are opulent and sumptuous, featuring, for instance, grand entryways, double staircases, chandeliers, scattered mirrors with gilt frames, overstuffed furniture, and the layering of fabrics, rugs, and window coverings, all in colors and patterns popular prior to modernism. Other postmodern homes, inspired by "country living," incorporate wood furnishings that are distressed, combination living room/kitchens, small-floral-print fabrics, and other characteristics of rural houses. Others still combine these aesthetics and more to produce a grandmother's house/flea market/pop culture/anything goes aesthetic. Fantasy is back, supplanting the modern concern for function, purism, and structural "honesty." This shift in interior design is illustrated by French designer Andrée Putman's 1996 redesign of Manhattan's Morgan Hotel—which she first designed in 1984 in a high-tech and minimal style using black leather, gray, and white—in what she describes as her "no color" color scheme, featuring antique armchairs with well-worn leather in the lobby, corduroy chairs and wool sofas in beige-on-beige guest rooms, and bar stools of wood from fallen Central Park trees for the basement bar.[69]

Whereas the opening up of spaces in the modern house reflected a desire to break with the past, the partitioning of spaces in the postmodern house perhaps reflects a desire to rekindle the past. If the opening up of spaces engendered a sense of emptiness, void, and meaningless, the partitioning of them would perhaps bring meaning back. And if the flowing space suggested and facilitated the elimination of social differences, perhaps enclosed space would vindicate and reassert these distinctions during a time of pervasive insecurity. A place for everything and everything in its place. Nonetheless, the trend has not been towards recreating premodern interior spaces wholesale, but towards a best-of-both-worlds compromise between these and the modernist open plan, particularly for the kitchen, living room, and dining room areas.

This partitioning of domestic space has paralleled a larger partitioning of urban space, as retribalization and nostalgia have lent renewed vigor to traditional identity markers. The reassertion of national, regional, ethnic, and political boundaries and groupings (especially evident during the Persian Gulf War and in the war in the Balkans) suggest that history has not in fact ended—that we have not transcended the dueling dualisms characterizing modernity—as Francis Fukuyama postulated.[70] Such expressions of the need to anchor ourselves in time and space in order to withstand universalizing forces is reminiscent of the "geopolitical" reflexes of the 1930s. Martin Heidegger, for instance, called for "rootedness in place and environmentally bound traditions as the only secure foundation for political and social action in a manifestly troubled world."[71]

A third response to contemporary fear is escapism, characterized either by a retreat from the larger community (privatism) or a flight into collective or personal fantasy worlds that actively disregard the problems of real life, or what cyberists refer to in shorthand as "RL." Retreating and fleeing are reactions to the blurring of public and private realms, the continued decline of meaningful public space, and the resultant fragmentation of city life and city form. As Kathleen Stewart writes,

> There is no clear "inside" or "outside" anymore, no private and public spheres of life. We build public space as fantasy environments to roam around in—malls, theme parks, every town modeled as a postmodern village of the imagination... "the country" becomes just an urban space with more room."[72]

Kenneth Galbraith has described this condition as one of "private affluence and public squalor."[73] Richard Sennett attributes the decline of the public realm to changes "that began with the fall of the *ancien régime* and the formation of a new capitalist, secular, urban culture."[74] He explores the psychological implications of this decline, saying,

Western societies are moving from something like an other-directed condition to an inner-directed condition—except that in the midst of self-absorption no one can say what is inside. As a result, confusion has arisen between public and intimate life.

This self-absorption, he says, "obscures the continuing importance of class in advanced industrial society" and leads us "to undervalue the community relations of strangers, particularly those which occur in cities."

The French philosopher Jérome Bindé maintains that the widespread desire to live in an individual house can be understood in the context of

the postmodern moment where everyone is returned to himself. To his little games, to the scenery of his daily life, to his narcissistic anxiety of "being liberated."... The individuals of societies in crisis, disoriented by the sudden devaluation of unanimous credos (capitalist "abundance" or socialist "emancipation") become thus refugees in a rediscovered opium, in this padlocked garden where one would like to forget the snubs of real History.[75]

Privatization, Bindé maintains, involves "the search for stability in an unstable and anxious universe, without imaginary landmarks to anchor oneself," "the simulated regression towards the past, evoked like a maternal and appeasing specter which one knows very well no longer exists, never existed, but in which one would very much like to believe." He says,

A little like the Carnivals used to suspend...sexual prohibitions and social hierarchies, our collective postmodern rites ritually raise the prohibitions to guide and favor the privatization of existence. But at the same time they confirm and reinforce the narcissistic and anxious insularity of this individual sphere, always frustrated, always unsatisfied.

For Bindé, privatization is not

the adventuresome conquest of a mode of civilization along with new relations of production. Far from being a conquest, or an offensive ideological arm of the avant-garde and social revolution, this privatism functions like a refuge, a retreat, a redoubt whence the aggressivity of [those] who defend it.

Those ardent proponents of the free-market economy will not achieve the minimum state intervention they seek, says Bindé, "but its opposite: maximum state intervention...and maximum bureaucracy" through the expansion of the military-industrial complex and of transnational corporations.

The impulse to privatize is epitomized by the growth of gated communities, residential developments with patrolled entryways and a clear separation from other neighborhoods, usually by a secure fence. The clear spatial and social distinctions provided by the gated community have replaced the erstwhile clear social distinction provided by "vertical segregation"—which became blurred with the advent of the elevator, making all floors equally desirable—with horizontal segregation. The number and size of these socially homogenous ghettos has expanded as mass transit has become more extensive. This segregation allows a certain ignorance regarding social differences, which, in turn, allows for the generation of myths, and negative stereotypes about people who are not familiar.

Privatism is also manifest in the appropriation of public spaces by private agencies. Such spaces are found in the inward-turning shopping mall, which has abandoned the central city for the suburbs and whose fortresslike exterior surrounded by a moatlike parking lot turns its back entirely on its surroundings. Other examples include the indoor "atriums" of corporate office buildings; theme parks in which "Main Street" and other recognizable features of the past are reproduced at seven-eighths their actual scale, scrubbed clean of their real contexts, and commercialized; and franchises and chain stores that offer consumers familiarity wherever they may be.

All of these places are patrolled by sophisticated security systems, which largely influence their design as well as regulate who enters and what activities transpire there. In these more recent forms of public space, participation is singularly focused (as opposed to the diverse roles of traditional public spaces) and almost always consumer oriented, limited to those with the ability to purchase.

Older public spaces have also been appropriated and controlled through increases in the signage designating who should be using the space and when ("We have the right to refuse service to anyone"), in curfews and police sweeps in transportation terminals and parks, in both public and private police forces, in gating, and in the antigrowth mentality. While certain parks, plazas, and commons remain places to escape from loci of production and consumption, their traditional social component invariably has been compromised, because the rising tide of fear has transformed them into controlled and guarded places. These so-called "public" spaces have become places of exclusion as well as inclusion.

Michel Foucault's concept of disciplinary space offers one interpretation of this evolution. Foucault posited that evolving technologies of power serve to maintain the status quo. Based on the seventeenth- and eighteenth-century political rationality of *raison d'état*, "biopower" began to inform the disciplinary technologies employed by elites.[76] For the exercise of biopower, visibility was essential. Spectacles of terror and punishment as well as those of patronage and benevolence acted as a kind of "natural policing."[77] To enhance visibility and to organize individuals in space, architects and their clients designed buildings and cities accordingly. As disciplinary strategies have evolved to the present, visibility of the ruled has continued to increase, but that of the rulers has decreased. This is because, as Foucault remarked, "power is tolerable only on condition that it mask a substantial part of itself. Its success is proportional to its ability to hide its own mechanisms."[78] This evolution was foreshadowed by Bentham's Panopticon, described above, which is widely regarded as the paradigmatic example of disciplinary space.

As the expression and exercise of power has become less and less visible over the last few centuries, its influence has become more difficult to discern . . . and to resist. Whereas the plaza—or *place* in French—brought displays of power to the public until the nineteenth century, today's *place*-lessness renders the exercise of power more elusive and thus insidious. It is everywhere and nowhere, assumed ubiquitous or, alternatively, assumed absent.

On the urban scale, this new ordering of power is manifest in a sort of centrifugal urbanism—a movement out of central cities. One example of such defensive, disciplinary, or escapist urbanism is the splintering of the Parisian university in the wake of the student uprisings of May 1968. The university was not only factioned into a number of smaller ones, but many of these were located outside of the central city and designed to incorporate little or no public space for spontaneous—or even planned—student gatherings. A concurrent French example is the building of five new cities in the outer suburbs of Paris, which both gentrify Paris and mollify the radical politics of the inner suburbs. A parallel example in the United States, though initiated by the private sector, is the massive movement of corporate headquarters from central cities to more controlled suburban "office parks" or "corporate campuses" (allowing management better control of labor) as well as the "edge cities" of which they form an integral part.

Disciplinary space is also encountered on a smaller scale in, for instance, atrium buildings, which could be regarded as evolved heirs to the Panopticon where the center is occupied by a void rather than a supervisor. One such example is New York University's Bobst Library (designed by Philip Johnson in 1972), in which the void discourages improper behavior, whether the stealing and abuse of books or physical assaults. The erstwhile supervisor is rendered superfluous as library users become their own guardians. This disciplinary strategy is less blatant than earlier ones, and so are the disciplinary agents. Is it the architect, the client (NYU), or library users who are exercising the control?

The exercise of power today, then, is disguised and difficult to identify because it is not localized, because its agents are rarely self-aware, because it is largely internalized, and because it therefore goes largely unnoticed. The elusive quality of power has made people feel like ever smaller and insignificant cogs in a giant machine whose workings are incomprehensible. As our sense of control over

Activities that once occurred in the public realm have been usurped by more private realms as leisure activities, entertainment, information centers, and consumer services are increasingly accessible from home via the television or computer.

our world has diminished, our fear of the unknown and unpredictable "other"— variously defined—has grown, leading to distrust, paranoia, and the proliferation of racism, hate crimes, neo-Nazism, and other xenophobias. As Alberto Moravia has pointed out, we have become terrorists as well as terrorized.[79] In the end, a growing perception of greater equality among people both nationwide and worldwide—plied largely by the various mass media—accompanies and legitimizes growing inequalities.

Consequently, rather than nip the sources of fear in the bud, the more common reflex has been avoidance and self-protection. Activities that once occurred in the public realm have been usurped by more private realms as leisure activities, entertainment, information centers, and consumer services are increasingly accessible from home via the television or computer, or, if one leaves home, in the strictly controlled uni-functional settings of the shopping mall, theme park, or variants thereof. The contemporary built environment contains increasingly less meaningful public space, and existing public space is increasingly controlled by various forms of surveillance and increasingly invested with private meanings.

The other kind of escapism—that into fantasy worlds—is most obvious perhaps in the rapidly expanded possibilities for networking on line and its potential for identity creation. This is exemplified by the "cyberdelic counterculture," for whom the computer is specifically regarded as a means for escaping from the humdrum of everyday life.[80] The ability to "reside" in virtual space and multi-user dungeons (MUDs) allows for multiple (virtual) identities. Such experimentation with other identities, worlds, and ecosystems can potentially assist the search for solutions to contemporary problems (through, for instance, software programs such as SIM-City and SIM-Earth), but it can also contribute to blurring the real and the virtual, a fragmentation of the personality, and an overabundance of options that ultimately discourage engagement with the real world.[81]

This kind of space is also apparent in the more passive relationship with the television screen, which Americans watch an average of six hours per day. While the amount of time people spend watching TV has grown, program content ironically has become increasingly "reality-based," with situation dramas, news magazines, and talk shows that portray something approximating the "Real World," which happens to be the title of a popular cable program that ostensibly records everyday lives without scripting. Movie studios have been capitalizing on our obsession with insecurity by producing such films as *Primal Fear* (Paramount Pictures), which, at the time of this writing, is number one at the box office, and *Fear* (Universal Pictures). Booksellers, meanwhile, report that consumers are in "pursuit of safety" in their selection of reading material. As a result, "celebrity-driven" books—which are written by people who are already known or which have a TV or movie tie-in—are by far leading the sales pack. In the June 1996 *Publishers Weekly*, for instance, the best-selling nonfiction book was by basketball star Dennis Rodman, and four books based on the TV hit "The X-Files" were selling briskly.[82] "Formula-driven" books, whether suspense, horror, adventure, romance, or self-help, are also key to satisfying consumers' pursuit of safety.

With our hold on reality and our sense of community increasingly tenuous, it seems that we devote our more traditional moments of escapism (reading, watching TV and movies) to living out our fears in the safety of home or cinema, to seeking answers, or to generating a sense of community—a group of significant others—who may be fictional characters or people we will never meet. Our sense of adventure unabated, but frustrated by our fear of engaging in the real world, we turn to the screen (both interactive and passive) to learn about how other people in other places contend with the vicissitudes of life.

The escapist reflex results in two opposing tacks of self-presentation, that of display and that of concealment. In clothing fashion, the desire to conceal oneself is evident in the vogue for baggy clothing that not only conceals one's body, but, potentially, one's sex, ethnicity, and social class. In contrast, the body-hugging, skin-baring styles allowed by synthetic fabrics such as lycra display one's strength and prowess for combating the *Blade Runner* world out there. The popularity of body modification—through body building, plastic surgery, piercing, and tattooing—enhances this image while blurring the distinction between what is natural and what is created, between human and machine. This fascination with cyborgs could be construed as a means of contending with the fear of increasingly intelligent and influential machines. Meanwhile, the popularity of the four-wheel-drive road warrior vehicle, especially in cities, expresses both the desire to conceal oneself and to display one's strength and power. This is epitomized by the Hollywood vogue for the HUMVEE (human military vehicle), which was recently released in a civilian edition called the Hummer, available for $45,000–$75,000. Arnold Swhwarzenegger purchased the very first one. While the Hummer may be "the ultimate in body armor,"[83] the safety value of all cars today is a major selling point and covers a wide range of options from alarms to car phones, built-in car seats for children, and unbreakable glass.[84]

Like clothing and cars, homes also aspire to conceal and display. Sometimes a single feature, such as an elaborately appointed gateway that conceals what is inside while displaying the residents' ability to do so, accomplishes both. Other means for displaying strength and prowess include signage warning trespassers not to enter and/or indicating "armed response" to intruders, turnstiles in housing projects, and ostentatious facades and front yards. Means for concealing include squatting in abandoned buildings, building shantytowns from discarded materials on abandoned lots, and, of course, constructing fences and barriers of all kinds. For the poor, such strategies can be resourceful and creative means for improving lives. For the rich, they may represent "stealth wealth," a desire to hide one's possessions during a time when the gap between rich and poor continues to grow.

Joining home decorating's fascination with the past has been a fascination with other cultures, or the exotic. This appropriation of other times and places in one's own home staves off the boredom of sameness through adventure in the unknown while, at the same time, taming this strangeness through artful placement and unique usage of artifacts. More cynically, it provides by association a showplace for displaying one's travel experience, discriminating eye, and power of purchase.

Outside the home, the escapist reflex is apparent in the growth of leisure and recreational industries and in the increased building of megastructures such as theme parks, stadiums, and convention centers. It is also apparent in the centrifugal urbanism described above: the continuing residential suburbanization (despite gentrification) as well as the movement of company headquarters away from central cities and efforts to recreate a sense of urbanity within them. In the late 1970s, for instance, Kevin Roche designed the General Foods Headquarters in Rye, New York to include "office neighborhoods" and a "Main Street" with newsstands and a restaurant. In the arguably non-urban city of Los Angeles, a number of recent office complexes, such as the one designed by Frank Israel for Propaganda Films, aspire to bring the city into the workplace instead of vice versa.[85] The apotheosis of escapist urbanism is found in the proliferation of "edge cities" during the 1980s, abnegations of the central city and the unique quality of life it promised.

Among architects, the escapist tendency has been manifest since the 1970s in the preoccupation with facadism and photogenic design as well as in a design attitude that abnegates social responsibility. Alexander Tzonis and Liane Lefaivre have described this tendency as "narcissistic," suggesting "an act of regression due to acute frustration"[86] with the prevalent urban design approaches of the 1960s. This narcissistic turn, they contend, reacts to the naive attitudes of scientism and populism and disregards or denies context entirely. Instead it is preoccupied with the purely visual features of architecture (formalism), the fascination with the evocative power of drawings and models ("graphism"), the tendency to view design solely as an object of gratification (hedonism), the conviction that the architect is the supreme judge of the quality of the built environment (elitism), and the rejection of the functionalist aesthetic as well as the very idea of function itself (antifunctionalism).[87] This tendency led Ada Louise Huxtable to exclaim,

> The most fundamental change in architecture today is one of attitude. Scratch a postmodernist and you will find an apostle of architecture for art's sake, something that would have had any respectable and responsible architect drummed out of the profession not too long ago.... With the renunciation of traditional social responsibilities as beyond his capacities or control, the architect has finally been freed to pursue style exclusively and openly...without apology or disguise.[88]

An outcome of this tendency has been the production of "hyperreal" environments comprised of "simulacra." Jean Baudrillard applied the term "simulacra" to describe

> the generation by models of a real without origin or reality, a hyperreal. The territory no longer precedes the map, nor survives it. Henceforth, it is the map that precedes the territory—PRECESSION OF SIMULACRA—it is the map that engenders the territory.[89]

Simulation, as distinct from resemblance, has no original or referent, for the model replaces the real "as exemplified in such phenomena as the ideal home in women's or lifestyle magazines, ideal sex as portrayed in sex manuals or relationship books, ideal fashion as exemplified in ads or fashion shows,"[90] and so on. With hyperreality, the simulations come to constitute reality, leading to what Baudrillard has called "the death of the subject." When something is produced artificially such as a simulated environment (Disneyland being the prototype), it does not come to be regarded as "unreal, or surreal, but realer-than-real, a real retouched and refurbished."[91]

A hyperreality does not even have any pretense to accurately recall a particular past or place, but to produce an environment that transcends its sources of inspiration. As Umberto Eco explains, hyperreal environments must be absolutely fake in order to be better than anything real.[92] David Harvey has observed that in theme parks "it is now possible to experience the world's geography vicarious-ly, as a simulacrum," in a way that conceals "almost perfectly any trace of origin, of the labor processes that produced them, or of the social relations implicated in their production."[93] In a contemporary—and somehow unnerving—twist, these simulacra have become reality, particularly via mass media and theme parks, since many more people visit the simulacra of Africa and China presented in Disney World than actually visit these foreign lands, and for them the simulacra are Africa and China more than the far-off places themselves. Daniel Solomon has astutely observed, "If history were the victim of the first generation of post-war development, reality was the victim of the second."[94]

Much of our postmodern landscape, then, can be considered "hyperreal," particularly master-planned communities, shopping malls, theme parks, and entertainment palaces. Some of these are commendable for the quality of life they offer, the quality of their architecture and urbanism, their level of showmanship, and the opportunities they provide for relaxation and good times. But the exis-tence of such hyperreal environments side by side with places of desperation and people who are unable to share in the hyperreal benefits certainly engenders shame, resentment, and fear in the haves and have-nots alike. To the extent that these fantasy worlds disguise real problems and thereby diminish the potential for resolving them, they contribute to exacerbating them.[95] In addition, the "search for a fantasy world, the illusory 'high' that takes us beyond current realities into pure imagination"[96] can distract architects and urban designers from the actual program. This is apparent in some buildings by "starchitects" and their epigones, works that blatantly ignore client requests, including budget constraints, and ele-vate fiction, finesse, and fantasy above function.

The deconstructivist trend in architecture, so critical of the escapist tenden-cy of postmodern urban design, has attempted to express the messiness of the contemporary world. But deconstructivism's lack of a social agenda, its extreme cynicism, as well as its consequent coziness with elite benefactors have conspired to produce the ultimate architecture of fear, places that are not assuring, con-ducive to contemplation, or nurturant. It is not surprising that despite the media attention devoted to deconstructivism, its actual impact on the landscape and the urban design profession is negligible. Rather, it seems more of a passing fancy of some designers dissatisfied with the bulk of what is being produced and seeking alternatives, commissions, and notoriety.

A final response to postmodern insecurity has been a spiritual one. With the faltering of faith in the modern project, there has been a (re)turn to spiritu-ality and mysticism throughout the Western world. In the tradition of earlier thinkers such as Immanuel Kant and Friedrich Nietzsche, a number of recent observers of the human condition have called for a spiritual turn to mollify the harshness of the modern world. This tendency is found across the spectrum from writers as diverse as Roland Barthes, Jacques Derrida, Jacques Lacan, Michel Foucault, Julia Kristeva, Charles Jencks, David Griffin, and Charlene Spretnak. Spretnak suggests turning to wisdom traditions such as those of the Buddha, Native Americans, Goddess spirituality, and the Semitic traditions, which can

> help us to nourish wonder and hence to appreciate difference, the unique subjectivity of every being and community, thereby subverting the flattening process of mass culture. Such awareness keeps hope alive. It protects consciousness from becoming so beaten down that it loses a grasp of what is worth fighting to defend.[97]

Griffin describes this spiritual turn as a move from disenchantment to "reenchantment."

Champions of the potential for new communications technologies, although they apply hyperrational means, often sound much like those with explicit spiritual messages.[98] Self-described "technopagans" actually do see the computer as a tool for connecting with some larger entity, perhaps to God.[99] With the replacement of a communications zeitgeist for a labor zeitgeist, Jurgen Habermas has observed, the post-Enlightenment secular utopian impulse, so prevalent in the eighteenth and nineteenth centuries, has virtually disappeared, appearing—when at all—in a religious guise.[100] Perhaps this return to a more mystical or religious utopian vision reflects a reconception of space whereby symbolic space or cyberspace is privileged over physical space, which has been largely neutralized.

Shelter or Storm?

Postmodern urban design trends have their counterparts in intellectual trends. Regionalist urban design recalls attempts to introduce multicultural themes into academic curricula. The nostalgia among urban designers bears interesting parallels to neoconservative crisis literature and the "cultural literacy" campaign, which bemoan the decline of order in contemporary society and invoke a return to an idealized past, morality, or canon. And the escapist and privatistic reflexes may be detected in poststructuralism's assertion that there is nothing but cultural construction in human experience (for example, Derrida's "there is nothing outside the text"), in its understanding of things we share like language and culture as "prison houses" from which we must escape, and its valorization of autonomy and control.

In contrast to these largely insular academic debates, however, the debate surrounding urban design affects the shape of our environment and is tested by

The nostalgia among urban designers bears interesting parallels to neoconservative crisis literature and the "cultural literacy" campaign, which bemoan the decline of order in contemporary society and invoke a return to an idealized past, morality, or canon.

those who live in it. Do these urban design efforts achieve their goals, particularly that of diminishing danger and providing a sense of security? Or does the concerted effort to plan for spontaneity, to invent traditions, and to design for diversion and escape subvert this intent? The answer is not clear-cut.

Certainly, the popularity of neotraditionalist and regionalist urban design and of "themed" environments bespeaks a certain satisfaction with them. But the concerted effort among urban designers to respect differences and to design with regard to historical and regional contexts can itself become a style. This defeats its very purposes of being anti-universalistic, preserving "distinction," and celebrating pluralism. And even when a certain past or place is effectively recreated, will the colonial North American past or the preindustrial European village provide inhabitants who have different cultural traditions with a sense of roots and security? In addition, the pretense of designing preindustrial spaces for a postindustrial society denies important changes that have taken place and does not always correspond to contemporary needs and tastes.

Strategies such as gating, policing and other surveillance systems, and defensive urbanism do provide certain people with a limited sense of security. But such settings do not, according to recent studies, always diminish actual danger. And they also contribute to accentuating a more general sense of fear by increasing paranoia and distrust.

The escapist nature of all these undertakings—behind gates, into the past, other places, or fantasy worlds—may emit signals that the present is too unsavory and must be actively suppressed. For urban designers, this escapism may also reveal a refusal to acknowledge their own changing role in society and their desire to return to a time when they were less in the thrall of the state and private developers. Ultimately, however, this attitude may render urban designers accomplices to the banes of capitalist urban development and contribute to exacerbate their own weakened position as well as the problems of the built environment that they are trying to remedy.

Reconstructive Approaches to Urban Design

Within this climate of fear and urban design that amplifies or succumbs to it, there are indicators of what a non-defensive—or offensive, living, proactive, or reconstructive—urbanism might be. This is reflected primarily in the growing attention towards protecting the environment, expressed in terms of "growth management" or "sustainable design." Such design intervenes so as not to deplete natural resources or impose hardship upon people, and so as to enhance both the physical and social landscapes. Urban designers sensitive to the fragmentation of the built environment increasingly have been attempting to "mend seams" among the various urban design professions and between these and their constituents. This has resulted in new forms of collaboration producing novel results, as in the efforts by Andres Duany and Elizabeth Plater-Zyberk, Peter Calthorpe, and William Morrish and Catherine Brown to effect changes in policy as well as public opinion regarding the potential value of urban design.

Likewise, a number of urban design initiatives have been engaged in mending seams—or healing the scars—of modern interventions, such as railroads and highways built with little consideration for the surrounding communities and natural landscapes. This work involves reusing abandoned transit corridors, designing new ones, and redesigning existing urban and suburban fabrics, sometimes in collaboration with local communities. While these efforts share the neo-traditionalist emphasis on enhancing the public realm, they are not necessarily intent upon emulating past townscapes, but consider instead contemporary lifestyles and aspire to retain the valuable elements of modern urbanism and architecture. Rather than direct their focus on the traditional center, they are more often concerned with the edges between the city, suburb, and countryside, between neighborhoods, between functional uses, and between the more metaphorical edges of disciplines, professions, and local communities.[101] In some instances, these initiatives aspire to eliminate the traditional center in an effort to do away with the social inequalities it supports.

Conclusion

Contemporary insecurity has elicited a reassertion of cultural diversity, a nostalgia for an idealized past, an infatuation with mass imagery, a flight into fantasy worlds, a marked privatism, and a spiritual turn. In urban design, these tendencies are primarily manifest as historicisms, regionalisms, and allusions to mass culture. With the exception perhaps of the spiritual turn, the seen-it-all done-it-all sophistication of these responses has engendered a blasé attitude and a studied ironic response. In its extreme, this attitude has led to a disengagement, a retreat from asking questions and from acting. Although touted by some as the only responsible course given the circumstances of the contemporary world, this tendency also recalls the saying of the ancient Chinese philosopher Wang Yang-Ming, "To know and not to act is ultimately not to know."

Modern architecture and urban planning sought to assuage the fear generated by industrialization by rationally resolving current and future problems of "disorder" in the physical landscape. But instead of applying the industrial mode of production and machine imagery toward producing universal solutions for housing a more egalitarian society, the landscapes produced by modernism became, in the words of Liane Lefaivre, "synonymous with inhumanity, desolation, and devastation."[102] Modern architectural theory suffered from a confusion of terms that succeeded in preserving the architectural profession at the cost of exacerbating the crisis to which it was trying to respond. By deifying the machine while trying to transcend the fashion cycle and by paying lip service to a social and political agenda while insisting on the architect's role as an artist who acts independently, the modern movement succeeded only in offering a Band-Aid solution to the ills plaguing the modern city and the architectural profession rather than a cure. The profession of urban planning, meanwhile, diverged from its initial agenda to become primarily curative rather than preventive or formative. It was largely relegated to a rearguard position with a social agenda as only an impossible ideal or an "imperialistic" and undesirable end.

Consequently, those few who still carry the "modern" torch, who are forward looking and interested in designing for a "new" society, tend to be denigrated, especially in the United States. Proposals for buildings without ornament or for towers in a park rather than preindustrial-looking townscapes are often condemned as fascistic. And even where an idealistic desire to make a better world persists, the ability to do so is diminished because of the thoroughly transnational nature of power. Postmodern urbanism has sought to improve upon the shortcomings of modernism and to respond to the peculiar nature of fear that it attended and in part caused. But postmodernism has failed to retain the merits of modernism and has fallen into many of its same traps.

The misdirection of both modern and postmodern urban design can be traced to the early part of this century when architects contended with industrialization and when urban planning emerged as a profession. As the industrialization and bureaucratization of the building process threatened the architecture profession with extinction, it resorted to elitism. Rather than redefine its creative task to adapt to a changing political economy, it presumed environmental determinism in an effort to distinguish and thereby preserve itself. The lack of collaboration between architects, planners, and social scientists—as well as ineffectual efforts to collaborate—derives in large part from similar atavistic desires to maintain one's turf. The urban planning profession and the social sciences, both of which were sparked by the mounting problems engendered by industrial capitalism, diverged as planners focused on the modern city (the container) and social scientists focused on modern life (the contents). And the architectural profession largely divested itself of its traditional concerns with city building and with social concerns. The resultant division between thought about the container and thought about its contents facilitated the growth of the modern industrial city in a fashion that has suited the patrons of building more than the majority.

In the process, fear—along with the efforts to cope with it by referring to an idealized past, an exoticized other, a fantasy world, group cohesion, or oneself—has intensified. Amidst the less satisfactory urban design repercussions of this—especially the privatization and theme-park-ing of cities—some promising efforts have arisen to create living places as opposed to defensive generic spaces. If we are to effectively target the sources of dissatisfaction with the places in which we live, propose solutions, and implement them, we must learn from these efforts and initiate others that combine a respect for the past with a concern for the future and a reflexivity with a turning outward.

Building Paranoia

Steven Flusty

Twenty years ago, I was given a premonition of what Los Angeles would be like in the 1990s. My grandparents visited our house, in what was then the far western suburbs of Los Angeles, after returning from a cruise to Rio De Janeiro, Brazil. The stories they told me would have seemed unbelievably dystopian were it not for the fact that I then believed that grandparents do not lie. They spoke of how the houses of the rich Brazilians were surrounded by high walls topped with broken glass. The concierges of apartment buildings carried automatic weapons. The city's outskirts were packed with cardboard and corrugated metal shanties. Children in ragged clothes slept on the sidewalks and ate out of garbage cans in alleys.

My parents still live in that same suburban house, purchased twenty-eight years ago. For eighteen of those years, the house remained much the same. I would pass through a front yard open to the street, unlock and rotate the doorknob, and walk in. Over the past decade, however, the simple act of entering the residence has grown dauntingly complex. Next to the door is a small metal plate with an illuminated red L.E.D., warning of the presence of an activated alarm. Upon disengaging the dead bolt and opening the front door, I have thirty seconds in which to deactivate the alarm by entering a sequence of digits into a small keypad in the entry hall. Should I forget the number, or should the hall be too dark to work the keypad within the prescribed time, a shrieking siren wakes the neighborhood. Next, the dead bolt must be reengaged and a separate switch, located elsewhere in the house, must be tripped to deactivate pressure pads strewn beneath the floor and contacts embedded into the interior doorways. At that point the house's interior becomes safe for passage and the alarm may be safely reactivated as a perimeter defense. At any time, the alarm may be intentionally activated by hitting "panic buttons" sprinkled throughout the house at strategic locations. The exterior of the house, once illuminated only by a porch light, now basks in the glare of multiple 150-watt security lights in the back and side yards, switched on from dusk to dawn by photoelectric sensors.

My parents' house is one of the neighborhood's less obtrusively secured. Many feature lawn signs cautioning passersby of armed response. Some include security lights controlled by motion detectors set to blind anything that moves on the adjacent sidewalk and street. A few have installed spike-topped perimeter fences with remote-controlled, chain-driven gates to allow automobile access without having to exit the vehicle. Patrol cars carrying private security officers pass through the street late at night, watching over only those homes whose owners pay an additional service fee.

This neighborhood transformation did not occur all at once. It was a long, incremental process that only after some ten years has become obvious. A few residences took action in response to specific incidences. Most, however, have reacted to a pervasive sense of insecurity. It is an insecurity at odds with the neighborhood watch maps showing this portion of Police Reporting District 1091 largely free of the *X*'s and *R*'s marking sites of residential and street burglaries.

Meanwhile, three blocks away, people in ragged clothes sleep in the bushes by the side of the freeway and eat from garbage cans behind the supermarket.

"Blockhomes," my term for secured residents like my parents', are one component in the ongoing remaking of L.A.'s landscape as an intrusively nervous place. As we safari through this landscape of elite communities over the next few pages, I will point out a number of these components and try to come to some conclusions about how they add up. Despite the fact that we will be wandering around Los Angeles, the things we will observe could be in Sao Paulo, Manila, indeed any of the long-established colonial cities or newly emerging world cities. Specifically, we will be hunting down interdictory spaces—spaces designed to intercept and repel or filter would-be users. To date, I have found it convenient to distinguish five species:

Stealthy space—space that cannot be found, is camouflaged or, more commonly, is obscured by such view impediments as intervening objects or grade changes (for example, the Poets' Walk Garden of Citicorp Plaza at Seventh and Figueroa streets, concealed behind an office tower, a department store entrance kiosk, and a flight of escalators).

Slippery space—space that cannot be reached, due to contorted, protracted, or missing paths of approach. Such a strategy is costly, as it may require obfuscating numerous routes of access extending well beyond any single site. Justifying this expense, slippery space provides public-relations benefits in that it may be blamed on preexisting topographical constraints as a means of defraying criticism (for example, California Plaza's Watercourt at 2nd–4th streets and Grand Avenue, looming over Olive Street with no readily apparent means of access from the streets below).

Crusty space—space that cannot be accessed, due to obstructions such as walls, gates, and checkpoints (for example, the Los Angeles County Museum of Art's grounds and sculpture garden at Hancock Park, once open to one another and the surrounding greenswards but now encircled within a series of high wrought-iron and chain-link fences).

Prickly space—space that cannot be comfortably occupied, defended by such details as wall-mounted sprinkler heads activated to clear loiterers or ledges sloped to inhibit sitting (for example, the 380-square-foot park wedged into a southwest-facing pocket between the sidewalk and the Ronald Reagan State Office Building at Third and Spring streets, boasting sparse shade, a highly reflective pavement, and backless benches with seating heights at a leg-numbing twenty-four inches).

Jittery space—space that cannot be utilized unobserved due to active monitoring by roving patrols and/or remote technologies feeding to security stations (for example, the Biddy Mason Pocket Park in the Broadway-Spring Center, a secured through-block connection featuring guarded rest rooms and seventeen video cameras monitoring the park's sitting areas and public sidewalks abutting the park entrances).

In the field, of course, we are unlikely to spot these spaces in isolation. Rather, they tend to be deployed simultaneously, so as to form distinctly unfriendly mutant building typologies. The "blockhome," for instance, is often embedded in an extended jittery perimeter of alarms, video observation cameras, and security lighting. Fast becoming the Angeleno residence of choice, blockhomes are most apparent in gentrifying areas, where new wealthier residents feel threatened by the established poorer community. Venice Beach is dotted with blockhomes forced into compact bunker and tower forms by the expense of beach-adjacent property. The high-style architectural tastes of the area's new residents have resulted in oddly angled concrete walls, Cor-Ten steel gates, and tall, tilted courtyard enclosures collaged of stucco and frosted glass. Witty references to the preexisting community, such as a miniature white picket fence set before a windowless corrugated metal studio/house (as in Dennis Hopper's house) and a home stealthily retrofitted into the unrestored shell of an existing dilapidated house (complete with an address number spray-painted like graffiti across the housefront), abound.

This trend is not confined to locations in flux. In established and affluent foothill neighborhoods like Royal Oak, neighborhood homes sprout such features as crenellated walls and fences comprised of unscalable vertical piping. Some homes include exterior video cameras to communicate the identities of visitors prior to admission through remotely controlled driveway gates. Others employ prickly plantings in "security-oriented gardens" beneath windows and surrounding the property. In areas such as this, the entire neighborhood may be rendered slippery and jittery.

Just five blocks west of my parents' house, Calabasas is an affluent residential community priding itself on its "old west" charm. Most of publicly accessible Calabasas, though, is not somewhere to linger in but to pass through, as the streets are a pointedly inhospitable place to sojourn. Throughout the past decade, these hills have been covered with over 800 homes contained within four walled and gated residential complexes, or "luxury laagers." The public roads of Calabasas Park are confined within a continuous lining of cinder-block walls punctuated only by occasional guardhouses and remotely activated gates. As the luxury laagers face private internal streets, little effort has been made to landscape the public rights-of-way, leaving the spaces between the laagers very prickly—unshaded, hot, and forbiddingly barren. We would see the same thing in all the new hillside developments ringing the L.A. Basin.

These developments sell exclusion. Advertisements tout security features with the Dragnetian brevity of "gated with twenty-four-hour drive-by security" (an entirely novel use of the ominous "drive-by" moniker) or florid prose like, "as you drive through the wrought-iron gates, past the uniformed guard, and over the rushing stream, you will be transfixed by…" There is also novelty, like one moated development's "deep twenty-five-acre lake provides total security for the owners of the spacious high-rise condominium homes."

Jittery beneath a crusty shell, sealed luxury laagers with checkpoint entries and private internal security patrols may now be found throughout the L.A. area and beyond. This proliferation has led to an explosion of typological permutations providing high-security residential units in a wide range of prices. High-density multiple-building apartment complexes are refitted with metal fencing stretched between the structures to block access to internal streets. Medium-density stealthy suburban town houses are set atop tall berms landscaped so heavily that you would never know there were houses up there. Back in Calabasas, low-density clusters of exurban mansions are accessed by passing through sentried forecourts augmented by video cameras to record visitors' license plates.

One thing we have probably noticed since our walk began is the eerie absence of people, like in one of those "Twilight Zone" episodes where some poor rube wanders around a depopulated theme park. We could try to find ourselves some locals to hang out with. Unfortunately, we are not likely to find any in the very few open spaces we have passed. Public open space has come under assault as privatization has reacted opportunistically to public sector penury. The Propo-

Strong point of sale
Eastern Hollywood, California

Luxury laager
Calabasas, California

Crusty space
Labrea Tarpits and L.A. County Museum of Art
at Hancock Park, California

Dennis Hopper House
Venice, California
Brian Murphy, architect

sition 13 property tax "revolt," declines in sales tax due to consumers' loss of purchasing power, the late 1980s collapse of the local real-estate market, and reduced federal assistance have created a state budget deficit of $11 billion, reflected in Los Angeles as a budgetary shortfall of $500 million. As a result, legislators have called for the discontinuation of fiscally burdensome functions of public space and the transfer of potentially profitable functions to the private sector. Such public facilities as parks and libraries have been debilitated by shrinking tax revenues and declining income from user fees, first losing programs, then maintenance, and finally closing entirely.

Traditional public spaces are increasingly supplanted by privately produced (although often publicly subsidized), privately owned and administered spaces for public aggregation,[1] that is, spaces of consumption or, most commonly, malls. In these new, "post-public" spaces, access is predicated upon ability to pay. People without purchasing power, goods that cannot be mass marketed, more-than-passive activities, and ideas narrowly perceived as inimical to the owner's sensibilities (and profit margin) are unaccommodated or ejected by private security as

Traditional public spaces are increasingly supplanted by privately produced (although often publicly subsidized), privately owned and administered spaces for public aggregation, most commonly malls.

quickly as they are manifested. Exclusivity rules here, ensuring the high levels of control necessary to prevent irregularity, unpredictability, and inefficiency from interfering with the orderly flow of commerce.

The first thing we notice is a new running fence enclosing the mall parking lot, limiting points of access. Spaces of consumption cannot seal themselves off completely, as they are dependent upon customer access for sustenance. Even so, they have imposed tight controls over use, becoming "strong points of sale." The smallest strip mall is a tightly nested series of crusty, jittery, and prickly spaces. The fenced parking lot itself is watched over by armed security guards. Pay phones have been removed to discourage vagrants, and some convenience stores have installed exterior speakers blaring Muzak to drive away adolescent head-bangers. Fast food outlets, equipped with video cameras at pay stations and drive-through windows, feature outdoor eating/playground areas surrounded by outward curving steel bars. Loading docks large enough to enclose delivery vehicles whole are accessed through steel doors set into concrete parapets and watched over by guard towers.

The interior promenades of some larger malls are unremittingly jittery, remotely monitored by both private security and police in on-site substations. One mall substation in Baldwin Hills serves as a base for 200 police officers; another bay immediately across the promenade houses a municipal courthouse. These substations have become central institutions in affluent suburban malls, where the role of shopping as community social focus has provided a site for police contact with the general public. Here, the substations serve as the public hub for community policing and neighborhood watch operations.

Since the 1992 L.A. uprising, this "make-my-day" shopping has undergone accelerated research and development paying special attention to thwarting looting and arson. Wood-frame structures, flammable and easily breached, have been replaced by single or double walls of concrete masonry. Roof lines have been raised to deflect fire bombs thrown from street level. Display windows have been filled in, or set into concrete bulwarks three feet above sidewalk level to prevent automobiles ramming through to the interior. Glass entries have been replaced with armor-plated roll-down doors, pre-graffitied to discourage taggers.

A few blocks east of the still-smoldering wreckage of L.A.'s multicultural mythos, we arrive at Bunker Hill. Bunker Hill was twenty blocks of disintegrating, Victorian, low-income housing until the early 1960s, when it was disconnected from the surrounding street grid, plugged into the freeway, and razed for redevelopment. Now Bunker Hill is the Central Business District, covered in high-rise "citidels" to give L.A. that *sine-qua-non* world city skyline. "Citidels" are the corporate control centers of the global econo-cultural web, the properties administered by management companies competing with one another to attract corporate tenants.

I would take us up Bunker Hill, but the hill's designers are not too keen on pedestrians coming up from down below (except as janitors), so we cannot get there from here. The entire hill is slippery, separated from the adjacent city by an obstacle course of open freeway trenches, a palisade of concrete parking garages, and a tangle of concrete bridges linking citidel to citidel high above the streets. Every path we try confronts us with the blank undersides of vehicular overpasses, towering walls studded with giant garage exhausts, and seating cleverly shaped like narrow sideways tubes so as to be entirely unusable. We could attain the summit from the south, but only by climbing a narrow, heavily patrolled stair "plaza," studded with video cameras and clearly marked as private property. But ignoring the fact that, in the world beyond this text, we would probably find ourselves inadvertently walking onto a freeway offramp (I know I have), we will traverse the plaza on the hill.

The plaza reflects both a shared consciousness between developers and public institutions of the value of user-friendly urban designs and a differing conception of to whom those benefits should accrue. By providing spaces where "office workers will find outdoor areas for noontime relaxation,"[2] attractive site amenities are seen as integral to this competition. Municipal agencies, meanwhile, see plazas as developer-funded additions to the city's open space inventory. Thus attempts are made to extract plazas from private developers in exchange for subsidies provided through below-market-rate land sales or leases, tax abatements, and density bonuses. In negotiations with developers, municipal agencies have been successful in linking public subsidies to the provision of habitable open spaces, in no small part because such spaces enhance the value of the project to the developers. Municipal agencies have not, however, been terribly concerned with assuring right of public access to these spaces. Thus, public subsidies have often been expended to create plazas accessible only at the discretion of private owners; plazas sit stealthy behind hedgerows and grade changes, jittery with blue-blazered private security. Most have small bronze plaques at the property line reading, "Private property. Right to pass by permission, and subject to control, of owners. Sec. 1008 civil code." Inside the plazas we would find malls uniformly equipped with eateries, express mail posts, dry cleaners, and gift shops to relieve office workers of the need to leave the premises. The malls are lushly planted and ornamented with water features. They are graced with high-art plaza-turds signed by some of the best plop-artists. And, once again, they are nearly inaccessible to us.

As we have wandered the streets intent on our destinations, there are some interesting bits that have escaped our notice. I would like to call our attention to a couple of these, starting with the omnipresent whir of helicopter rotors. Across the city, police helicopters maintain a continuous vigil overhead with the aid of gigantic block numeral coordinates painted atop buildings and busses. One helicopter keeps watch over each of the city's three patrol areas at any given time. These helicopters, originally developed for military applications, can cross the L.A. Basin in eleven minutes at a speed of approximately 140 miles per hour. They are equipped with the Spectrolab Nightsun illumination system, producing 30 million peak beam candle power, and the Forward Looking Infra-Red (FLIR) sensing system, capable of detecting body heat at a distance of 1,000 feet, a lit match at 4,000 feet.

We also have not bothered to look closely at the lampposts, freeway signage, and transmission towers, despite the fact that they have been looking at us. Video cameras have become standard equipment at major intersections across the city. Set in bulletproof casings more than forty feet above street level, the cameras are equipped with remotely controlled pan, tilt, and zoom capabilities. They feed to a control center beneath City Hall. These cameras are part of the $300 million Automated Traffic Surveillance And Control (ATSAC) system undergoing installation citywide. ATSAC cameras are presently used to determine the specific cause of traffic delays indicated by in-pavement sensors. Police spokespersons and the mayor's office, however, have been careful not to deny an interest in using the cameras to keep watch over the streets, sidewalks, and adjacent properties. This is not surprising, given that the local police department increasingly shares the rest of the city's love affair with electronic media. Cameras, video recorders, and computer terminals are being installed in LAPD patrol vehicles, enabling mobile street-level surveillance and the instantaneous gathering and transmission of such intelligence as video still images. In essence, the entire region has become jittery space.

So how should we read these symptoms, visible to any peripatetic? Diagnoses require consideration not just of what has happened to us over the course of our excursion, but also of what has not. In all likelihood, we have not been run over or mugged. We have not been verbally abused by beggars, shot by gang members, or had our throats slit in our own driveways by some disgruntled ex-athlete. What we have experienced is ex-aerospace workers pan handling in front of pastel marble-clad office buildings, vendors of pirated cassettes and chili'd mangos on the sidewalks in front of overcrowded Spanish revival apartments, billboards and store signs plastered with Spanish, Hangul, or Amaric, and a handful of streets in very poor neighborhoods partially obstructed by unattended police barricades.

The statistics and their ramifications fill in the picture. The population of Los Angeles County increased by nineteen percent to about nine million in the last decade. This mushrooming population cannot sprawl anymore since the infrastructure is too overburdened, so estimated densities in some residential areas have reached those of Manhattan. Population growth has created demand rendering real estate prohibitively expensive for a majority of Angelenos, even in the current depressed market. Resulting land pressures have crowded higher-density development into neighborhoods of traditional, albeit less affordable, suburban homesteads previously isolated along quiet avenues. Development is swallowing up open land: portions of the mountains, beaches, and the few major public parks.

The impact of the increasing demand for limited real estate has been exacerbated by the loss of over half a million jobs since the 1990s began, due to the continued outmigration of industrial investment for more easily exploited locales and the post-cold-war decrease in subsidization of the area's warfare industry. This collapse of the labor market's demand exacerbates the impoverishing effects of more than a decade of upward income redistribution under "trickle down" economic policies, corporate capture of mobile capital, and the resultant expansion of low wage/low skill service work, temporary office or day labor, and the burgeoning informal economy.

The shrinkage of the labor market has increased already substantial differences in quality of life between the city's highly visible elite and expanding poor neighborhoods. It has deformed the geography of resource flows within the city to replicate the distributional inequities of the world economy in general. Thus, portions of L.A., like most world cities, have joined the global economy's exploited and neglected periphery despite being wholly contained within the city itself. Further, in the absence of affordable land and opportunities for significant economic advancement, the parks and streets of neighborhoods in L.A.'s internal periphery have become either the rent-free and accessible sites of informal sector market transactions in "illegally" vended commodities (narcotics and prostitution) or unauthorized temporary sites of homeless encampments.

Reflecting patterns of human displacement throughout the emerging world system, L.A.'s demographic globalization has been a fundamental aspect of its population increase. Los Angeles is the affluent world city most frequently and widely represented (and misrepresented) in electronic media, and the fastest growing on the American continent's West Coast since the 1980s. It has thus become the destination of choice for a disproportionate slice of the planet's estimated one billion immigrants, drawn from regions arrayed around the Pacific Rim and beyond.

There are more Iranians in L.A. than in any city outside of Tehran. Armenian is the first language in pockets of Los Feliz. An Ethiopian three-block stretch of Fairfax now seeks formal recognition as Little Addis. It is the geographical links to Latin America and Asia, however, that have most reconstituted the region's demographics. The "Latin" population is fast reestablishing its long lost majority, comprising 37.8% of the county population as of the 1990 census. It is said that the region boasts more Mexicans than any city outside Mexico City, more Salvadorians than any city but San Salvador. The Asian population has nearly doubled over the past decade to over 10% of the county population. There has emerged a Little Saigon spread across an area half the size of Ho Chi Minh City itself, and a roughly seventy-block swathe of Mid-Wilshire rechristened Koreatown in the map books. Each of these populations brings with it cultural conceptions of urban life differing from the rapidly outmigrating suburban Angeleno ideal.

Previously permitted to settle only in demographically homogeneous, less desirable locations, immigrant communities are more recently atomizing across the L.A. Basin. This dispersion has been facilitated by anti-discriminatory housing policies, by the affordability of clusters of commercial and residential structures depreciated by age, and by the evaporation of local employment bases. Further, many newcomers are of comparatively affluent merchant classes and bring with them assets permitting greater locational choice. An expanding constellation of Little Indias, although concentrated in Artesia, includes outposts from Hollywood to the central San Fernando Valley, with a new Vishnite temple back in Calabasas. New Chinese immigrants have largely bypassed Chinatown; five of the region's incorporated cities are now majority Asian with a preponderance of Cantonese speakers.

Rising population in a limited area, concentrating wealth and poverty (what I like to call the "new world bipolar disorder"), and increasing cultural segmentation at regional and neighborhood levels are producing in Los Angeles, as in other world cities, a densely packed heterogeneous population manifesting dramatic juxtapositions of privation and opulence. This has served to erode the spatial and

Street gangs use spray paint while homeowners associations use neighborhood watch signs; either way we are talking informal militias.

ideological dominance of an aging, predominantly white "native" elite. The resultant drastic shift in the balance of cultural influence is complicated by the fact that no other group has yet emerged with a sufficient preponderance of members and/or resources to establish itself as the new majority. Lacking such a majority, no one group is empowered to determine new behavioral standards.

With the decay of previously established cultural standards, and the absence of widely accepted new ones, a wealth of differing ways of life has surfaced, each with its own rules governing spatial use and interpersonal contact. The result is a fluid urban matrix in which likely outcomes of encounters are unpredictable and territorial clues are misread or ignored, causing social friction as individuals and groups continuously encroach upon one another. In response to the uncertainties of a fragmented and dynamic urban milieu, social groups form into "defended neighborhoods" in order to segregate themselves from "danger, insult, and the impairment of status claims."[3] The defended neighborhood is characterized by a homogeneous social group exerting dominance within its boundaries in reaction to perceived threats of territorial violation by outsiders. Street gangs use spray paint while homeowners associations use neighborhood watch signs; either way we are talking informal militias.

In short, the security obsession now pervading our cities is fueled in large part by fears of complex social change and inequitable resource distribution. The concomitant Angeleno "war on crime" may be interpreted as a means of forcibly maintaining, reconstituting, or at least salvaging a challenged and possibly collapsing social consensus while simultaneously protecting the perquisites of that consensus's established beneficiaries. Segmentation of the socio-spatial realm is the critical means to this end.

The luxury laager may thus be seen as the territory of a social group possessing the considerable resources required to assert its spatial claims with walls and mercenaries. Luxury laagers are therefore not intended to exclude merely crime, but a wide range of behavior deviating from the community norms. This overriding concern with conformance to behavioral standards is demonstrated by the fact that residents are subject to covenants, conditions, and restrictions (CC&R's) forbidding such "low class" deviations as painting one's home a color objectionable to the architectural committee, working on one's vehicle outside of one's garage, using overstuffed or other indoor furniture on patios or front lawns, or putting one's garbage cans out early.

Similarly, the blockhome may be interpreted as an attempt by those unwilling to submit to the conformity of the laagers, but unable to afford large lots of their own, to substitute blank walls for wide lawns as a means of establishing a comfortable distance from outsiders. Walls need not even be high for the symbolic exertion of spatial dominance to the owner's satisfaction; many blockhomes' perimeter fences are five feet tall or less with blunt spikes, and interrupted by easily scaled support columns.

It is the unenviable task of the strong point of sale, if it is to survive, to draw prospective tenant merchants and customers into a setting that, by virtue of accessibility to a variety of social groups, precludes the ability of tenants or customers to enforce their own social norms. To resolve this contradiction, the strong point of sale acts to reassure visitors against the likelihood of unpredictable encounters by itself becoming the arbiter of behavioral standards even more conservative than those of the luxury laager.

Like luxury laagers, the plazas of citidels are configured more for the symbolic defense of status then for the physical protection of occupants. This status, however, is not held by individuals within, but must be attained through exhibition to such external constituencies as other businesses and the consuming and investing public at large. The plaza is regarded as a front yard reflecting upon the tenant corporation's aesthetic sensibility and management competence. Thus, management and tenants view a plaza's white-collar user mix adulterated by vagrants or a janitor's family on a picnic as a loss of prestige before the "business community," and a resulting loss of clientele.

Taking a broad perspective on these proliferating spaces of control, it becomes apparent that the sites in which daily life and face-to-face interaction take place—the streets, parks, bazaars, and plazas—are being sacrificed to redundant zones of oversight and proprietary control. This threatens the free exchange of ideas engendering a progressive society. It creates an impediment to the cross-cultural communication necessary to knit together diverse publics. It is a rejection of the individual's right to space in which to be.

In my opinion, what is most ominous about the places we have visited is this: one's permitted passage inside or willingness to step outside is determined by one's actual or apparent affluence. Thus, by employing space as the medium for securing status, we are building material barriers between individuals on the basis of wealth. As the world economic system constitutes a commercial society, access to wealth in the world city is largely a function of professional occupation. Thus, the physical segregation of the world city by criteria of affluence functions to divide society into rigid groups reflecting and reinforcing the local division of labor, while simultaneously impeding mobility and contact between these groups. Therefore, we are not merely witnessing the installation, component by component, of infrastructure restructuring the city into electronically linked islands of privilege embedded in an erratic police state matrix. We may also be observing a warning sign that, in the emerging world cities, class is solidifying into caste.

This essay is adapted from Building Paranoia: The Proliferation of Interdictory Space and the Erosion of Spatial Justice. *Los Angeles: Los Angeles Forum for Architecture and Urban Design, 1994.*

The Search for a Place in the World

Richard Sennett

The word "new" is one of the most abused in the English language. But we are today at the beginning of a truly new economic era. It has transformed both the work people do and the places where they live in ways that, a mere twenty years ago, would have seemed unimaginable. The great corporate bureaucracies and government hierarchies then appeared to be securely entrenched, the products of centuries of economic development and nation building. Commentators spoke of "late capitalism" or "mature capitalism," as though earlier forces of growth had now entered an end-game phase. Now a new chapter has opened; mammoth government and corporate bureaucracies are becoming both more flexible and less secure institutions. They employ new technologies to connect globally, while ridding themselves internally of layer upon layer of managers and skilled workers. The character of work has thereby shifted away from fixed functions or clear career paths towards more limited or shifting tasks. Work is ceasing to provide the worker with a stable identity.

Thanks to these economic changes, place has changed its meaning. The identity of places has weakened, becoming more hybrid in composition because of the impact of global labor migration. In this sense, the power of place has weakened, as the emerging economic network evades the controls of national or local geography. In an earlier generation, social policy was based on the belief that nations, and within nations cities, could control their own fortunes; now, a divide is opening between polity and economy.

These great changes in modern capitalism have had equally profound cultural consequences. For instance, it is already apparent that in the midst of material growth, many working people are experiencing a heightened sense of personal failure, believing themselves useless, peripheral, or over the hill at an early age. Fear of sudden vulnerability infects even those making their way in the new economy, reinforcing the sense that work is no secure framework for the self. If the new economic order erodes feelings of self-worth in the marketplace, it also erodes individual institutions that protected people against the market.

As a result, people are seeking compensation from the places in which they live: personal standing locally if not on the job and a sense of community cohesion and stability, which are absent in corporations that are continually repackaged and resold. This *pas de deux* between labor and place is, to be sure, neither certain in its movements nor necessarily beautiful to behold. Because places large and small are not self-determining, they may in fact be unable to provide the social compensations people seek. And if neighborhoods, cities, or nations become defensive refuges against a hostile world, they may provide symbols of self-worth and belonging through practices of exclusion and intolerance.

Yet out of these great economic transformation we are now experiencing, something better might grow. Work is a problematic frame for the self, since it tends to equate worldly success with personal worth. And failure is not necessarily a disastrous experience; people often learn their limits by failing at something, or come to pay attention to those whom they previously used merely as instruments of their own will. Of more civic consequence, troubled fortunes may lead people to see themselves as something other than economic animals, to put a certain distance between themselves and their natural circumstances.

This was Hannah Arendt's hope a generation ago, when she made, in *The Human Condition*, her famous distinction between labor and politics. She hoped that in urban life, with its large scale and impersonality, people could conduct a civic existence that did not merely reflect, or depend on, their personal fortunes. Today, the uncertainties of the new economy argue more than ever for a selfhood, as well as civic behavior, unchained from the conditions of labor. Yet the places in which this might occur can neither be cities of the classical kind, which Arendt admired, nor can they be defensive, inward-turning localities. We need a new kind of city life to cope with the new economy.

The age of high capitalism—which for convenience's sake can be said to span the two centuries following the publication of Adam Smith's *The Wealth of Nations* in 1776—was an era that lusted for sheer quantitative growth, but had no trouble dealing with growth's consequences. This involved, in part, a fear of risk. Few of Smith's contemporaries in London or elsewhere in Europe wished to cast on the uncharted seas of unregulated commerce; they wished the government to stand behind them, as it had in the past. Even in America, as Oscar and Mary Handlin showed in *Commonwealth*, a magisterial study of the evolution of the colonial American corporation, privatizing innovators wanted somehow to stop the free spin of the wheel of fortune. Yet economic growth created a different human problem for the servants of the new masters.

The structural complexity of the new economy impoverished the quality of everyday labor. Adam Smith argued that the division of labor promoted by free markets would make for a more complex society; society, he said, would become a honeycomb of tasks. Yet work experience became more routine in the process, condemning individual workers to a numbingly boring day spent repeating one small job.

In the nineteenth century, critics of high capitalism could see no easy way to end this trade-off between qualitative, experiential impoverishment and structural increase and complexity. In Karl Marx's view, no reform could divorce economic growth from the impoverishment of labor, save a revolution.

This paradox of experiential impoverishment and structural development is seen to have ended in the emerging political economy, but it has in fact become more acute. Modern technology promises to banish routine work to the innards of new machines, and does so. It could therefore be argued, from a strictly technological point of view, that the division of labor is coming to an end, and with it one human evil of the old order. In reality, however, the new technology frequently "de-skills" workers who now oversee, as the electronic janitors of robotic machines, complex tasks the workers once performed themselves. More brutally, the division of labor now separates those who get to work from those who do not; large numbers of people are set free of routine tasks only to find themselves useless or, at best, under-used, especially in the context of the global labor supply. Geography no longer simply separates the skilled First World from the unskilled Third World; for instance, computer code is written efficiently in Bombay for a third of the cost of that in IBM home offices.

The specter of uselessness now shadows the lives of educated middle-class people, compounding the older experiential problem of routine among less-favored workers; there are too many qualified engineers, programmers, and systems analysts, not to speak of too many lawyers, MBA's, and securities salesmen. The young suffer the pangs of uselessness in a particularly cruel way, since an ever-expanding educational system trains them ever more elaborately for jobs that do not exist.

Enthusiasts for the new economy are, as they say in California, "in denial" on this subject. In a popular classic about modern corporations, *Reengineering the Corporation*, the authors Michael Hammer and James Champy defend "reengineering" against the charge that it is a mere cover for firing people by asserting that "downsizing and restructuring only mean doing more with less."[1] The "less" in the last sentence reverberates with the denials of an older Social Darwinism: those who are not fit will somehow disappear.

The imagined corollary of uselessness is a dispensable self. Instead of the institutionally induced boredom of the assembly line, this experiential deficit appears to lie within the worker, who has not made him or herself of value to others, and so could simply disappear from view. And personally failing to be of value has, in turn, great social implications in a skill-based economy. What Michael Young feared in his prophetic essay, *Meritocracy*, has come to pass; as the economy needs ever fewer, highly educated people to run it, the "moral distance" between mass and elite widens. The masses, now comprising people in suits and ties as well as in overalls, appear peripheral to the elite productive core.

Some tough-minded economists argue that current forms of unemployment, under-employment, de-skilling, and welfare parasitism are incurable in the emerging order, since the economy indeed profits from doing "more with less." What I wish to emphasize is that the classical model of growth offers no solution to these human deficits, neither through providing more consumer goods nor through further division of labor. Put simply, the market does not nurture the dignity of the worker.

All epochs of economic change are destabilizing, and insecurity cuts deep into the fabric of civil society. Basic social bonds like trust, loyalty, and obligation require a long time to develop; you cannot instantly create loyalty the way you can form a new corporation—by fiat. And time equally shapes the sense that one's experience is more than a series of randomly arising, personally uncontrollable events.

In the previous capitalist era, people had to struggle hard, both personally and civically, for such security. The progress of nineteenth-century capitalism was anything but steady and linear, instead lurching from disaster to disaster in the stock markets and in irrational capital investment. A certain kind of character type—appearing in the pages of Balzac but also in the more mundane annals of finance—fed on these crises, thrived on disorder, and, most of all, possessed a capacity for disloyalty. For every responsible capitalist like Andrew Carnegie, there were hundreds of Jay Goulds, adept at walking away from their own disasters. Less powerful or more responsible beings could hardly flourish under these conditions.

Max Weber's famous image of modern life confirmed in an "iron cage" belittles stability as an achievement in the lives of ordinary people. For instance, the service ethic of steady, self-denying, life-long effort Weber evoked in *The Protestant Ethic and the Spirit of Capitalism* allowed his less-favored contemporaries to purchase a home, and home-ownership in the nineteenth century became one of the few bulwarks against the capitalist storm, as well as a source of personal and family honor.

Weber feared the rise at the beginning of the twentieth century of large national bureaucracies and corporations that made use of the service ethic, earning the loyalty of those whom they made secure; he doubted that loyal servants would make objectively minded citizens. Yet petty bureaucrats, time-servers, and the like derived a sense of status and public honor from their stations in bureaucracies. T. H. Marshall, the intellectual father of the modern British welfare state, understood this well; however static big institutions may be, they provide their members with a scaffolding of mutual loyalty and of trust that events can be controlled, which are prerequisites of citizenship.

The current rush to take apart this institutional architecture is undoing the civic dimensions of durable time. Take loyalty. In the emerging economy, as economic institutions increasingly replace permanent workers whenever possible with temporary workers, and as people increasingly do shifting, task-central jobs rather than pursue stable careers guaranteed by bureaucracies, loyalties to institutions diminish. Loyalty requires that personal experience accumulates in an institution, and the emerging political economy will not let it accumulate. Indeed, the profitable ease with which international capital today assembles, sells, and reassembles corporations erases the durability of institutions to which one could develop loyalty or obligations.

Of course, it is always wrong to imagine that the past can be simply wiped away, even by such a chameleon economy. What has been carried into the present are a set of subjective values, values for making personal time coherent and durable, and these intersect with the new economy of work in particularly disturbing ways.

The Victorians founded their sense of self-worth on life organized as one long project; the German values of formation and the English virtues of purpose were for keeps. Careers in business, military, or imperial bureaucracies made the life-long project possible, grading work into a clear sequence of steps. Such expectations devalue the present that is in constant upheaval and that may tempt an individual into byways or evanescent pleasures. Weber thus described future-orientation as a mentality of delayed gratification, but Lionel Trilling saw this Victorian ordering of time more largely as a question of will, strength of will that can eventually make order out of present chaos.

Yet this is only half of the experience of a life project. It leaves out the subjective past and emphasizes success rather than failure. In *Thus Spake Zarathustra*, Friedrich Nietzsche wrote, "Powerless against what has been done, he is an angry spectator of all that is past. The will cannot will backwards."[2] But Nietzsche's contemporaries did bend the will backwards in time.

The Victorians bent consciousness backwards to compose out of the dislocations accidental changes of direction or unused capacities of a life record for which one had to take personal responsibility, even though these events might have been beyond the actual control of the person who experienced them. Sigmund Freud remarked that such feelings of responsibility are modern sentiments, in

> The destruction of institutional supports, at work as in the welfare state, leaves individuals only their sense of responsibility; the Victorian ethos now often charts a negative trajectory of defeated will.

contrast to those of earlier ages in which people felt their life histories to be in the hands of the gods, God, or blind fortune.

Today, these late-Victorian values of personal responsibility are as strong as they were a century ago, but their institutional context has changed. The iron cage has been dismantled so that individuals struggle for security in a seemingly empty arena. The destruction of institutional supports, at work as in the welfare state, leaves individuals only their sense of responsibility; the Victorian ethos now often charts a negative trajectory of defeated will, of having failed to make one's life cohere through one's work.

Twenty-five years ago, for the book *The Hidden Injuries of Class*, I interviewed workers in Boston who, like Nietzsche's "angry spectators," knew that work was beyond their control, yet took responsibility for what happened to them. In that generation, a catastrophe in the economy that caused a worker, say, to lose his home roused this double consciousness of being an angry spectator and a responsible agent. Today, by contrast, the processes that help the economy to expand put workers in this double bind.

Take what happens when career paths are replaced by intermittent jobs. Many temporary workers have a dual consciousness of their work, knowing such work suits obligation-resistant companies, yet nonetheless believing that if only they had themselves managed their lives differently, they would have made a career out of their skills, and so be permanently employed. The new economic map that devalues life-long career projects has shifted the optimal age curves of work to younger employees (from the late twenties–middle fifties to early twenties–early forties), even though adults are living longer and more vigorously. Studies of dismissed middle-aged workers find them both obsessed and puzzled by the liabilities of age. Rather than believing themselves to be faded and over the hill, they feel that they are more organized and purposeful than younger workers. Yet they still blame themselves for not having made the right moves in the past, for not having prepared.

This legacy of personal responsibility deflects anger away from economic institutions. The rhetoric of modern management indeed attempts to disguise power in the new economy by making the worker believe he or she is a self-directing agent; as the authors of *Reengineering the Corporation* declare, in the emerging institution "managers stop acting like supervisors and behave more like coaches."[3]

In his *Oration on the Dignity of Man*, the Renaissance philosopher Pico della Mirandola declared "man is an animal of diverse, multiform, and destructible nature"; in this pliant condition "it is given to him to have that which he chooses and to be that which he wills."[4] Man is his own maker; the chief of his works is his self-worth. In modernity, people take responsibility for their lives, because the whole of it feels as though it is of their own making. But when the ethical culture of modernity, with its codes of personal responsibility and life purpose, is carried into a society without institutional shelters, there appears not pride or self-worth, but a dialectic of failure in the midst of growth. Is there any way in which this burden could be lightened?

Having a place in the world makes the human animal a social being. Ideally, we might want to imagine a city as Hannah Arendt did, as a place for forming loyalties and responsibilities, relieved of the burdens of material circumstance and its subjective interpretation. But such an ideal place bears little resemblance to any form of modern community.

In a community, people try to compensate for their dislocations and impoverished experience in the economy with communal coercion and illusion. Though I could not prove it statistically, I am convinced that the rise of the religious right in American suburbs, a movement now spreading toward the city from its traditional small-town base, correlates to an increased feeling of threatened fortunes. More obviously, many current building projects are exercises in withdrawal from a complex world, deploying self-consciously "traditional" architecture that bespeaks a mythic communal coherence and shared identity in the past. These comforts of a supposedly simpler age appear in the New-Englandish housing developments designed by the American planners Elizabeth Plater-Zyberk and Andres Duany, in the efforts undertaken by the Prince of Wales to reproduce "native" English architecture, and in the neighborhood renovation work undertaken by Leon Krier on the Continent. All these place-makers are artists of claustrophobia, whose icons, however, promise stability, longevity, and safety.

One might say that these fantasy communities, like the Christian suburb or the urban neighborhood that discriminates against immigrants, are reactions to real injuries. And one might conclude that Arendt's ideal city is condemned to remain a far-off dream, the likely scenario for our own time being that as people suffer more in the economy, they will increasingly seek the comforts of place on these terms—which are those of a closed system. Yet I am not quite so pessimistic.

For one thing, localities can act on the economy rather than defensively react to it. The emerging corporations present themselves as having cut free from local powers; a factory in Mexico, an office in Bombay, a media center in lower Manhattan—these appear as mere nodes in a global network. Localities fear that if they exercise sovereignty, as when a business is taxed or regulated locally, the corporation could as easily find another node in Canada if not Mexico, in Boston if not Manhattan.

The split between polity and economy, however, may be remediable. Already we are seeing signs that the economy is not as indifferent to location as has been assumed; you can buy any stock you like in Dubuque, Iowa, but cannot have a stock market in the cornfields; the ivy-hung cloisters of Harvard may furnish plenty of raw intellectual talent, yet lack the craziness, messiness, and surprise that make Manhattan a stimulating if unpleasant place to work. Similarly, in Southeast Asia, it is becoming clear that local social and cultural geographies indeed count for a great deal in investment decisions.

Businesses, like their workers, are not self-directing free agents; the possibility thus exists for making communal demands on the economy. One way to do this would be for a locality to contract with investing corporations to assure jobs for a certain number of years in exchange for tax relief and other benefits. Another would be to enforce strict workplace rules on age discrimination. What matters, it seems to me, is more the will to act than a specific magic policy bullet, since so far politics have tended to behave like weak supplicants rather than necessary partners with needs of their own.

There is also reason to hope that strong communities need not be condemned to turn inward. Much innovative city planning has recently focused on how to counter claustrophobia and open communities up to one another. For instance, "active edge" planners have sought to direct new building away from local centers and towards the boundaries separating communities; as in some experiments in east London, the aim is to make the edge a zone of interaction and exchange between different groups. Another strategy is to diversify central spaces; planners in Germany are similarly exploring how pedestrian zones in the centers of cities can regain light manufacturing.

Such urban strategies do not seek to determine a specific outcome. They do make assumptions about the process of change: in the case of the active-edge planners, that the more people interact, the more they will become involved with those unlike themselves; in the case of the central zone planners, that the value of place will increase when it is of more than commercial worth. They attempt to translate Hannah Arendt's celebration of the diverse, socially engaging ancient agora into contemporary spaces.

Lurking in these hopeful experiments is the embrace of what makes a city a city—its impersonality. One great theme in the literature of modern urban culture—from Charles Baudelaire to Louis Aragon to Walter Benjamin to Jane Jacobs—finds in crowds a peculiar antidote to selfhood with all its burdens, a release into a less personalized existence. That release has a particular value in terms of social class and material fortune; density and equality have an affinity in daily experience.

Of course, no one could argue that an impersonal city life will extinguish either the reality of or the sentiments aroused by economic failure. Nor has innovative city planning for live edges or mixed centers focused on the problem of durable social relations. Concern for long-term human relationships in the city has been left to visual and social reactionaries—who have hijacked the term "place making"—whereas finding new forms of durable human connection should be the very crux of confronting the emerging political economy. But the relief to be found in dense networks of streets, pubs, playgrounds, and markets—which are far more lively places than the Prince's fantasy villages—cannot be treated as inconsequential. Such dense forms of civil society do affect how people think of themselves as citizens; as the late Henri Lefebvre put it, sensing one's "right to the city" helps people feel entitled to other rights.

Place as a remedy for the ills of work poses a large and illuminating challenge to the new material order. The economy does not "grow" personal skills and durable purposes, nor social trust, loyalty, and commitment. Economic practice has combined, however, with a durable cultural ethic, so that institutional nakedness coexists with the will to take responsibility for one's life. The forms of polity we need to invent must somehow help people to transcend both elements of that combination. Place making based on exclusion, sameness, or nostalgia is socially poisonous and psychologically useless; a self weighted with its insufficiencies cannot lift that burden by retreat into fantasy. Place making based on more diverse, denser, impersonal human contacts must find a way for those contacts to endure.

Baudelaire famously defined modernity as the experience of the fleeting and the fragmented. To accept life in its disjointed pieces is an adult experience of freedom, but still these pieces must lodge and embed themselves somewhere, in a place that allows them to endure.

This essay was previously published as "Something in the City: The Spectre of Uselessness and the Search for a Place in the World" in Times Literary Supplement, *22 September 1995, 13–15. Reprinted with permission from* TLS.

Multiplication + Subdivision
A Paradox of Danger and Safety

Jane Harrison

The focus of this study of the American suburban landscape is the area around U.S. Route 29 (named after the 29th U.S. infantry division, which fought in the Normandy invasions) as it passes through Albemarle County, Virginia. This area was selected because here the transition from farmland to suburb is in its early stages. This is an example of the fiction of safety and the devices that are deployed in the complex construction of this fiction, a paradoxical equilibrium negotiating nostalgia and novelty, property and place, independence and communality, seclusion and exposure, isolation and proximity, and danger and safety—a play of appearances.

The piece is composed of seven sections organized in sequence:
- *Faictions*—definitions
- *Real Property: Veins + Patches = Taxation*—plan of segment of Albemarle County cut by U.S. Route 29 identifying 29/210 subdivisions
- *X*—photographs of Dunlora
- *Taxonomic Subdivisions*—subdivision road plans/phonetic annotation
- *Thruways + Dead Ends*—photographs of thruways and cul de sacs
- *Fond*—Hollymead crime map of eighteen-month period beginning January 1994
- *Shoot*—still choreography (performed by Bunty Matthias)

Crime coding used by Albemarle County Police

ABDN	abandoned vehicle	ASLT	assault	DRUG	drug
ACC	accident	BURG	burglary	DSOR	disorder
ANML	animal problem	DMST	domestic	DVI	driving under the influence
ALRM	alarm	DOG	dog problem	FOND	found property
HR	hit and run	LARD	larceny from vehicle	MENT	mental
HUNT	hunting violation	LARF	larceny from bike	MISC	miscellaneous
INFO	information	LARI	larceny—all others	MPJ	missing juvenile
ITOX	intoxicated person	LITT	littering	MP	missing person
MVI	motor vehicle violation	PARK	parking violation	SEXO	sex offense
MVTH	motor vehicle theft	PRLR	prowler	SHOT	shots fired or heard
NOIS	noise	ROBB	robbery	SLCT	solicitor
ODOW	open window	ROHZ	road hazard	STLK	stalking
SUIA	suicide attempt	TAMP	tamper with vehicle	VAND	vandalism
SUSC	suspicious circumstances	TRAF	traffic	WARR	warrant
SUSP	suspicious person	THRT	threat	WEAP	weapon
SUSV	suspicious vehicle	TRES	trespassing		

Faictions/Faictions/Faictions of Safety

fact

fækt
an event or thing known to have happened or existed

a piece of information

a truth verifiable from experience or observation

an actual event

a proposition that may be either true or false in reality or actuality (as in a matter of fact)

an inescapable truth especially an unpleasant one (as in a fact of life)

the truth (as in the matter of the fact)

faction

fækt ʃən
a group of people forming a minority within a larger body

a dissentient group

strife or dissension within a group

a television program, film, or literary work comprising a dramatized presentation of actual events

fiction

fɪk ʃən
literary works invented by the imagination

an invented story or explanation

a lie

the act of inventing a story or explanation

something assumed to be true for the sake of convenience, though probably false

of

ɒʌ
comes from *af*

comes from *aba*

comes from *ab*

comes from *apo*

safety

seɪftɪ
the quality of being safe

freedom from danger or risk of injury

the defensive player furthest back in the field

subdivision

sʌbdɪ vɪʒən   the process, instance or state of being divided again following
upon an earlier division

a portion that is the result of subdividing

a tract of land for building resulting from subdividing land

a housing development built on such a tract

division

dɪ vɪʒən   the act of dividing or state of being divided

the act of sharing out, distributing

something that divides or keeps apart, such as a boundary

a difference of opinion, especially one that causes separation

a mathematical operation, the inverse of multiplication

army	a major formation containing necessary arms to sustain independent combat
biology	a major taxonomic division of the plant kingdom
horticulture	any type of propagation implants in which a new plant grows from a separated part of the original
logic	the fallacy of inferring that the properties of the whole are also true of the parts
music	the art of breaking up a melody into quick phrases

multiplication

mʌltɪplɪ keɪʃən   comes from *multiplier*

comes from *multiplicare*

comes from *multus* = much, many + *plicare* = fold

an arithmetical operation defined initially as repeated addition

the act or process in animals, plants or people of reproducing
or breeding

the act of increasing or causing to increase in number,
quantity or degree

replication

rɛplɪ keɪʃən   comes from *replicate*

comes from *replicatio* = a folding back

comes from *re* + *plicare* = unroll

a reply or response

a plaintiff's reply to a defendant's answer

the production of exact copies of complex molecules that
occurs during the growth of living tissue

repetition of a procedure, such as a scientific experiment, in
order to reduce errors

Real Property

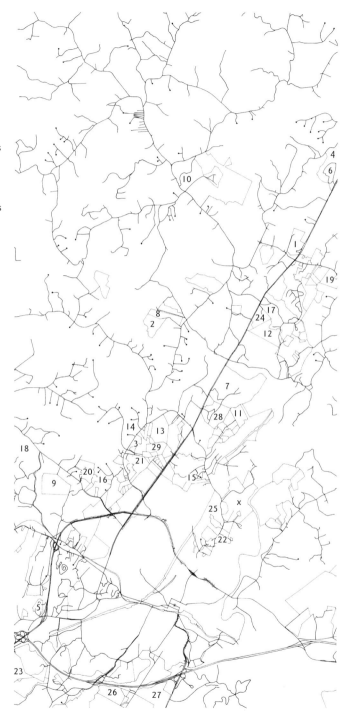

1 airport acres
2 ardwood
3 birnam wood
4 briarwood
5 buckingham
6 camelot
7 carrsbrook
8 clover hill
9 colthurst farm
x dunlora
10 earlysville heights
11 fieldbrook
12 forest lakes
13 four seasons
14 gardencourt
15 greenbriar heights
16 hessian hills
17 hollymead
18 inglecress
19 jefferson village
20 montvue
21 oak forest
22 rio heights
23 sherwood farms
24 terrybrook
25 village square
26 willoughby
27 willow lake
28 woodbrook
29 wynridge

x

εəpɔːt eɪkəz   bxːnən wʊd   bxkɪxəm   kləʊvə hɪl   kaːz brʊk   xːlɪz vɪl haɪtz

     aːd wʊd   braɪə wʊd   kæmɪlat   kaːz brʊk   kəʊlthxːst faːm

fiːld brʊk   fɔː siːz n   griːn braɪə haɪtz   holɪ miːd   dʒɛfəs n vɪlɪdʒ

   farɪst leɪkz   gaːd n kɔːt   hɛsɪən hɪlz   ɪxg lkrɛs

mant vjuː   ʃxːwʊd faːmz   tɛrɪ brʊk   wɪl´ʊbiː   wʊd brʊk

   əʊk farɪst   rɪo haɪtz   vɪlɪdʒ skwɛ́   wɪl´ʊ leɪk   wɪn rɪdʒ

Taxonomic Subdivisions

Thruways + Dead Ends

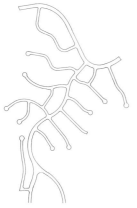

Fond

Powell Creek Drive x burglary = re
Powell Creek Drive x burglary =
Powell Creek Drive x driving under influ
Powell Creek Drive x suspicious circ
Powell Creek Drive x misce

Sourwood Place x annoying phone call = report
Sourwood Place x noise = handled by officer
Sourwood Place x vandalism = unfound
Sourwood Place x suspicious circumstances = gone on arrival
Sourwood Place x motor vehicle violation = report
Sourwood Place x assault = handled by officer
Sourwood Place x vandalism = report
Sourwood Place x accident = handled by officer
Sourwood Place x burglary = unfound
Sourwood Place x soliciting = handled by officer
Sourwood Place x animal = gone on arrival
Sourwood Place x annoying phone call = handled by offic
Sourwood Place x larceny of bike = repo
Sourwood Place x vandalism = u
Sourwood Place x fra
Sourwood Place
Sourwood Place x liquo
Sourwood Place x lar
Sourwoo

Easy Lane x suspicious cir
Easy Lane x suspic
Easy Lane x
Easy Lar
Easy
E

Lampkin Way x road hazarc
Lampkin Way x warrant =

Golden Tree Place x suspicious vehicle = handled by officer
Golden Tree Place x prowler = handled by officer
Golden Tree Place x soliciting = handled by officer

Hollymead Drive x driving
Hollymead Drive x motor vehicle
Hollymead Drive x miscellane
Hollymead Drive x suspicious cir
Hollymead Drive x annoying phone calls = h
Hollymead Drive x driving under influen
Hollymead Drive x stalking
Hollymead Drive x suspicious person = handled k
Hollymead Drive x larceny = handled by
Hollymead Drive x motor vehicle violation = handled by
Hollymead Drive x road hazard = handled by off
Hollymead Drive x accident = handled by off
Hollymead Drive x vandalism = gone on arr
Hollymead Drive x vandalism = gone on arr
Hollymead Drive x suspicious vehicle = handled by
Hollymead Drive x assist a citizen = handled by
Hollymead Drive x disorder = handled b
Hollymead Drive x driving under influence
Hollymead Drive x accident = gone
Hollymead Drive x road hazard = refer to oth
Hollymead Drive x vandalism
Hollymead Drive x vandalism
Hollymead Drive x accident =
Hollymead Drive x accident =
Hollymead Drive x motor vehicle violation = be c
Hollymead Drive x motor vehicle violation =
Hollymead Drive x dog problem =
Hollymead x accident =
Hollymead Drive x accident = unf
Hollymead Drive x trespassing = handled by c

Hollymead Elementary x motor vehicle violation = gone on arrival
Hollymead Elementary x suspicious person = unfound
Hollymead Elementary x dog problem = report
Hollymead Elementary x miscellaneous = handled by officer
Hollymead Elementary x open window = handled by officer
Hollymead Elementary x vandalism = unfound

Hollymead School x miscellaneous = report
Hollymead School x accident = handled by officer
Hollymead School x miscellaneous = handled by officer
Hollymead school x suspicious circumstances = handled by officer
Hollymead School x suspicious person = gone on arrival
Hollymead School x vandalism = report
Hollymead School x shots fired or heard = unfound
Hollymead School x suspicious vehicle = handled by officer
Hollymead School x vandalism = report
Hollymead School x vandalism = report
Hollymead School x vandalism = handled by officer
Hollymead School x motor vehicle violation = gone on arrival
Hollymead Square x vandalism = handled by officer
Hollymead General x noise = unfound

cious vehicle = unfound
e x assault = report
wood Circle x unauthorized use = report
Gatewood Circle x noise = unfound
Gatewood Circle x assault = handled by officer
Gatewood Circle x assist a citizen = handled by officer
Gatewood Circle x miscellaneous = handled by officer
Gatewood Circle x suspicious circumstances = gone on arrival
Gatewood Circle x tampering with vehicle = handled by officer
Gatewood Circle x larceny of bike = report
Gatewood Circle x assist a citizen = handled by officer
Gatewood Circle x suspicious circumstances = handled by officer
Gatewood Circle x assist a citizen = handled by office
Gatewood Circle x assist a citizen = handled by officer
Gatewood Circle x accident = report
Gatewood Circle x miscellaneous = report
Gatewood Circle x sex offense = report
Gatewood Circle x assist a citizen = handled by office
Gatewood Circle x assist a citizen = handled by officer
Gatewood Circle x cat problem = report

d
y officer

ed by officer
unfound
nces = unfound
d
s = gone on arrival
= unfound
/ = report
ssing person = report
suspicious person = handled by officer
e x missing person = report
ne x suspicious person = handled by officer
Lane x missing person = report
sy Lane x prowler = report
sy Lane x suspicious circumstances = report

Gatewood Circle x noise = handled by officer
Gatewood Circle x noise = handled by officer
Gatewood Circle x missing person = handled by officer
Gatewood Circle x missing juvenile = unfound
Gatewood Circle x missing juvenile = handled by officer

Hollymead x miscellaneous = handled by office
Hollymead x missing person = canceled
Hollymead x abandoned vehicle = handled by officer
Hollymead x larceny = report
Hollymead x found property = report
Hollymead x threats = handled by officer
Hollymead x found property = handled by officer
Hollymead x driving under influence = be on look out
Hollymead x suspicious vehicle = handled by officer
Hollymead x motor vehicle violation = unfound

Allen's Way x abandoned vehicle = handled by officer
Allen's Way x noise = handled by officer
Allen's Way x noise = handled by officer

Poe's Lane x animal problem = handled by officer
Poe's Lane x alarm = handled by officer
Poe's Lane x suspicious circumstances = handled by officer
Poe's Lane x noise = report

report
eport
port
r
on look out
by officer
ficer

Raven's Place x suspicious circumstances = unfound
Derby Lane x annoying phone calls = report
Derby Lane x larceny from vehicle = report
Derby Lane x trespassing = handled by officer
Derby Lane x hit and run = report
Robin Lane x suicide attempt = report
Robin Lane x dog problem = canceled
Robin Lane x suspicious circumstances = handled by officer
Robin Lane x threats = refer to other agency
Robin Lane x road hazard = refer to other agency
Maiden Lane x larceny from vehicle = report

Drive x accident = report
ad Drive x assisting a citizen = handled by officer
ead Drive x motor vehicle violation = report
ymead Drive x assist a citizen = handled by officer
Hollymead Drive x accident = report
Hollymead Drive x suspicious circumstances = handled by officer
Hollymead Drive x accident = report
Hollymead Drive x accident = handled by officer
Hollymead Drive x assisting a citizen = handled by officer
Hollymead Drive x disorder = handled by officer
Hollymead Drive x annoying phone calls = handled by officer
Hollymead Drive x suspicious circumstances = handled by officer
Hollymead Drive x suspicious person = gone on arrival
Hollymead Drive x suspicious vehicle = gone on arrival
Hollymead Drive x vandalism = report

ABDN	ASLT	DRUG
ACC	BURG	DSOR
ANML	DMST	DVI
ALRM	DOG	FOND

Shoot

HR	LARD	MENT
HUNT	LARF	MISC
INFO	LARI	MPJ
ITOX	LITT	MP

Shoot

MVI	PARK	SEXO
MVTH	PRLR	SHOT
NOIS	ROBB	SLCT
ODOW	ROHZ	STLK

Shoot

SUIA	TAMP	VAND
SUSC	TRAF	WARR
SUSP	THRT	WEAP
SUSV	TRES	

Shoot

Divided We Fall
Gated and Walled Communities in the United States

Edward J. Blakely and Mary Gail Snyder

The Gating of the American Mind

It has been over three decades since this nation legally outlawed all forms of discrimination in housing, education, public transportation, and public accommodations. Yet today, we are seeing a new form of discrimination—the gated, walled, private community. Americans are electing to live behind walls with active security mechanisms to prevent intrusion into their private domains. Increasingly, a frightened middle class that moved to escape school integration and to secure appreciating housing values now must move to maintain their economic advantage. The American middle class is forting up.

Gated communities are residential areas with restricted access such that normally public spaces have been privatized. These developments are both new suburban developments and older inner-city areas retrofitted to provide security. We are not discussing apartment buildings with guards or doormen. In essence, we are interested in the newest form of fortified community that places security and protection as its primary feature. We estimate that eight million[1] and potentially many more Americans are seeking this new refuge from the problems of urbanization.

Economic segregation is scarcely new. In fact, zoning and city planning were designed in part to preserve the position of the privileged by subtle variances in building and density codes. But the gated communities go further in several respects: they create physical barriers to access, and they privatize community space, not merely individual space. Many of these communities also privatize civic responsibilities, such as police protection, and communal services, such as education, recreation, and entertainment. The new developments create a private world that shares little with its neighbors or the larger political system. This fragmentation undermines the very concept of civitas, organized community life.

The forting-up phenomenon has enormous policy consequences. By allowing some citizens to internalize and to exclude others from sharing in their economic privilege, it aims directly at the conceptual base of community and citizenship in America. The old notions of community mobility are torn apart by these changes in community patterns. What is the measure of nationhood when the divisions between neighborhoods require armed patrols and electric fencing to keep out other citizens? When public services and even local government are privatized, when the community of responsibility stops at the subdivision gates, what happens to the function and the very idea of democracy? In short, can this nation fulfill its social contract in the absence of social contact?

Gated Communities Today

Since the late 1980s, gates have become ubiquitous in many areas of the country, and now new towns are routinely built with gated villages while entire incorporated cities feature guarded entrances. While early gated communities were restricted to retirement villages and the compounds of the super rich, the majority found today are middle to upper-middle class. Higher end tracts within planned communities are now commonly gated. They seem to be more common in larger tracts, as there are more units over which to spread the cost of walling, gating, and constructing and staffing guardhouses. For similar reasons, they also are common in multifamily and higher-density developments, where unit costs are often low enough to place gates within the reach of the middle class. It is estimated that one-third of the communities developed with gates are luxury developments for the upper and upper-middle class, and over one-third are retirement oriented. The remainder are mostly for the middle class, with a growing number for working-class communities.

The gates range from elaborate two-story guardhouses manned twenty-four hours a day to roll-back wrought iron gates to simple electronic arms. Guardhouses are usually built with one lane for guests and visitors and a second lane for residents, who may open the gates with an electronic card, a punched-in code, or a remote control. Some gates with round-the-clock security require all cars to pass the guard and issue identification stickers for residents' cars. Unmanned entrances have intercom systems, some with video monitors, for visitors asking for entrance.

Along with new residential developments, existing neighborhoods are using barricades and gates with increasing frequency to seal themselves off. Since the 1950s, there has been a constant move away from the traditional city grid pattern to suburban cul-de-sacs and non-connecting streets. Urban street closures attempt to recreate this suburban pattern in the older grid, altering access and the ability of outsiders to penetrate.

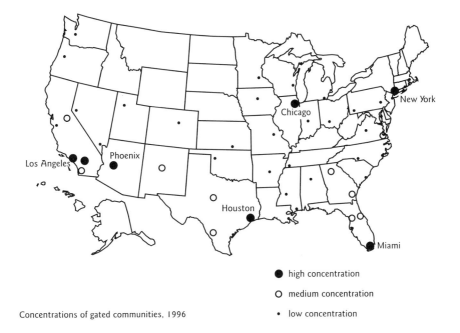

Concentrations of gated communities, 1996

● high concentration

○ medium concentration

· low concentration

Gated communities are part of the trend of suburbanization. There is no doubt that Americans have given up on the old style of urban living for the large private spaces and small public spaces of the suburbs. A majority of people now live in suburbs. The old central cities are losing their position as the most powerful place in the metropolitan hierarchy, as not just residency but industry, commerce, and retail shift their balance to the suburbs. Driven by high costs, crime, and other urban problems, the expansion of the suburbs is likely to accelerate in the 1990s as development moves ever farther out, supported by and leapfrogging beyond the new economic centers of the edge cities.

Gating is not a universal American phenomenon. It is very geographic. It is a metropolitan phenomenon, and a southwestern, southern, and southeastern phenomenon. At the moment, it is less a midwestern or northern phenomenon. But even in these regions, gated communities are emerging around big cities. In terms of absolute numbers, California is home to the most gated communities, with Florida ranking second. Texas runs a distant third. Gated communities are very common in metropolitan New York, Chicago, Phoenix, and in Miami and other southern seaboard cities. They are also found in Arkansas, Colorado, Hawaii, Iowa, Kansas, Louisiana, Maryland, Massachusetts, Michigan, Minnesota, Missouri, Nevada, Oregon, Oklahoma, Virginia, Washington, and Wisconsin.

The Developers

For developers, gated communities can be a marketing angle, another way to target specific submarkets, or, in some areas, a necessity to meet demand. Southern California builders report faster sales in gated communities, and quicker turnover means thousands in additional profits per unit. With their often elaborate guardhouses and entrance architecture, gates provide product differentiation and clear identity in a crowded and competitive new home market. Also, whenever a significant recreational feature such as a golf course or lake is part of a development, the gate controls access and assures buyers their amenity will be theirs alone.

The developers of gated communities see themselves as providing security. The elderly have been targeted for gated communities since the 1970s, and gated second home complexes are also well established. Those seen in need of walls now also include empty nesters, who are likely to be away on long vacations frequently, and double-income families, in which no one is home during the day. Security is viewed as freedom not just from crime, but also from such annoyances as solicitors and canvassers, mischievous teenagers, and strangers of any kind, malicious or not. According to our survey, among those gated community association boards that think they experience less crime than the surrounding area, most believe that the gate is the reason.[2]

The Context: Housing Segregation Patterns

There is little doubt that urban problems are the stimuli for this wave of gating. The drive for separation, distinction, exclusion, and protection is fueled in part by the dramatic demographic change in many of the metropolitan areas with large numbers of gated communities. High levels of foreign immigration, a growing underclass, and a restricted economy are changing the face of metropolitan areas like Los Angeles, Miami, Chicago, and New York at a very rapid pace. Many of the other places with large numbers of gates, such as Oregon, Arizona, and Nevada, are destination states for the increasing numbers of white Californians fleeing the state.

The need for gates and walls is also created and encouraged by changes in the social and physical structure of the suburbs. The suburbs are becoming urbanized, such that many might now be called, in Mike Davis's term, "outer cities," places with many of the problems and pathologies formerly thought to be restricted to big cities. America is increasingly separated by income, race, and economic opportunity. Suburbanization has meant a redistribution of the urban patterns of discrimination. Minority suburbanization is concentrated in the inner ring and old manufacturing suburbs. The Los Angeles area is an example of the new archetype of metropolitan spatial segregation, in which poverty is no longer concentrated in the central city, but has moved to the suburbs. This segregation by income and race has led groups within the hyper-segregated environment to wall and secure their space against the poor, as in Pacific Palisades on the California coast, to protect wealth, or, as in Athens Heights in inner-city South Central Los Angeles, to protect property values.

Structural segregation, when seen in the metropolitan context, leads to distinct gating phenomena. Those feeling threatened by creeping poverty have two options: to fort up in place, or to move to a perceived safe zone and fortify there. Those who fort up in place are the wealthy who have homes in desirable locations on the ocean or near downtown, or the working and middle class without the resources to move. Their gates are installed either at the resident's initiative or the developer's. Those who move to a safe zone are the residents of the subdivisions and new towns of the outer suburbs and exurbs. They intend to get as far away as they can and then fortify their new position to keep it safe from future threats.

Types of Gated Communities and Rationales for Gating

Gated communities can be classified in three main categories based on the primary motivation of their residents. First are the lifestyle communities, where the gates provide security and separation for the leisure activities and amenities within. These include retirement communities and golf and country club leisure developments. Second are the elite communities, where the gates symbolize distinction and prestige and both create and protect a secure place on the social ladder. These include enclaves of the rich and famous; developments for the very affluent; and executive home developments for the middle class. These two categories are examples of gating motivated by a desire to invest in and control the future through measures designed to maximize the internal life of the residents. The intention is also in part to artificially induce community in an ersatz, homogenous neighborhood, where physical security and social security are enhanced by both sameness and controlled access.

The third category is the security zone, where the fear of crime and outsiders is the foremost motivation for defensive fortifications. Here existing neighborhoods are retrofitted with gates or barricades. This category includes the inner-city perch, where gates attempt to protect property and property values and sometimes to wall out nearby crime; the suburban perch, where gates are installed as once quiet suburbs urbanize; and the street barricade areas where mazes of blocked streets are created to reduce access and deter outsiders. Here the residents erect fortifications to regain control of their neighborhood and so that changing conditions do not overwhelm them. By marking their boundaries and restricting access, these places often try to build and strengthen the feeling and function of community.

Social Values: Resident Motivations

The three major categories of gated communities—lifestyle, elite, and security zone—all reflect to varying degrees four social dimensions or values: a sense of community, or the preservation and strengthening of neighborhood bonds; exclusion, or separation from the rest of society; privatization, or the desire to replace and internally control public services; and stability, or the need for homogeneity, predictability, and similarity.

	LIFESTYLE	ELITE	SECURITY ZONE
SENSE OF COMMUNITY	tertiary	tertiary	secondary
EXCLUSION	secondary	secondary	primary
PRIVATIZATION	primary	tertiary	tertiary
STABILITY	secondary	primary	secondary

The lifestyle communities attract those who want separate, private services and amenities, and who are also seeking a homogenous, predictable environment. The elite communities draw those seeking a stable community of similar people where property values will be protected; concerns of separation and privatization of services come second. Within the security zone, neighborhoods are trying to strengthen and protect a sense of community, but their primary goal is to exclude the places and people they perceive as threats to their safety or quality of life.

Lifestyle Communities—Gates of Paradise

The lifestyle communities were the first mass-market gated developments, springing up in sunbelt retirement areas such as Florida, Southern California, and Arizona. They include two types: retirement communities and golf and leisure developments. The residents say that their primary motivation for choosing to live in these development is the amenities provided. Many of these communities are marketed to golfers, retirees, and empty nesters. Carefree living, an active lifestyle, or member-only golf and country club facilities are highlighted. The security measures attempt more to establish control than to protect against criminals.

One such lifestyle community is Mission Hills Country Club, a sprawling development centered around a lush golf course; the vista from nearly all of the narrow internal roads is of greens and palm trees. It is located in Rancho Mirage,

Lifestyle community

Elite community

Security zone

one of the wealthier of the small contiguous towns of California's Coachella Valley, where Palm Springs is located. There are three gates into the walled development, each with a staffed guard house, and a private security firm patrols twenty-four hours a day. These security arrangements protect a prestigious community for active retirees, where each individual subdivision is run by its own board.

Residents say the social life can resemble that of "Peyton Place." Many volunteer at local charities, but finding people to volunteer for board duty, like community associations everywhere, can be difficult, and getting cooperation between the fifteen boards is next to impossible. But in the end, these retirees did not come to Mission Hills to find a small town community. They came for manicured greens, the built-in social life, the many amenities. This is the list of the affluent retiree: "The gate, the golf, the tennis, the ability to drive around in a golf cart...there are many days when I never move my regular car. It's a different lifestyle, and I bought *the lifestyle*."

Elite Communities—I Have a Dream

Gates not only protect leisure amenities and lifestyle enclaves, but economic and social status. The elite communities are perhaps the most traditional type of gated community in the United States, having their roots directly in the walls and gates that the very richest have always had. Now, however, the merely affluent, the top fifth of Americans, also have barriers between themselves and the rest of us, and so can the upwardly mobile middle class. These developments feed on exclusionary aspirations and the desire to differentiate. The services of gate guards and security patrols add to the prestige of exclusivity; residents value the simple presence of a security force more than any service they may actually provide. Except for some of the oldest developments, the elite communities tend toward ostentatious entrances and showy facades. Although they lack the recreational amenities of the lifestyle types, they do have carefully controlled aesthetics and often enviable landscapes and locations.

When you enter the southern California elite gated community of Marblehead, you are entering a place of dreams—the dream of Mr. and Mrs. Executive America. They want good schools, nice homes, streets in which kids can play, and friendly neighbors. And Marblehead is just that—a nice community. It is a suburban housing tract of middle-class homes that would look like any other tract anywhere except for the gate and the guard. The residents we met were clear right off that Marblehead was no friendlier, no more of a community, or even safer than any other suburban community: "It is just like any other place."

The gates do give the area a prestige that is attractive to young executives, but they have been less than effective at slowing traffic or keeping out crime. The gate guards are lax, hired only to monitor traffic, and no one is willing to pay the cost for improved levels of security. The community has burglaries and other mild vandalism, just as anywhere else. Gangs from nearby San Clemente have entered the development from an adjacent park, and teenagers who live inside have also been a source of trouble. The speed at which residents drive within the gates is a contentious issue. Marblehead seems far from the crime and traffic of the city, a protected suburban cocoon, but it has many of the same problems inside the walls as exist outside them, and the people who live there know it. "You can run but you cannot hide."

Security Zone Communities—Valleys of Fear

Possibly the fastest growing type of gated community is the security zone, characterized by the closed streets and gated complexes of the inner-city, suburban, and street barricade perches. Poor inner-city neighborhoods and public housing projects are using security guards, gates, and fences to keep out drug dealing, prostitution, and drive-by shootings. Other neighborhoods, frightened by spillover crime from nearby areas, are obtaining city permission to take their streets out of public use, limiting access only to residents. In the inner suburbs, in areas both near to and far from high crime areas, existing communities tax themselves to install security gates. Whether crime is acute or infrequent, the threat actual or only perceived, the fear is very real.

The security zone community of Whitley Heights is a part of old Hollywood, a historic film and artist colony. It has only two entrances—one from Hollywood Boulevard on the south and the other from the Hollywood Bowl parking lots on the north. The contrast between the flatlands of Hollywood Boulevard and Whitley Heights on the hill above could not be greater, despite the few short blocks that separate them. Over the years, Hollywood Boulevard became the site of prostitution, drug dealing, and other urban ills, and the people on Whitley Heights began thinking of gates, despite the fact that there was little crime on the hill itself. But no matter how strong the fear and the perception of crime, cars were perhaps an even greater concern to those on the hill. The residents of the apartment buildings below were parking their vehicles on the hill, and commuters were using it as a convenient shortcut when the freeways were jammed with cars. In 1986, the community decided to gate off their streets. "Gating was not propelled by any high increase in crime, but a sense that we could not control our community," explained Bob, a former board member. Gates were to control "who got up here."

As citizens divide themselves into homogenous, independent cells, their place in the greater polity and society becomes attenuated, increasing resistance to efforts to resolve regional, let alone municipal, problems.

Opposition emerged from the neighbors in the apartment buildings on the other side of the new gate. Calling themselves CAGE, Citizens Against Gated Enclaves, they filed a lawsuit to keep the public streets of Whitley Heights from being closed. They claimed the gates were an exclusionary, elitist slap in the face; Bob thinks they were just upset that they would lose their parking spaces. Even when completed, the gates stood open, hostage to the lawsuit making its way through appeals. Finally the California Supreme Court ruled in CAGE's favor: the gates to Whitley Heights may not ever be closed. To those on the hill, the fight was to save their community, or at least their part of it. To those in the flatlands, the fight was to keep the hill dwellers from dividing the Hollywood community with fences. In the end, the cost was high, and not just in money and time. The battle exhausted the community of Whitley Heights; the board collapsed, and street parties and other events that had been held for decades have been abandoned.

Fortress Mentality

Walled cities and gated communities are a dramatic manifestation of the fortress mentality growing in America. Gates, fences, and private security forces, along with land-use policies, development regulations, and other planning tools, are being used throughout the country to restrict or limit access to residential, commercial, and public areas. These turf wars, while most dramatically manifested by the gated community, are a troubling trend for land-use planning. As citizens divide themselves into homogenous, independent cells, their place in the greater polity and society becomes attenuated, increasing resistance to efforts to resolve regional, let alone municipal, problems.

Movements to gate public streets in Los Angeles and other large cities and the dramatic growth of the private security industry are indicative of the fortress mentality. Proponents support street closures as an effective crime deterrent that helps reduce traffic, curb white flight to the suburbs, and maintain neighborhoods and homeownership. Opponents point to exclusion, the displacement of crime and traffic, and negative impacts on neighbor's property values.

Citizen Who

Privatization is the new means by which local communities, burdened with an increasing share of the costs of schools, roads, police, housing, and other services, pass off previously public roles. Privatization here refers not to the hiring of private firms by government to provide public services, but to privatized government, the replacement of public government and its functions by private organizations who purchase services from the market. Private communities are providing their own security, street maintenance, recreation facilities, and garbage collection. An entirely parallel, private system exists to provide schools, playgrounds, parks, and police protection for those who can pay, leaving the poor and less well-to-do dependent on the ever-reduced services of city and county governments.

Privatization of a wide range of traditionally public goods and services is fueled in part by the declining levels of services provided by localities across the country. In areas where citizens feel let down by local government, it is not surprising that those who can afford to turn to private service provision do. Even in the most affluent suburbs, however, where crime is nearly nonexistent and street repairs occur promptly, Americans are turning to self-provision of services, privatizing their streets and buying security and other services on the private market. Here the issue is less one of replacing failing city services than controlling residential space. In a gated community, the swimming pool, the street, and the tot lot is private, used only by residents and their invited guests, fully under their control.

Residents of gated communities are in essence taxed twice, once through local property taxes, and again through homeowner association fees. A few communities are revolting against this double taxation, asking for rebates on the cost of the public works and public safety services they provide for themselves, despite the fact that they volunteered for it when they bought their property or gated their streets. They are taking care of themselves, they say, and have no desire to contribute to the common pool serving their neighbors in the rest of the city. In areas where gated communities are the norm, not the exception, this perspective has the potential for severe impacts on the common welfare.

Social Contact and the Social Contract

Gating is an extension of the separation and distinction that the covenants and restrictions of suburban tracts already provide, acting as an additional way to define boundaries, guarantee property values, and effectively prohibit neighborhood change. Exclusionary segmentation imposes social costs on those left outside; it reduces the number of public spaces that all can share, and thus the contacts that people from different socioeconomic groups might otherwise have with each other. Gated communities are themselves a microcosm of the larger spatial pattern of segmentation and separation. The growing divisions between city and suburb and rich and poor are creating new patterns that reinforce the costs that isolation and exclusion impose on some at the same time that they benefit others. Suburbanization has been instrumental in dividing up the gains and losses of economic restructuring, allowing the winners to protect their position through geographic separation and further exacerbating differentials in income and wealth.

The issues of social exclusion, privatization, and segmentation that gated communities bring up raise concern that without social contact, the social contract that underpins the health of a nation will be damaged. Certainly the move to gate private reserves has impacted commitment to public spaces. In Laguna Beach, the California Coastal Commission has been fighting gated communities for years over the lack of public access to the beaches that their multimillion dollar homes overlook. The beaches are public, but the gates to the private streets built along them preclude any access to the coves along the rocky coast. Cities across the nation are involved in similar battles as those with privileged access to natural resources try to exclude the rest of the public from sharing them.

Divided We Fail

Recent demographic changes are dividing, not diversifying, the nation. Metropolitan areas have become increasingly spatially pluralistic and segregated in terms of race, class, and land values, and these spatial patterns are apparently being recreated on a national scale. The unprecedented volume of foreign immigration in the 1980s was concentrated in seven states: New York, New Jersey, Illinois, Massachusetts, Florida, and California, most of which experienced significant white out-migration.

The divided city is becoming a sharper reality. As the middle class flees not just the city but the inner suburbs and even entire states, and as walls are built to help protect those who try to stay behind, poor neighborhoods are increasingly isolated from the municipal land, labor, and social markets. In a sense, the poor inner-city neighborhoods form a new land and social pattern. They are not responsive to the regular real-estate market. Even the reduction in land values does not attract buyers or lenders. Consequently, the fate of these neighborhoods cannot rest on the workings of market forces as in previous decades.

The trend toward privatized government and communities is part of the more general trend of fragmentation, and the resulting loss of connection and social contact is weakening the bonds of mutual responsibility and the social contract. We no longer speak of citizens, but rather of taxpayers, who take no active role in governance, but merely exchange money for services.

Gated communities manifest a number of tensions, between notions of civic responsibility and exclusionary aspirations rooted in fear and protection of privilege; between the trend toward privatization of public services and the ideals of the public good and general welfare; and between the need for personal and community control of the environment and the dangers of creating outsiders of fellow citizens.

Forts or Communities

Our analysis of the new fortress communities is depressing in several respects. First, walls, street patterns, and barricades that separate people from one another reduce the potential for people to understand one another and commit themselves to any common or collective purpose. Second, the very foundations of citizenship are rooted in sharing. Finally, protection from violence and other criminal activity largely depends on the active vigilance of fellow citizens. We are interdependent. Walls, gates, and other barriers, as Peter Marcuse says, are "second best solutions."[3] No solution that denies the problem has great longevity. Surely, walls are only temporary measures at best. Anyone who wishes to penetrate such an environment can and will. Our field work and analysis of local studies provide no evidence of any general permanent reductions of crime in walled security areas. Gates and fences are not impenetrable to the serious criminal, and they do nothing to reduce crime arising from residents. Unfortunately, most crime is committed by locals who know their victims. If walls do not protect, if they do not build better neighborhoods, and if they do not bolster civic life, are they worth it? Moreover, if they fail these tests are there any other alternatives?

Building Better Communities

Enormous national resources have been expended on building housing units and expanding the suburbs. However, the inadvertent price we paid for this explosion in housing stock was an absence of attention to the configuration and organization, both physical and social, of the community structure. Now the residents of suburbs and cities turn to separate gated enclaves in an attempt to thwart crime, reduce traffic, and create livable neighborhoods. However, there are other means to these ends, means that also build community. And without community, we have no hope of solving our social problems or ever really gaining control of our neighborhoods.

One remedy to revive our communities is neotraditional design, the "new urbanism" of Peter Calthorpe and of Andres Duany and Elizabeth Plater-Zyberk. Neotraditional design is based on the notion that community means face-to-face contact and interaction. In contrast to gated communities, it focuses on street patterns and designs that bring people together rather than isolate them. A prominent feature is the open, traditional American street pattern that provides privacy and security without barriers.

In Europe, the concept of "slow streets" has taken hold to reduce traffic and increase livability. These streets are narrowed, curved, and landscaped to make them pedestrian-friendly and to reduce automobile speeds to a crawl. The residential streets become a sort of community courtyard, where children can play, adults interact, and everyone can keep an eye on the street for suspicious or dangerous activity.

Ever since Jane Jacobs's *The Death and Life of Great American Cities*[4] urban designers and planners have recognized that "eyes on the street"— the social control of a tightly knit community—are basic defenses against crime. Today, programs like neighborhood watch and block safe houses offer ways for families in suburbs and cities to build community and reduce crime. Overall, these socially based mechanisms are more effective than additional hardware like gates. Where physical design is employed, as in Oscar Newman's "defensible space,"[5] the physical environment is intended to facilitate and encourage these social, communal responses. Gated communities, in contrast, offer fortification and hired guards, relieving residents of any need to feel responsible for maintaining the safety of their neighborhoods.

One of the most important elements in democratic societies is respect for and maintenance of heterogeneity. Communities need all age groups and lifestyles to remain viable places. Gated communities, however, tend to be homogeneous economically and by age. This lack of diversity makes the communities brittle and too easily harmed by a single trauma. A more diverse community can protect itself as each group assists the others.

Maintaining diverse communities can be achieved. Some cities, like Shaker Heights outside of Cleveland, work hard to maintain their diversity through active community programs that attract and retain their residential base. This type of program can be introduced in any community. Active citizen organization effects community behavior in many tangible ways, ranging from improving community relations to reducing crime. Another approach is the development of active community volunteer programs supported by local governments. Miami has developed a network of community service centers that act like miniature city halls and give residents a sense of comfort and governmental concern and presence. As a result, residential stability is increased with the resultant impact of stronger community organizations.

Neighborhoods in the Region

Good neighborhoods exist in good cities. Good cities are supported in good regions. Some areas of the country, such as Portland, Oregon and Minneapolis/St. Paul, Minnesota, have few gates and walls. In part, this is because of a much more active regional approach to dealing with urban needs and problems. These areas have developed regional approaches aimed at protecting neighborhoods and making quality of life central to economic well being.

Regional development does not mean regional government. Rather, it requires regional analysis of problems and the implementation of regional policies and infrastructure to meet housing and community needs. Portland's emphasis on regional transportation and regional land use has led to both rational and livable environments, while Minneapolis/St. Paul's tax and burden-sharing approaches continue to provide quality living environments at a reasonable price. This is not to say these places are perfect or do not have crime, walls, or gates. However, we must acknowledge that no neighborhood, area of a city, or city can survive on its own outside of the regional economic and social framework.

Community as Bedrock

We have been concerned here with the notion of community within a particularly residential framework. Our research has provided us with evidence that the social structure of a community is more important than its physical features in combating crime and maintaining quality of life. As a result, we advocate a much stronger, deeper national commitment to community building that goes beyond bricks and mortar, and attention to the social effects and impacts of the physical structures we build. We need a commitment to develop neighborhoods and communities that are racially and economically integrated, safe, and connected to the larger society. There is too little effort, philanthropic or governmental, aimed at discovering how we can build better social space. We must engage this question for the health of our neighborhoods, our cities, and our nation.

Walls of Fear and Walls of Support

Peter Marcuse

Do walls in the city provide security—or do they create fear? Walls of course provide an elemental security, literally: security against the elements, against wind, rain, cold. As soon as it goes beyond that simple statement, the matter becomes more complicated. Do walls provide security against attack, a protection of privacy? That depends. And it depends not so much on the composition of the walls themselves, as on their social role. Armory walls in New York City are thick and strong, but when an armory is used as a homeless shelter, its walls intimidate and confine, rather than defend. Are the police lawless, and do they break in without a warrant? Does the landlord have the unlimited right to enter to inspect in the lease? Then walls are no protection of privacy. And privacy is in any event very culture-determined; what appears intolerable overcrowding to some is normal sociability to others, and among some peoples merely turning their backs to others provides the sense of privacy for which others require a room of their own.

Walls and Boundaries

All walls are boundaries, but not all boundaries are walls. Some orthodox Jewish communities define the limits of Sabbath travel by tying ribbons around trees and poles along the routes they need to take. Little picket fences form the boundaries of front yards in suburbia. Developers of multifamily housing have found many ingenious ways of delimiting private, semiprivate, and public spaces in their projects without using walls. So have office designers, in open layouts; movable partitions become a social, more than a physically effective, barrier that protects one work-station from overlapping with another. Moving up the scale, jurisdictional lines among municipalities, or among districts or states, in the United States are effective for many purposes, such as taxation and provision of services, but they are represented by signposts, not by walls. National boundaries are rarely represented by walls. Even in Israel, the idea of building a wall along the boundary with the Palestinian West Bank evoked horror, and in the United States the proposal to reinforce the boundary with Mexico with a fence produced widespread shock and derision. The responses to the Berlin wall proves the point.

For walls produce and reflect fear as well as security. Anyone who has visited a concentration camp knows of the feelings that their first glimpse inspires in a visitor; it challenges the imagination to reproduce the feelings such walls inspired for the inmates. Prison walls and jail cell walls are no different. And what is one to make of the steel shutters behind which storekeepers seek to protect themselves against break-ins, or the tiny windows in concrete-block exteriors where jewelry merchants display their wares to the outside? Such walls reflect, rather than inspire, fear, but they are walls created by fear nonetheless. The same may be said of the gated communities that are proliferating in the western and southern United States, and in other countries as well. Granted they may be pleasingly designed, covered with shrubs and flowers, inviting to look at. But their function, certainly as symbol and generally in reality, is to exclude the unwanted, those feared by their residents. Not only the elderly in retirement communities or the rich in country-club estates want such fear-inspired protection; when public housing residents want walls or fences around their developments, it is not to identify them or signal their high status, but to protect themselves from the fear inspired by drug dealers or vandals. Such walls are walls of fear as well as walls of security.

The fear that walls inspire or reflect is sometimes unwitting, but is often their very purpose. This includes not only walls that confine, as prison walls, but also walls that dominate, as the walls of the citadel, the palace, and the fortress. We have just to think of the images of the castle in the movie version of Franz Kafka's story, or in the Gothic romances of the nineteenth century. In the opening scene of Rainer Fassbinder's *Berlin Alexanderplatz*, Franz walks out the massive gates of the prison in which he had been incarcerated and momentarily turns back with a start from the unfamiliarity of the outside world he glimpses to seek the protection of the walls in which he had been confined; the striking image shows the ambiguity of the role physical walls can play. In each of these cases the walls are designed as clear physical statements, as definitions both of what is within them and what is outside. Their meaning shifts with the social circumstances of their use. And it is the meaning of walls, their boundary function, rather than the simple physical form they take (except as that form relates to that function), that is the focus of this article.

The Two Sides of All Walls

Walls are boundaries, then, but they are a particular form of boundary. All boundaries suggest divisions among individuals and activities, within or among societies, or between groups and peoples. Everything has boundaries, for all life and the spaces it occupies are bounded. Boundaries say nothing about the relations of those on opposite sides; they can be friends and neighbors sharing values and resources, or bitter enemies. "Boundaries" is thus a neutral, if not a deceptively bland, term. Walls that act as boundaries, however, can suggest a particular set of relationships between those on the opposite sides of the boundary: separation, distance, fear, tension, hostility, inequality, and alienation. They are two-sided in their purpose: at once creating and seeking to defend against the impact of division. A little white picket fence may bound a peaceful front yard in the traditional small town in the United States, or define the limits of a real-estate lot; an eight-foot-high wall with barbed wire in Johannesburg's white northern suburbs may similarly be built along a lot line, but its meaning is quite different. Both walls do more than simply state ownership and define territoriality; both give a clear if opposite message about the relationship of those inside to those passing by.

The distinction between the various meanings of walls lies then in their shifting purpose. One may imagine that walls were not really needed within the Garden of Eden, just as clothes were not needed. But the Garden of Eden, if medieval paintings are to be believed, did have a wall around it; indeed, etymologically, a garden is an "enclosed place," and the word for "garden" and the word for "fence" or "wall" are directly related in many languages (as, indeed, is "town" with "*Zaun*," the German word for "fence"). When Adam and Eve were expelled from the garden, gates were closed behind them. The wall around the garden and the gates that controlled access to it were no longer meant to protect those that formerly lived within them, but to exclude them. They represented an inequality between the power that controlled the gates and those excluded by them. The intervention of a snake had converted walls that had been for protection to walls of exclusion.

Anthropological literature suggests that walls around the places where one or more families dwelt were first used for purposes of social identification, each household having a similar definition. At some point walls were used as protection against threats from the outside, whether from beasts or hostile human marauders. No one can object, on moral or social grounds, to walls built for such purposes. They served basic human needs, and their social role was positive. Only aggressors could complain. But, since these early days, walls have come to play a more ambiguous and increasingly divisive role. They have become boundary walls. They have come to reflect, and to reinforce, hierarchies of wealth and power; divisions among people, races, ethnic groups, and religions; and hostilities, tensions, and fears. Their use has become aggressive as much as defensive; they

Boundary walls have come to reflect one of the chief characteristics of our historical experience: that those who oppress are themselves limited by their oppression.

have imposed the will of the powerful on the powerless as much as they have protected the powerless from superior force. They have isolated more than they have included.

In the process, boundary walls have come to reflect one of the chief characteristics of our historical experience: that those who oppress are themselves limited by their oppression, those that imprison are themselves imprisoned, that power dehumanizes those that exercise it as well as those against whom it is exercised. Since most of us are neither at the very top nor at the very bottom of the hierarchy of our societies, most of us will simultaneously oppress and be oppressed, imprison and be imprisoned, and be both protected and limited by the walls of the cities in which we live. Walls today represent power, but they also represent isolation; security, but at the same time fear. They are a second-best solution to the problems of our societies. They have always been a second-best solution; one might indeed speak of an ideal society, one of peace and freedom, as a society without any walls other than that minimum needed for shelter and privacy: without boundary walls. But we have come to accept this second-best solution as the best we can do. We accept walls that divide people and rigidify the relations among them as inevitable. They pervade our cities, they are visible (or block our sight) wherever we look, they symbolize status, rank, and power (or its lack), they are taken for granted and accepted as desirable, in one form or another, by everyone.[1]

I want to argue that the key to understanding the meaning of the boundary function of walls is an examination of the relationship between those on the two sides of the wall. That relationship is, today, likely to be one of inequality, one of superiority and inferiority, domination and subordination, benefit and cost. But, because even in a hierarchically structured society very few are at the extreme ends of the hierarchy, because most are higher than some but lower than others, because those that benefit pay some of the costs and those that pay most of the costs derive some benefit also, walls will be two-sided in their impact, not only because they separate those on their two sides from each other but also because they reflect domination for some, subordination for others. They will rarely if ever reflect unlimited power, or total powerlessness, to either side. Their very existence bears evidence to the limitations, the insecurities, the fears, that lead to their construction by those to be protected, at the same time as they may impose even greater limitation, insecurity, and fear on those outside their ambit.

Will the history of walls as boundaries bear out this understanding of their meaning?

The History: Overview

The oldest, longest standing, and most famous wall of all is probably the Great Wall of China. Built by the Emperor Ch'in Shih Huang Ti in the years after 228 B.C., it was eventually almost 1,500 miles long, between 18 and 30 feet high, topped by a road over 10 feet wide, and dotted with more than 25,000 watch towers. It was built for defense against invasions from the north, and much of it is still standing, not only visible to tourists but also perhaps the man-made object most easily identified by satellites.

Yet it never fulfilled its expected role. Large invading armies were able to open gaps in it, through which their troops could pour; only small raiding parties were kept out. If it protected, it did so not because of its height or its defenses, for individual warriors could scale it with relative ease; only their horses could not get over it.[2] It protected against small dangers, but not against large ones.[3] Like the Maginot Line the French built against the danger of German invasion more than 2,000 years later, it may have rendered those who built it more vulnerable to attack than they had been, for by placing their faith in a physical wall they undermined those strategies that might in fact have been more effective in their defense.

Masada's walls, in and on a mass of rock in the desert near the Dead Sea, were created by nature, although fortified by men and women. We think of them today primarily as the scene of the last stand of Eleazor and the Jews who retreated to it in A.D. 70 to resist Roman conquest. At that time they were defensive walls, within which those who had no choice but to trust in them committed suicide rather than surrender when they were breached. But the same walls had also served Herod over 100 years before as an outpost to extend his power against the Parthians.

The walls of the cities the Romans built are perhaps the classic example of city walls that are at the same time walls of aggression and walls of defense. They were built by the invading armies of Rome to protect the "civilized" communities the Romans founded from attack by the barbarians, but they were built on the lands of those barbarians, and might as justly be viewed as means of consolidating conquest as of protecting civilian life.

The walls of medieval cities reflected the exact distribution of power within medieval society. A typical pattern was the citadel on the hill (the fortress through which the temporal and spiritual lords dominated the city) surrounded at its base by the residents of the city (its workers, merchants, and crafts people), in turn surrounded by a city wall separating them from the agricultural serfs and laborers outside. The frequent location of the Jewish ghettos, outside those walls but immediately adjacent to them, likewise symbolized both the rejection of Jewish communities by, and their necessity to, the dominant society.

In towns established for commercial rather than political reasons, city walls could play a more two-sided role. For the crafts and trading community within the city, the use of walls for military defense was accompanied by the use of those same walls for economic benefit, since they permitted the dominant guilds to control entry, to regulate commerce, and to set the rules for business activity within their precincts. If they were an unwelcome necessity for defense, they were also a very useful instrument of control and enrichment.

The advent of the bourgeois epoch effectively ended the history of city walls in most of the world. Partly, this was because of the industrial revolution; with powerful artillery, walls could not stand a concerted onslaught for long.[4] As powerful an influence, however, was the ascendancy of capitalism and the advent of liberal democracy. Power no longer had to be exercised with the symbolism, or the reality, of superior force behind it; the combination of a new economic and political freedom meant that hierarchical relationships of power and wealth could be put in place, protected, and enhanced through more subtle means than walls of stone. Technological and socioeconomic changes combined to make city walls obsolete. Napoléon probably represents the historical turning point; after his sweep through Europe, city after city demolished its walls, often replacing them with representational boulevards, parks, or highways. Vienna and Paris are among the best-known examples.

Today, boundaries around cities, when they are visible at all, are physically permeable. They may be green belts, deliberately established and owned by the government. They may be sporadically created by zoning restrictions, the exact boundary hard to see in the gradual slope of height and use limitations. They may be a highway laid along the city's legal boundary, as the Périphérique in Paris, or a beltway defining a metropolitan area, as in Washington, D.C. They are social boundaries, walling in or walling out more by the nature of the activities and the structures on each side of them than by their physical presence itself.

Today, the walls, the physical walls of division, are inside the city rather than around it—or, more accurately, within the metropolitan area, which is an economically integrated whole but internally divided. The modern urban area, in its complex uses of walls, far surpasses anything known in previous centuries.

Anyone who has lived in a modern metropolis can conjure up the following images without difficulty:[5]

•Battery Park City, surrounded on three sides by water, best accessible across a major roadway by an enclosed pedestrian skywalks from the World Trade Center, a haven of planned security in an unruly city;

•One enclosed mall-like complex after another built in the heart of a central business district, whether in New Haven or Atlanta, or simply an atrium space suggesting an openness that is in fact carefully exclusive;

•Wide curved walls of stucco surrounding a restricted residential area just outside a California city, with a manned gatehouse controlling entry from the outside streets;

•A landscape of barbed wire topping the roofs of buildings on the Lower East Side of Manhattan;

•Public housing projects in New York City surrounded by fourteen-foot-high chain link fences behind which youngsters play ball;

•A model middle-income community in Los Angeles or in Miami, whose street entrance (impossible to tell whether it is private or public) has a barrier arm next to a watchhouse;

•An eight-foot-high wrought-iron fence, embellished with ornamentation at the bottom and prominent outward-turned spikes at the top, surrounding the common grounds of a cooperative apartment development at its street side, the fence protecting its recreational grounds;

•Buildings burnt out in the low-income "riot zone" of Los Angeles, similar buildings destroyed by Hurricane Andrew south of Miami, and buildings abandoned by the owners as no longer profitable to rent in the South Bronx, all with walls on the verge of collapse and gaping open windows long since exploited by looters and vandals, now occasionally offering a minimum of shelter to a squatter;

•The enclosed Renaissance Center in Detroit, standing bright and tall at the edge of the city center, visible for miles around, separated by light-years from the scenes of earlier riots nearby, in stark contrast to an old and run-down set of low buildings, partly empty and abused, surrounding it at its base;

•The Martin Luther King Plaza, built by African Americans in the Watts area of Los Angeles after the riots of 1964, now with a heavy but open cast-iron fence around it, protected by the National Guard during the recent disturbances;

•Union-sponsored housing on New York's East River, surrounded by high fences topped by razor wire;

•Village Green, a prize-winning, integrated, liberal community in Los Angeles, replacing its inconspicuous fences with sturdier ones with "Private Property" posted on them, and now guarded by a private security patrol;

•Suburbs, building their walls of space between themselves and the cities on which they depend, limiting access by the avoidance of public transit and public services;
•"Edge cities," insulated by walls of distance from the heterogeneity of real cities, providing a congenial environment for living, shopping, sometimes even working, for their one-class residents.

What Walls Divide: The Clarity of Hierarchical Lines

We can draw some general conclusions from this proliferation of walls. The key lies in the concept of hierarchy, what Nathan Glazer calls "horizontal lines of division," as opposed to vertical ones.[6] Horizontal lines differentiate people by quantity of an attribute, most simply by power and wealth, rather than by kind or characteristic, as religion or color or sexual preference. Very crudely and schematically, the horizontal lines of division, those that divide a city into hierarchically ordered parts, might be listed as creating five separate residential cities. In the typical large city of the United States today, the following distinctive types of quarters can be found; while each type is represented in multiple neighborhoods, those neighborhoods fall into an ordered pattern, which forms essentially separate cities within the city:[7]

The *dominating city*, not really part of the city but enclaves or isolated buildings with luxury housing, is occupied by the top of the economic, social, and political hierarchy. In the United States, the dominating city tends to be all white and disproportionately Anglo-Saxon Protestant.

The *gentrified city* is occupied by the professional, managerial, and technical groups, whether yuppie or muppie, often dinks (double income, no kids). Ethnically it is relatively open, being to an extent a meritocracy, but since access to education is unequally distributed, whites are heavily over-represented.

The *suburban city*, sometimes single-family housing in the outer city, other times apartments near the center, is occupied by skilled workers, mid-range professionals, and upper civil servants. Ethnic characteristics will vary widely by location; African Americans and Latinos are under-represented, immigrant groups separated.

The *tenement city*, sometimes areas of cheaper single-family housing but most often rentals, is occupied by lower-paid blue- and white-collar workers, and generally (although less so in the United States) includes substantial social housing. Most immigrant groups cluster in the tenement city, although individual members will leave it as their circumstances improve; African Americans and Latinos are over-represented in most tenement cities in the United States.

The *abandoned city* is the end result of trickle-down, places left for the poor, the unemployed, and the excluded, where in the United States home-less housing[8] is most frequently located. Here the poorest of the poor, and overwhelmingly African Americans and Latinos, are concentrated.

Such a schematic description should not, of course, be taken as a scientific taxonomy. Boundary lines between these cities, these quarters, the walls of the modern city, are dynamic; in the extreme case, as perhaps in Los Angeles, the lines may shift from block to block, street to street, as one group moves in and another moves on or out, and only social or ethnic characteristics may separate one quarter from the other. But, for the residents of the tenement and the abandoned cities, the Koreatowns and the Watts and the barrios of Los Angeles, for instance, they are distinct communities, separated by socially palpable walls.

The physical characteristics of walls are not decisive as to their meaning. Rather, the key questions is: Who is on which side of the wall? Does the wall perpetuate power, or defend against it? Does it reinforce domination, or shield vulnerability? Does it strengthen hierarchical relationships among people, or does it pave the way towards greater equality?

Morally these are, it seems to me, the most important distinctions. For the wooden stockades built by Native Americans around their settlements may resemble the sharp pointed walls erected by the United States army around its forts when it came in to "pacify" them; yet one wall was for defense, the other for aggression. In today's cities, the poorer residents of the Lower East Side of Manhattan, of Kreuzberg in Berlin, and of the area around the University of Southern California in Los Angeles wish to keep the gentrifiers out as much as the residents of the suburbs and luxury housing of these cities want to keep the poor out; yet the two desires are not equivalent morally. One represents the desire of those poorer to insulate themselves from losses to the more powerful; the other represents the ability of the more powerful to insulate themselves from the necessity of sharing with, or having exposure to, those poorer. One wall defends survival, the other protects privilege.

Walls of the type I have described can thus be tangible or intangible, physical or social or economic, official or customary. Walls are usually thought of as being of stone or concrete or barbed wire. But topographic divisions, highways, and freeways can be just as much walls; the old phrase "on the other side of the railroad tracks" references a clearly visible and functional physical barrier. Walls can also be of price and status, of rule and prejudice. These perhaps are even more effective, for intangible walls can be internalized by force and custom, their causes and functions hidden, their maintenance costs reduced. Sometimes boundary walls are simply inscribed on a map and enforced by law or official practice: the red lines drawn around minority areas in United States cities in the 1930s, where mortgage loans were refused to anyone living in these "red-lined" areas, effectively created ghettos; the curfew line drawn in Los Angeles during the uprisings in April of 1992 reflected, but reinforced, a similar ghettoization.

There is thus no room for a fetishism of physical walls. But walls can, I believe, usefully be defined by their purpose and the parties they serve. Types of walls may be grouped according to the following taxonomy:

Ramparts, castle walls, in my use symbolically are named after the fortifications surrounding the medieval citadels. A citadel[9] is defined by the Oxford English Dictionary as a "little city... a fortress commanding a city, which it serves both to protect and to keep in subjection." Today walls of domination, expressing superiority, typically are physically represented by superior height in the skyscraper apartments and penthouses that have replaced the mansions of the upper class in the city and that are now protected by technologically developed walls, gates, and security devices. They generally embody representative architecture, the architecture of wealth and power. Such walls may be underplayed, for similar representative reasons, in the offices of a government wishing to portray itself as democratic;[10] or they may be deliberately overpowering, as in the official buildings of fascist governments; or they may be treated as businesslike and internalized, as routine and sensible precautions in an irrationally dangerous world, as they are at all major airports and in the business districts of London and New York City. Ramparts, small and large, physical and human, pervade the world of those with much to lose. They defend against those below them in the hierarchy. They define what I have called the *dominating city*.

Stockades, as I use the term, are named after the walls of pointed stakes typically used in the early history of the United States. Their function is similar to that of the Roman walls of aggressive superiority built around the settlements created by the Roman Empire in the lands of the "barbarians." Unlike ramparts, which protect a position already well established, stockades are used to expand territory, to intrude on hostile ground; stockades, indeed, are likely to be attacked. The market may be the instrument of aggression, or the aggression may be direct and physical; in either case, it is clearly unwelcome. In the relatively tame context of gentrification in New York City, stockades both protect "pioneers" and secure their invasion. The analogy, suggested by Neil Smith, is appropriate for the process of creating the *gentrified city*.[11]

Stucco walls, often gated, sometimes of glass, is a fitting term for the walls that shelter exclusive communities whose residents are socially, economically, and politically established, but not at the very top of the hierarchy. Here fear of those below is attenuated by distance and status, but a symbolic demarcation remains necessary to reinforce a security often buttressed by governmental measures such as exclusionary zoning. Here walls exclude for reasons of status and social control, symbolically protecting privilege and wealth from the threat of physical intrusion. Unlike ramparts, whose walls are likely to be understated but dramatically effective when needed, walls in the *suburban city* are likely to be pretentious; they are intended to denote comfort, security, and the superiority of those behind them to the world outside.

Barricades are walls sometimes defined, as for immigrant quarters, simply by the language of street signs and spoken words, sometimes by the color of the skins of the residents, sometimes by the age and limited pretensions of the housing, sometimes by the social symbolism of the sign that says "public housing" or the architecture of unornamented blank walls that spells "project." These walls may define the *tenement city*, but they may also surround the trailer park of migrant workers or the limits of a stable squatter settlement. But here the walls, if erected by their residents for protection, cohesion, and solidarity, are reluctant, abashed, perhaps even undesired. For the residents of the *tenement city* are used to seeing other people's walls aimed at keeping *them* out; walls more often mean to them "keep out" or "watch out," rather than "you are safe inside." At best, for their residents, the attempt is to make them visible enough to serve their function, but transparent enough not to reflect hostility or exclusivity. At worst, for these walls are as two sided as all boundary walls, they hem in, limit, demarcate areas of private disinvestment and official neglect.

Prison walls is the obvious term for walls of confinement, walls defining ghettos and prisons and camps for the temporary warehousing of the unwanted, walls built for the control and reeducation of those forced to live behind them. These are the physical walls of the ancient ghettos, the social and economic walls surrounding the modern ghettos, the brick walls of Andrew Cuomo's transitional homeless housing in New York City, and the barbed wire surrounding the camps of Cuban and Haitian refugees in the southern United States. Often reinforced by ostentatious public actions, they are the walls that racism has erected around the African-American ghettos of United States cities, walls of public housing, of highways, and of public institutions. These walls are entirely unwanted by those that are behind them; they are imposed from the outside on those believed to lack the power to resist. They define the *abandoned city*.

On paper, the parties divided by walls, the parts of the city walls divide, and the type of walls used to define each part, can be coherently described. The reality is always more ambiguous.

At the extreme ends of the spectrum, the purpose of walls will be unquestioned. At the upper end, whom *ramparts* help and whom they oppress is clear; at

Perhaps one way of defining a better society would be to speak of it as a wall-less society, a society in which the divisions among people were not equated with the walls between them.

the bottom, *prison walls*, ghetto walls, imprison, and everyone knows it. But in between, *stockades*, *stucco walls*, and *barricades* may all be deceptive in appearance, with different meanings for different people, and even for the same people. Barbed wire protects, but it imprisons; *stockades* protect the invader, but confine as well; *stucco walls* and wrought-iron fences provide a sense of identity, but reflect insecurity and betray vulnerability as well.

These ambivalences are not accidental. Most people are in daily contact with some above them and some below them in the ladder of wealth and influence; they need both, and are needed by both. Thus people may at different times defend and attack, need protection and want to aggress, wish to exclude but wish not to be excluded. Those are the inevitable results of living in a society that is hierarchically ordered; one's position in the hierarchy needs to be continually established, reinforced in all directions. Hence the necessity of walls that reflect such hierarchical status.

But hierarchy is not an inevitable part of social organization. We live in a society in which the prosperity of one is often based on the poverty of the other. That need not be so; we have today the resources, the skills, and the room to be able to combine justice with prosperity, mutual respect with efficient organization. Physical restructuring can help achieve such a society; attacking walls of fear, walls of confinement, will help. But it needs to be part of a broader effort to build a better society, physically, economically, socially, and politically.

All walls are to some extent boundaries, but all boundaries are not walls. Perhaps one way of defining a better society would be to speak of it as a wall-less society, a society in which the divisions among people were not equated with the walls between them. We have sometimes, in recent years, attempted to justify segregation and even ghettoization by saying that it can be a source of strength for those within the ghetto; it can produce solidarity, creativity, and bonds of mutual support that a less confined environment might not nourish. It is certainly true that ghettos have produced wonderful and heroic actions. But that is certainly no justification for the creation of ghettos. Those who have lost one arm or one leg can sometimes do wonders with the other; that is no reason to cut off an arm or a leg.

But then there are what some choose to call "voluntary ghettos," the Chinatowns, Lower East Sides, Koreatowns, and Harlems of American cities, the clustering together of immigrants from the same location in unique neighborhoods in their new country. In New York City today there are communities of Russian Jews, Vietnamese, Cambodians, Lebanese, and Guatemalans, just as in previous years there were neighborhoods of Japanese, Italians, and Jews. Residents in these neighborhoods do cluster together, help each other, support each others' businesses, share tastes in food and clothing, and celebrate the same holidays and festivals. I would not call such communities ghettos, precisely because their residents are not confined to them, but are there by choice. Residents can, and do, move out when they wish, and no one else who wishes to move in is prevented from doing so. They have in other words, no walls around them. They do not claim superiority; they claim only difference. Nor is inferiority communicated to them by those outside. They are free communities of affinity, of solidarity; it is of their essence that they are wall-less. The need to protect "turf" against strangers is not an inherent attribute of such neighborhoods, but a reflection of fears, insecurities, and tensions externally induced.

"Enclaves" is the word often used for such communities to differentiate them from "ghettos." But, mirroring the two-sided nature of boundary walls, all ghettos are in part enclaves, enclaves in part ghettos. A distinction by whether the walls around them are voluntary, whether the parties inside are there by choice or by force, does not work completely. For an immigrant group may form an enclave "voluntarily" because of the absence of any better alternative. And a group forced to live in a ghetto may develop a social structure and a set of interests dependent on continued separation, creating a positive incentive to maintain that separation. The ambiguities of purpose and of party are not easy to resolve.

Yet one policy conclusion seems clear. The key question, in the construction of cities and of communities within cities, is what the relationship of the people within them is to one another and to those outside. Walls reflect those relationships. If they are hierarchical, then boundaries will reflect power and status, and walls will reflect superiority and inferiority. If differences among people are differences only of kind, of preference, of history and tradition, then walls may in fact undermine hierarchy by fostering respect for difference. Such walls may require negotiation to meet the needs of those on both sides; if those negotiations are among equals, they become simply an inevitable aspect of living in an urban society. Walls that welcome and shelter are fine in their place, but not walls that exclude and oppress, or isolate and confine.

If we see walls as boundaries, all this becomes even clearer, and the lessons to be drawn from it become sharp. A boundary, whether represented physically by a wall, or socially by the representations of architecture and design, or purely by social and cultural differences as it is crossed, should protect and provide security. It should not denote a hierarchy or an inequality of wealth, power, or status on either side. Boundaries should invite their crossing; they should bring differences together at the same time as they support individual and group identities. If differences are nonhierarchical, are not of domination and subordination, interaction across the boundary will be voluntary, peaceable, and expansive. It is the exclusionary and oppressive character of boundaries, and the walls that are likely to represent them, that inspires fear. Such walls, in a decent society, should be unnecessary.

Mirrors

Kevin Sites

As a television journalist I have done only two stories focusing specifically on architecture. But in those two stories I was exposed to the beautifully simple concept that architecture, unlike any other art form, allows us to not only express the transcendence of our hopes and the prison of our fears—but also to live in them. That is to say, we build our shelters of mirror as well as mortar.

While working in Los Angeles, I learned about the famous architectural photographer, Julius Shulman, who, at eighty-one, was coming out of retirement to document the completed renovation of his favorite building, the Bradbury. Designed more than one hundred years ago by George H. Wyman, the Bradbury appeared from the outside to be just another semianonymous downtown brick box. But inside it seemed the most fascinating building in Los Angeles (it was inspired by a description of a futuristic utopia in Edward Bellamy's science fiction novel, *Looking Backward*). Since Shulman had an ongoing relationship with the Bradbury—he had photographed it in the 1950s for *LIFE* magazine—it seemed like the perfect feature story. It was ripe with narrative parallels, visual metaphors—and two interesting characters.

Shulman already had his large-format camera mounted on a tripod and slung over his shoulder, the way a carpenter carries a two-by-four, when I met him in the lobby of the Bradbury. He reminded me of Floyd the barber from *The Andy Griffith Show* but with the energy of Elvis in his early years. We videotaped him as he talked and recorded the "frozen music" of architecture.

"When I photograph the Bradbury it's almost like a religious experience," he told me. He spent the next two and a half hours peeling back the building's collective beauty, which helped me to see the magnificence of its individual elements. There was the mesmerizing floor-to-ceiling open space, which was the unifying aspect of the building surrounded by rings of floors. The glass eggshell ceiling filtered the intense Southern California sun into a soft whiteness. Elaborate black iron railings projected tree-branch-like shadows along the polished hardwood floors and Italian marble staircases. But the mechanical heartbeat within this organism of brick and wood, glass and iron, was the elevators. They were like open

Above and following:
Bradbury Building, Los Angeles, California
as photographed by Julius Shulman

canary cages of maple and metal that were hoisted and lowered by an exposed system of pulleys and weights, which were originally fueled by hydraulic pressure. And in the relatively short distance of only five floors they seemed to address the most nagging conflict of humankind by creating a space where science and religion seemed to peacefully coexist. This was accomplished by simultaneously possessing the man-made, industrial aesthetics of one of Captain Nemo's undersea inventions while ferrying their passengers on a swaddling sunlit ascension to the heavens.

As I watched him work, l discovered what set Shulman apart from other architectural photographers. He not only understood the building-block beauty of a structure, but also its inherent purpose—to provide a place for people. To photograph a building without people, I began to appreciate, was like taking a picture of an empty shoe; you can clearly see the design, but it is divorced from its function and meaning.

"Some of my greatest photographs were taken with people," Shulman said, "because they bring scale and life to a composition." He positioned people in archways and along staircases to create compositions where brick and marble absorbed a patina of life through human silhouettes and reflections. At the same time, his subjects were preserved and became a part of the Bradbury's art, a frame constructed from science and imagination.

When I put the story together, I decided to use only music to link the thoughts and images Shulman had shared with me. I thought the somber but ornate *Ave Maria* would be appropriate for the Bradbury's cathedral-like open space and Shulman's "near religious experience" remark. At the end of the story, Shulman said, "There is a line in all of my compositions that leads you into the picture." I played off that statement, and filmed Shulman walking down a shadowy corridor of brick and marble and dissolving into a setting from one of his 1950 black-and-white photographs of the Bradbury. It created the illusion that he had disappeared into the building. What I hoped would come across to viewers through Shulman's work and reflections was the transcendent power of architecture, its ability to allow us to live within the space and light of our own air.

The second half of my architectural education taught me that architecture's transcendent power also works in reverse. While it can be used to create cathedrals, it can also make cages. When open space is subjugated to the need for protective space, the celebration of our hopes through design gives way to the physical manifestation of our fears. Almost always, these take the shape of walls.

But aside from China's Great Wall, walls hardly ever get good press—until they come down. Architects know this, so rather than call them walls, some

When open space is subjugated to the need for protective space, the celebration of our hopes through design gives way to the physical manifestation of our fears.

describe their work as "defensive architecture." Defensive architecture has been around forever but started getting much more notice after the 1992 riots in Los Angeles. Santa Monica's Brian Murphy—who has been referred to as a guerrilla architect—turned the idea of residential curb appeal on its head by producing urban camouflage, structures that deter unwanted attention because of their unfriendly or impregnable look. It was Murphy's work that convinced me to do a story about how serious people were getting about their "walls."

When I began shooting the story, Murphy met me at one of his defensive home designs in Venice. He appeared to be such a lighthearted guy that I was surprised he was the mastermind behind such intimidating work. Wearing a baseball hat, T-shirt, shorts, and sandals, he walked me through a famous actor's home that was located in one of the area's most crime-ridden neighborhoods. The inside was spacious and light, with crisscrossing catwalks, large skylights, and a curved ceiling that resembled an upside-down boat hull still in the shaping stage. It was filled with expensive artwork, electronics, and even a forty-seat theater.

But if the inside said SoHo art house, the outside said North Jersey warehouse. It was a rectangle of unevenly cut corrugated metal with reinforced steel doors and unscalable pitched roof, all trimmed neatly in razor-sharp concertina wire. Murphy pointed to the metal face and said, "They would probably like to have a big bay window, but it just doesn't make sense here." Even the landscaping was gruff, with some cactus standing guard behind the front yard's small white picket fence, which Murphy threw in for irony. He said it had that "don't mess with me look." No hyperbole there. It was imposing enough from the ground, but from a helicopter it looked like an overturned tin pot or an armadillo hiding from a pickup truck. It was an effective architectural reaction to both real and perceived threats. No one touched the place, not even during the riots.

In addition to Murphy's work, my story also examined the growth of gated communities like L.A.'s popular Park Labrea development. Driving through the area it almost seemed like a film studio backlot with children playing on green lawns and suburban-looking streets just a mile or two from downtown skyscrapers. But these lawns and streets were separated from the rest of the city by high metal fences that reminded me of the walls that separated the Catholic and

Protestant neighborhoods in Northern Ireland. From the air, the towers of Park Labrea were giant Stonehenges, gathered together in a protective magic circle.

Gated communities are sometimes criticized for their exclusive nature. But as Murphy said to me in Venice, "We are animals and we *do* have survival instincts." Those survival instincts seem to have won out despite criticism, since many more gated communities are being developed in Los Angeles and around the country. But the tradeoffs are clear. By erecting walls around Park Labrea or any development, architects and designers might create safer environments, but they will also create more limited ones. We may succeed in locking crime out, but we will have locked fear in. Or, as Robert Frost put it more eloquently, "Something there is that doesn't love a wall...Before I built a wall, I'd ask to know/What I was walling in or walling out."[1] The story I eventually produced did not criticize the idea of defensive architecture, but did raise the issue that an increasing number of people are feeling the need to dig in for a less than comfortable future.

In my two brief journalistic ventures, it became obvious to me that in architecture's inherent purpose—-to create a place for people—cathedrals are preferable to even gilded cages, open space is better than closed, and in the mirror of architecture we look better in our hopes than our fears. What is not so obvious is in which reflection we can safely live.

The Fear of Architecture

Julius Shulman

The Tower of Pisa is now a source of fear—long after its designers
had envisioned its lofty levels, achieved by a brilliantly executed
eight-story spiral stairway, as a means of providing vistas of the land
for miles around.

The "dog door" is a control measure to alleviate the owner's fear—
the dogs could soil the new carpet in the adjacent bedroom.

above: The child in the scene is confronted by a horizontal fence. Her parents and the landscape architect preserved the view, which a vertical structure could have blocked, while curbing the potential danger of the adjacent steep slopes.

right: At the same site the design of a trespass-inhibiting fence with ankle-twisting rocks at its base is a product of fear. Ironically, the stimulation impressed by a client's sense of insecurity onto a design program often produces creative responses.

left: The anticipation of trespass through a doored wall of an adobe house in Santa Fe, New Mexico is tempered by the small door inset into the larger framed entry structure. People were forced, by the lowered doorway, to bend to gain passage. During earlier days of living in remote areas, inhabitants feared the dangers of intruders; a guard stationed behind the wall could strike the intruder's bent body as he passed through the boundary.

above: The scene is a daring spiraled airport parking structure designed by San Diego architects Tucker, Sandler & Bennett in 1965. The passengers and visitors, many of whom had a fear of flying, became fearful on descending, especially from the upper levels. The constant radius of turning and the low adjacent walls frightened them. This structure, although a design award winner, was, in the opinion of the fearful ones, a failure.

Even when the revolving doors of this Buenos Aires bank were locked, the building was susceptible to break in. The solution by the architects (to eliminate fears of the clients), was a steel, glovelike encasement secured on the interior.

Similarly, a bank's vaults highlight fear. The designers were confronted with a specification: if the massive entry was breached, a sliding
steel-barred gate would impede.

left: Architect Pierre Koenig assisted his clients in acquiring property for a home. Condition: a view with dramatic visual impact. The suggested site fulfilled the condition precisely. But how could a house be built on such a steep slope? Koenig sketched an overhanging steel and concrete system. Had the clients maintained (or retained) their uncertainty in their choice of sites, this classic house would never have been built. The photograph itself has appeared in practically every architectural magazine throughout the world as well as many books on architecture, thus helping to allay the public's fear of the structural capabilities of modern architecture.

above: Raphael Soriano, who designed my home and studio in 1947–49, lost many potential clients for their fear of what their friends would say about his factorylike buildings. My "factory" withstood the violence of the 1994 Northridge earthquake. The flexibility and monolithic properties of the steel-cradled structure absorbed the usual destructiveness of such a high-rated quake. No tumbling objects, no breaking glass, and no cracking walls occurred in the entire structure. Not a bad factory for a good life—we have no fear of architecture!

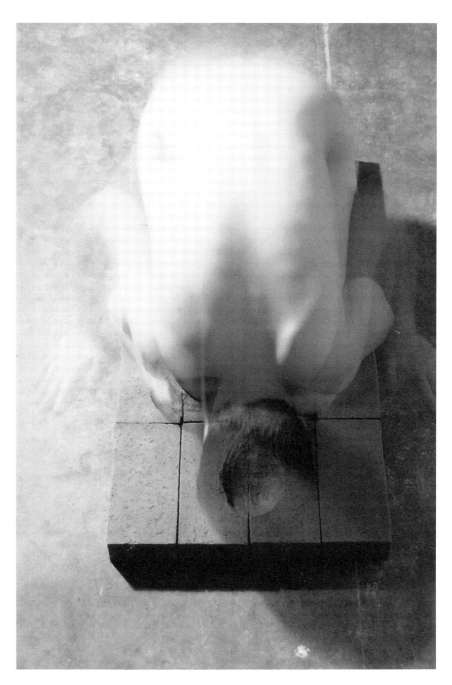

above and following:
Cayewah Easley, from the series *Body/Brick*, 1995

Abject Terror
A Story of Fear, Sex, and Architecture

Dora Epstein

In my tiny California grade school, its asphalt playground ringing loudly from the neighboring freeway, there were two distinct types of kids. We were desegregated, yes, but separate and unequal.

There were those like myself, those who lived in the Annex, with our detached single-family homes and detached sense of place, not quite El Cerrito, definitely not Richmond. We had a detached way of speaking, not up on the latest slang, and this had a way of magnifying our attachments—to the boundaries of our ten-square-block world, San Pablo Avenue to the east, the I-80 Freeway to the west.

And there were those who lived on the other side of the Tunnel, the Tunnel that provided daily access from the other side of the freeway, the Tunnel that separated the Annex suburb from the Richmond ghetto. Through the unlit, vibrating, echoing space, the Tunnel kids emerged in the morning and returned in the afternoon, as if the Tunnel were breathing them in and out. It was not that we feared the Tunnel kids (so tough, so cool, so bad-assed); we feared their beyond-world, their known that was our unknown, their forbidden "mean streets." And, most of all, we feared the dark passage, the Tunnel itself.

Whispering and wide-eyed, we told each other haunting stories about the Tunnel, like the time when some boys had a gang fight there, or, worse, when a girl our age was dragged into It and raped. And we dared each other to run from one side to the other just for a can of Coke. I did it once, breathless, to find only a grassy path and a big brown apartment building on the other side. I recognized it from countless car trips with my family as not so bad, but ran back scared all the same. The Tunnel had a way of doing that. The Tunnel stood for our every childlike, bogeyman, nightmarish, full-moon, monster-under-the-bed fear.

My tiny grade school is closed now, boarded up. Through chain link, the Tunnel's maw is "tagged" and smells of piss—I still will not go there, not for a can of Coke or anything. Having become a woman, having internalized a somewhat normative femininity, I fear it now more than ever. I fear rape. I fear assault and robbery. I fear bodily harm—from the rough grabbing of my wrist to the gunshot wound to my head. I fear mental and emotional harm—from the racial epithet to the trauma of bodily victimization. I fear violation—of my materiality, of my un/conscious, of my self. The Tunnel implodes my terrors.

There is a story to this fearing, this fearing that maps the cityscapes into places I will go and places I will not. As speaking subjects, sentient members of urban terrains, we can narrate our cartographies of avoidance, our fearing, far better than we can narrate how the fearing came to be. We know, can articulate, what we have deemed as "unsafe"—the strange, the unfamiliar, the supposedly violent "other" against which we have insulated and barricaded ourselves—and what we have deemed as "safe"—the lit, the populated, the orderly, or seemingly controlled to which we have clung. We felt justified when violence occurred in the realm of our "unsafe"; felt shock when it occurred in our "safe."

But...we do not know the beginning of the story, how the fearing was developed—how the *unsafe* came to be associated with *place*, how the *cartography of real and potential danger*, which informs conscious choices of daily access and movement, was formed.

This is a story of formations, constructions, of gender identity, of ideology and inequality, of spaces, places, and representations. This is a story of fearing.

Never Talk to Strangers

When I or else when you/ and I or we
deliberate I lose I/ cannot choose if you if
we then near or where/ unless I stand as a loser
of losing that possibility
that something that I have/ or always want more than much
more at/ least to have as less and
yes directed by desire

June Jordan, "When I or Else"

In between the distinctions between safe and unsafe, the distinctions between place and scape, is that which separates, that which forms distinctions. I move through the city in a particular manner because I have constructed a particular psychical reality made of distinctions, or powerful fantasies of distinctions, based on, not rational intentions or cognitions, but rationalizations of unconscious desires.[1] And, in their formation, these unconscious desires articulate a self, an I, my consciousness, in relation to and in opposition to an entire set of others, based

This space between consciousness and perception, which informs our inner world, our psychical reality, is not a material space. It is boundless, endless, without spatiality or temporality.

on the first other (the mother), my pre/post-Oedipal development, and my entrance into the symbolic order, replete with myths, metaphors, and knowledges for reading the representations of space, place, and time... my perception.[2] Or,

> The development of psychic structure begins with a basic self-feeling and self-structure, which includes relatedness to and aspects of the [M]other, and it continues through internalizations and splittings-off of internalized self-other representations to create an inner world consisting of different aspects of an "I" in relation to different aspects of the other.[3]

This space between consciousness and perception, which informs our inner world, our psychical reality, is not a material space. It is boundless, endless, without spatiality or temporality. But, from their formation as the unconscious, all material space and all relations are given meaning, indeed, given a politic.

With the name of the father, the entrance into the symbolic, prohibitions are absorbed, internalized as self-other representations. We learn not to desire our mothers (Oedipalization), and to instead accept the father as possessing the all-powerful signifier, to accept the dominance of the phallus. We learn a gendered position. We learn a normative/performative category of sex, male or not-male... abject female.[4] And, hence, our unconscious desires, the space between consciousness and perception, are injected with fantasies of privileged signifiers in which identities are associated with dominance and/or servitude, and places are associated with powerful cultural symbols. Thus it is that ideologies, and especially gendered ideologies such as that of the patriarchy, can be and are represented within the symbolic as "a limitless space which the desiring subject negotiates by predominantly unconscious transactions."[5]

These are the distinctions.

Wear Sensible Shoes

> This is the girl's mouth, the taste
> daughters, not sons, obtain:
>
> Adrienne Rich, "That Mouth"

In between the distinctions between male and female, between genders, is that which, like my tiny grade school, is a topology of abjections—separate, unequal, inherently unstable. Yes, gender is psychically constructed, not biologically given, but the question of our fearing remains with how femininity is internalized in a patriarchal society. It is not enough to say that one's entrance into the symbolic, into language as "he" or "she," ordains the abjections. Nor is it enough to say that women, as a distinct binaried category, have been taught to fear the public realm in order to keep themselves in the private realm. For no such clear boundaries exist. For women are terrorized in all spaces, in all distinctions, in all representations.

I turn to the Freudian model of sexual development, and then must turn away from its assumption that women are generally "successful" in their feminine construct, that women have overcome the difficulties of disassociating desire for the mother for heterosexuality, that the internalization of femininity is somehow complete—for this implies a tremendous, perhaps impossible, ideological alignment.[6] So, instead, I turn to the body as "the point of junction between the social and the individual,"[7] and understand that gender is a continual process based on experiences of normativity in which the body is materialized, qualified for cultural intelligibility as male or female.[8] And, thus, our corporeal materiality, our body, becomes the *a priori* site for struggles over power, for power's most immediate o/abjection.

In patriarchal fantasy, in patriarchal ideology, the body of woman stands for man's fears—reminding him of what is lost (the mother), what is lacking (the penis), and what is at stake (mortality). Propelled by his ever-wanting desire for prenatal wholeness, man views woman as death, a referent to his primordial lack, to his separation from the mother, to his acceptance of a much more phallically powerful father, indeed, to his ultimately fragmented humanity. Her womb has a view—beginnings and endings. Mostly endings, to men. The original gratification of food and pleasure, the suckled breast, can never be refound; loss is inserted as a type of death.

In patriarchal fantasy, in patriarchal ideology, male fears of female bodies are projected outward, relegating women to idealization or denigration, private or public, virgin or whore. This ideology ordains what femininity is. It ordains the stories, the myths, the rituals. It ordains the fears at the site of the body. How much of this femininity is absorbed, internalized?

These are the abjections.

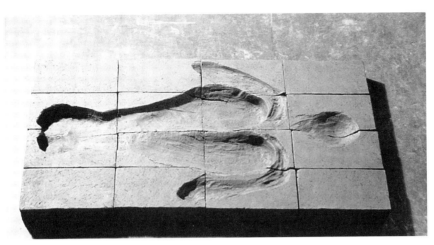

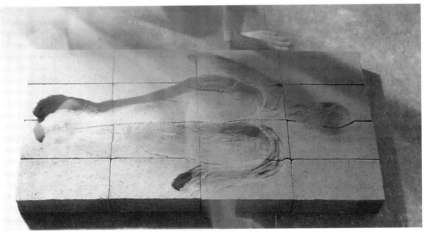

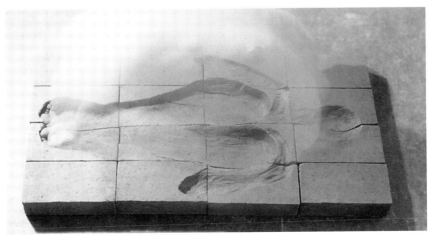

Never Make Eye Contact

I promised to show you a map you say but this is a mural
then yes let it be These are small distinctions
where do see it from is the question

Adrienne Rich, "An Atlas of a Difficult World"

I implicate architecture in this story. I implicate architecture in this fearing. I must, for architecture has been implicated for me.

The senses of spaces and places and cities, the very space that architecture inscribes, participates in our collective conscience. Or,

> The city's form and structure provide the context in which social rules and expectations are internalized or habituated in order to ensure social conformity, or position marginality at a safe or insulated or bounded distance (ghettoization). This means that the city must be seen as the most immediately concrete locus for the production and circulation of power.[9]

If ideology relies on representation, and it does, then architecture and the urban form it inscribes are advanced "technologies of representation."[10] They can stand for imprisonment on one side (of the Tunnel) and freedom on the other. They can stand for power in the hands of the few, and powerlessness in the hands of the many. They are representations, symbols, in their most solidified, monumental form: mortar and stone. They are the trauma of everyday life: flesh and blood.

There is a gap in the chain of signifiers, or else representation could not exist. This gap is the site of something (or things)—an *objet a*, a transitional object—through which unconscious desires are linked, not to the field of the other, but to a different fantasy, or phallic, scene. Here stands the building, here lies the city street—transitional objects of male desires. The built environment reverberates with the phallus—skyscrapers, walls, tunnels—and through these objects, patriarchal fears, bodily fears, become symptomized.

This is a way of rethinking the relationship between architecture and the political, a way of apprehending the implicit violence of architectural gestures. Here ego's aggressiveness, such as that which propels the patriarchal order, skews desire into dominance and servitude; here castration fantasies and pre-Oedipal longings turn unconscious desires into fears; here fears are realized, represented, and internalized.

I avoid spaces, places, certain buildings, certain streets. I construct a cartography of avoidance.

These are the implications.

Always Carry Protection

> The city bristles with malice.
>
> Mike Davis, *Fortress Los Angeles*

The city is armed. An architecture of fortification—iron bars and iron spikes, cinder blocks and barking dogs, razor-ribbon wires, deafening alarms—braces the structures from the threat of a supposedly violent other. Concrete bunkers shun the light.

"Where defenses are aggressively displayed they create bizarre, shunned streetscapes of distorted survivors and ruined losers."[11] And, where defenses peek through, let themselves be known, they let on that they are either suspect or victim, that you must also be armed.

I speak now of a postmodern cityscape, one that has been described as differing zones of security, as a frightening dystopia of fortification.[12] But, I also speak of a deep-seated hatred of the "modern" city whose carnival and diversity have always been viewed as a reason for fearing. Fear is considered a rational emotional response to the real and perceived menacing deeds and misintentions of strangers in public spaces.[13] We arm our buildings to arm ourselves from the intrusion of a public fluidity, and thus our buildings, our architectures of fortification, send a very clear message: "avoid this place or protect yourself."

This is social polarization. This is social control. We live, have lived, in fragmented cities—fragmented by the wastelands between the heterotopias of compensation and illusion, fragmented by the immediate and fluid boundaries between affluence and poverty, and fragmented by the mandates of zoning—because we are, as subjects and objects, fragmented beings. But, these cues of protection, these fortifications, tell a deeper story. "Sigmund Freud argued that the stronger the stimulus or shock (especially in the modern city), the stronger the screen erected in defense."[14] This shock must be tremendous.

What has happened to make us fear so much, to create a fearing so intense that the entirety of our built environment not only reinforces it but manifests it, to create a fearing so demanding that we limit our access and movement? Absorption here, internalization, is so terribly unnatural that we fear "strangers, the disorderly, the culturally alien, the morally corrupt, the disruptive."[15] All women are so when they are not-men.

Think here of the built environment as a text, a technology of representation, constituted by the same relations of power that produce knowledges, the reader of the text, and the reading. Power is at work—perpetually, culturally

But, this same fear is a liberator. It may be a dark passage, but also a way, a tunnel through to an understanding of fantasies and desires, of unconscious transactions, of ideological manifestations and bodily organizations.

shaping the subject; using representation as a text for the formation of the sexed subject, of sexuality, of sexual difference; using representation as a text for managing dread and pleasure, anxiety and desire. Thus, we have submitted—male and/or female—to a social order, to a directive that constructs our fear long before our bodies hit the urban terrain that has organized, and continues to organize, bodies and spaces in terms of concretes and absolutes.

This is where distinctions, abjections, and implications come together.

This is where fear is born.

Avoid Walking at Night

> Even tonight and I need to take a walk and clear
> my head about this poem and why I can't
> go out without changing my clothes my shoes
> my body posture my gender identity my age
> my status as woman alone in the evening/
> alone on the streets/ alone not being the point/
> the point being that I can't do what I want
> to do with my own body because I am the wrong
> sex...

June Jordan, "A Poem About My Rights"

Prohibition, taboo—the binaried opposition of biology and culture breaks down. At once, the physiology of fear is an instinctual reaction, a death-drive impulse to fight or flee, and a reaction to a cultured impetus, a representation of an ideology that fears otherness, a representation in which architecture is complicit.

But, this same fear is a liberator. It may be a dark passage, but also a way, a tunnel through to an understanding of fantasies and desires, of unconscious transactions, of ideological manifestations and bodily organizations. Though I speak here of gendered ideologies, I see other significations at work, the demands made by inequality and difference, the demands of the power of state, the power

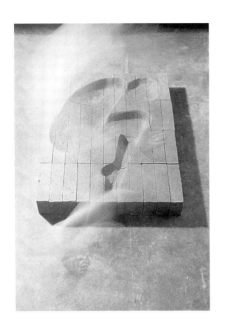

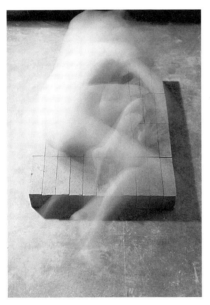
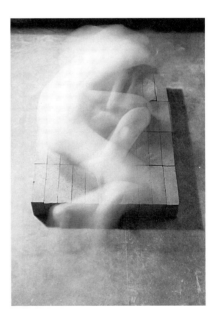

of ethnicity, the power of capital, and the power of knowledges that shape cultural symbolism, and the unconscious collective.

To liberate fear, we realize that identities are psychic, not social, leaving space for the subversion of binaries, concretes, and absolutes. I turn to Freud again to find the hysteric, hysterical fear. The hysteric dilemma: not knowing whether to identify as male or female, pointing to the inadequacy of a binaried identity. "She is disgusted . . . by the efforts to pin her down as a sexual body."[16] She lacks desire, identifies with lack, and here reveals the gaps in language, an incapacity to satisfy the ideals of symbolic ideologies and master narratives, a subversion of patriarchal norms. Can we learn from the hysteric? Can we take stances as urban hysterics?

To liberate ourselves from fear, we realize the fearing outweighs the actual victimization, the actual crime.[17] Ideologies change, can change, are open to re-signification.

There can be a new story.

Don't Panic

At my large university, grass expanses occupy the middle of a sprawling city. A topography of abjections spills into questions of temporality. The administration balks at the cost of installing more lights.

There are those like myself who hold silent vigil and march to take back the night. We have a way of speaking about our fears, our powerlessness, which has a way of magnifying our attachments to our gendered status, marginalizing our identities. We tell each other haunting stories in the name of empowerment. A woman near me sobs openly.

These are the stories, I tell myself, of the realities of women's lives. Curious, though, that we have come here to protest darkness when it is not really darkness that we fear. The trick of the dare is to pass from point *a* to point *b* without molestation, without harm or violation. The passage is implicated. The architectural body reverberates with the materiality of the lived body. They are rendered intelligible because of conscious and unconscious transactions of power.

To repeat: there can be a new story.

Inside Fear
Secret Places and Hidden Spaces in Dwellings

Anne Troutman

"I am a product of long corridors, empty sunlit rooms, upstairs indoor silences, attics explored in solitude, distant noises of gurgling cisterns and pipes, and the noise of the wind under the tiles."[1]

C. S. Lewis was a romantic. I am a claustrophobic. My house is too small, the walls are too thin or too thick or too many. I dream of fists flying, holes punched in the walls, of somnolent adolescents leaning threateningly on garden doors, of bums camping out on the front porch, of falling out of windows, of endless halls and countless rooms. I am constantly shifting furniture: I do not yearn for familiarity. My house will never be warm enough or cozy enough.

I grew up in a house stuffed with sentimental eccentricities: every object had a story, every story, a memory, and every memory, more objects. I could not dwell in the house; there simply was no room. And so I occupied its peripheries. Parts of me went into hiding. And there were many places to hide along the periphery: closets, halls, attics, window seats, drapes, back stairs, fire escapes, boiler rooms, basement, eaves, sheds, on the roof.

The dwelling is intimate, immediate, a resonant chamber, a mirror of the self, opening up in infinite perspectives, depth, and reflection. Soul, body, and dwelling are but expansions and projections of each other. For the house is not merely walls, doors, and windows, but a doorway to things beyond, a "capacity" of the senses and spirit. Finally, there is no distinction between outward and inward. We dwell in the home; the home dwells in us.

I do not believe the house is a safe place. For me, it is a collision of dream, nightmare, and circumstance, a portrait of the inner life. The primal shelter is also the site of primal fears. Its interiors are a map of the conscious and unconscious, with conscious securities and insecurities visible in the main rooms, and unconscious ones lurking in smaller, peripheral spaces. There is danger in the house. Though I passionately wish for calm nourishing warmth and spaciousness, "the promise of home," I am irredeemably caught in the house Edgar Allan Poe built: the one in which someone has been buried behind the wall, alive.

Within every image of the contented home, there resides the house
that anxiety built.

In the middle of the middle of the middle of the night ... in the middle of the middle of the middle of the room ... in the middle of the middle of the middle of your mind ...

In the middle of the land rises the fortification; in the middle of the fortification, the town; in the middle of the town, the castle keep; within the keep, stone walls, the tower; within the tower, walls, attic, eaves; within the walls, stairs and chambers, passages, panels, cabinets, a locked cabinet; within the cabinet.... Within the fortress walls, we believe ourselves safe from whatever lies without, but what of what lies within those walls—what is within the locked cabinet?

Closets, hallways, stairways, doors and windows, attics, basements, eaves, and cabinets expand and contract with fear and desire. They are the night side of the house, in which the identity and security of domestic life is symbolically tested. Incorporated within the house, they form another realm where daily life is displaced, condensed, fragmented.

Disturbing dreams and repressed fears transform surface into cavity, large into minute, the miniature into the overwhelming. These curious places become the refuge of the half-realized. Wishes, dreams, fantasies, fears, desires are the inhabitants of the internal boundaries of our everyday environment: the place of the other, the imagined, the double, the dream.

To get in or out of the back bedroom we have to pass through the linen hall. Narrowed by cabinets that reached upwards along one side, it seems longer than its fourteen feet. The high ceiling disappears in gloom. Only one cabinet towards the end, reserved for linens, smells sweetly of lavender. The rest of the cabinets are filled with old things in boxes and various containers that smell of metal, wood, and oil. The hallway contains a small vertical shaft for an old dumbwaiter that has long since fallen into disuse. The empty shaft, dark and smelling of dust and rope, is the locus of lost things, never to be recovered. It is in these long dusky hallways and cabinets with box latches that my memories of the losses and loneliness of late childhood resonate.

A parallel world inhabits the borders of my waking life. This parallel world is one of refuge and passage, quiet places in which to nest and dream, dark places in which to hide or from which to flee. They are the spaces behind, between and through which I enter the larger "rooms" of my daily life. They are spaces in which I am usually alone or on the way to somewhere else: the hall, the stairs, the closet, the attic. These spaces, internal to the house's structure yet external to its principal rooms, are the expanded boundaries of the house and my consciousness. They are condensed spaces, tight spaces, often storage spaces, repositories of the activities and memories just beyond and within the main episodes of my life. Without them, I am uncomfortably fastened to the present, limited to the surface.

The dwelling is a place where I may hesitate between worlds.

In my brother's closet there is a small rounded door, no taller than a small child. It is hidden behind all the clothes that are hung on the rack in front of it. The door sticks slightly when pulled and opens into the dark recesses of the eaves where we have our club. We set up our table and benches (old boxes) and store the necessary things to the right, along the length of the eaves as they stretch toward and behind my parents' bedroom, from which there is another small door, like our own, but one that we never use.

As a child, I explore these hidden spaces in order to explore my fears. From within the safety of the house, I can venture to its edges, its perimeters, and, undetected, experiment with facing my fears of the dark, of the adults, of a large noisy world. In the eaves I escape, I huddle, I frighten myself, I cry and whisper and laugh and plot. In this hollow between the self I know and see and the one I do not know and cannot yet see, but sense, I test my own limits and learn my own secrets. In these hollow walls dwells the unknown, the in-between, the impossible, the unseen. Exploring them, I am hero and master of the unknown; I stare fear in the face and survive.

The walls of the house are two feet thick and hollow to protect the house from the heat of the day. Every night, these walls come alive with scratchings, rustlings, and strange twitterings, charging the house with nocturnal life. We climb to the attic and peer down into the hollow darkness trying to see...

Physically, fear is signaled by feelings of constriction—the heartbeat quickens and shoulders, jaw, and stomach tense in readiness for battle. As Freud illustrated, instincts such as fear can be transformed, displaced, reversed, or sublimated. My feelings of fear sometimes erupt in constricted spaces that I remember or reinvent: the closet, the hall, the back storeroom, the narrow stairs leading down to the basement; or sometimes in large or empty spaces: disused rooms, attics and basements, an old storeroom, shed, or garage. The dwelling is part of my journey, my progress of feeling and experiencing.

The word "dwelling" itself contains in its root the sense of a transitional space. "Dwelling" has its origins in the Old English word *dwellan*, which means "to go astray, to hesitate, to delay." A dwelling is an *in-between* space, containing me as it divides me from the rest of the world; inside, it contains other *in-between* spaces, dividing and connecting my inner and outer selves, unconscious and conscious fears, fantasies, desires. Sometimes, within the protection of the house, the boundaries may be erased.

"Oh night without objects. Oh window muffled on the outside, oh, doors carefully closed; customs that have come down from times long past, transmitted, verified, never entirely understood. Oh silence in the stair-well, silence in the adjoining rooms,

Within the inner peripheries of the dwelling I may project feelings
and activities to which I cannot or will not allow access in the course
of my "normal" daily life.

silence up there, on the ceiling. Oh mother, oh one and only you, who faced all this silence, when I was a child."[2]

The innate desire for the primal shelter of "mother" is fraught with dangers of being cast into an unknown and frightening world outside of mother. The recovery of that infant/mother symbiosis is one of the promises of the comfortable dwelling, and its loss is one of its threats. Unlike actual dangers, which are identified as being outside the self, this anxiety lies *within* the self—and by extension, awaits us *inside* the dwelling.

Child psychiatrist D. W. Winnicott, in studying the period of life in which the infant separates from its mother, defined the concept of "transitional phenomena."[3] The emergent self of the young child is in a state of "me/not me." The child creates a "holding space" of fantasy to cope with its separation from the mother. Ideally, my dwelling is my holding space. It is one of the ways that I mitigate the influence and flux of the outside world—above all, it is a space, however large or small, in which I want to expand my sense of myself and my being. It is an emotional space; it is a psychological space. My dwelling is a place where I may hesitate between worlds; it is a place of *delay.* Marcel Duchamp described his work, *The Bride stripped bare by her Bachelors, Even,* as a "delay in glass"—an allegorical, psychological space, neither inside nor outside, without specific time or space, not a shelter, but a lens.

I live in a suburban tract house in Santa Monica, California. It is small and without detail; it has low ceilings, no basement, no attic or eaves and few closets. It symbolizes to me the absence of dwelling; it lacks the qualities I have come to associate with dwelling from my experiences, dreams, and memories since early childhood. Around it over the past three years I have cultivated several gardens. Now the garden is the shape of my home and the dwelling is merely the void in the garden, a window to the garden.

As a natural extension of the primal need for protection and nurture, the dwelling is also a defense against the primal fear of loss of protection. Occupying the territory between reality and illusion, the dwelling could be considered a creative "space" that defends the individual against the anxiety of being alone.[4] My experience of dwelling in dreams and in reality both reflects and mitigates this anxiety. The house is a transitional space—a combination of inner and outer, open and closed, celestial and temporal. It has an "illusory," malleable, adaptive character that assimilates unexpressed and unacknowledged anxieties and feelings of loss.

I am inside a small old house. It is picturesque, the kind that you would find in an English countryside village—a comfortable slouch of thatch and wood and stucco.

Spaces that feel terrifyingly empty or endless guard and contain
my anxieties.

As I explore it, I realize that it is empty, abandoned, and feel the emptiness of the rooms as a cold pressure drawing me deeper inside. I flee out the door and stand on the threshold, my gaze fastened on the door, feeling in its solid dark thickness the shape of foreboding.

Long hallways, dark staircases, and chimney flues are sometimes also the stage of this primal anxiety. Freud distinguished anxiety from fear (*Furcht*). Anxiety is a reaction to a perception of danger; fear requires a definite object of which one is afraid. He defined anxiety as an adaptive function—essential in humans and animals to their survival—in response to the flooding of psychic apparati with stimuli. He considered birth the first experience of anxiety, later the absence of the mother, whose presence is essential to the gratification of instinctual demands.

I am climbing upward through an endless series of rooms. The rooms become smaller, tighter, darker until finally I am within a wall, climbing an old staircase. It twists and winds and sometimes levels off, but always become tighter and more uncomfortable, until I can barely fit my shoulders through the next opening. Disheartened and afraid, I rest on the landing.

In the process of becoming separate, an infant develops the senses to mitigate the stimuli of the outside world. Psychological spaces, experienced as the locus of childhood insecurities and fears, grow into the adult's concept of the nature and meaning of certain space types. There may be some spaces—the endless room, the empty room, the dark ascending or descending stair, tight spaces (between walls, up the chimney, etc.), the door that should not be opened, sounding walls of unknown thickness, or uncomfortable proportion—that are archetypically horrifying.

"It had an unbelievably faulty design that left it chillingly wrong in all its dimensions, so that the walls seemed always in one direction a fraction longer than the eye could endure, and in another direction a fraction less than the barest possible tolerable length."[5]

It is within the *inner peripheries* of the dwelling—the hidden, disused, invisible, and newly discovered spaces—that we may project feelings and activities to which we cannot or will not allow access in the course of our "normal" daily lives, to which we may assign illicit behaviors and fantasies, anxiety and apprehension.

"For the door is an entire cosmos of Half-open. In fact, it is one of its primal images, the very origin of a daydream that accumulates desires and temptations: the temptation to open up the ultimate depths of being, and the desire to conquer all reticent beings. . . . At times, it is closed, bolted, padlocked. At others, it is open, that is to say, wide open."[6]

There will always be information of a hidden nature somewhere in the house.

In the houses of seventeenth- and eighteenth-century France, sets of parallel rooms separated public from private life. The earlier houses had two sets of *appartements*: one formal and one private. Later, three types of suites were established: formal, private, and intimate. The intimate spaces progressed in *enfilade* alongside the great formal rooms and were inaccessible to them except by separate entry from another hall. These spaces (later abbreviated into our closets and bathrooms, studies and dressing rooms) progressed from the outermost *vestibules* and *salons* to innermost *boudoirs* and *cabinets* in an erotic parade. They became famous historically as the site of court intrigues and seduction.

The mid-eighteenth-century erotic novel by Jean-François de Bastide, *La Petite Maison*, sensuously limns the seduction of a court lady by a Marquis through lush and explicit descriptions of a series of private rooms and their luxurious furnishings. *Salons, boudoirs, appartement des bains, cabinet d'aisance, cabinet des jeux, les ottomanes, les duchesses, les sultanes*—until deep in one of the innermost private *appartements*, the lady finally succumbs:

It was "*covered with heavy dark green silk, on which were arranged symmetrically the finest engravings of the illustrious Cochin, of Lebas, and of Cars. There was just enough light to be able to glimpse these masterpieces. The room was filled with sofas, daybeds, and chaises-longues.*"[7]

Once the visual is cloaked and other senses are introduced, another level of awareness is also ushered in. The hidden spaces—the dark spaces, spaces that feel terrifyingly empty or endless—guard and contain our anxieties. These hidden spaces are "assimilated" into the visible house; they are the other side of the existing walls, doors, stories, etc.—accommodations of the unconscious. Thus within every contented image of home, there resides the house that anxiety built and buried to counterbalance the security of the known self.

"*The interior is not only the universe, but also the sheath of the private man.... Covers and protective shields, all sorts of cases and covers are invented.... In the interior even the traces of the inhabitant are covered. The detective novel is born, which sets out to search for these traces ... the guilty parties in the first detective novels are not gentlemen, nor apaches, but bourgeois private citizens.*"[8]

Pieces of ourselves that are "split off" from our awareness appear as familiar, if frightening, strangers when encountered. Split off spaces in the dwelling often harbor those parts of ourselves, and provide us with a portrait of our unconscious. There will always be information somewhere in the house of a "hidden" nature that eludes consciousness.

The Winchester Mansion, built nonstop (twenty-four hours a day) over a period of almost forty years by Sara Winchester, heiress to the Winchester rifle

The dwelling is a trust of my known and unknown selves.

fortune, is a monument to the energy of anxiety. The house grew eccentrically to more than 160 rooms as the owner sought to confuse and accommodate the ghosts of the famous rifle's victims, by whom she believed herself haunted. Doors and cabinets open onto solid walls. Stairways lead nowhere. Chimneys stop short of the roof. Miniature doors lead into large rooms. Doors open into rooms without floors.

In various ways, secret spaces connect seductively to the scenes of our daily lives, sometimes by doubling. I grew up in New York City in what is referred to as a prewar "security" building. Ours was a sixteen-story masonry building built in the 1920s and manned by a contingent of doormen, elevatormen, servicemen, and superintendents. All the buildings that fill the Upper East and Upper West sides of Manhattan, however elegant or drab, have one thing in common: a double life. Behind, within, around the side of, and below the building's lobby, public entrance, elevators, and private apartments are a web of service "entries," backstairs, service elevators, and underground rooms for furnaces, plumbing, laundry, and storage usually accessible down wide, low, ill-lit hallways. The horizontal private apartments, linked by vertical voids of service stairways and elevators, ducts and pipes for water and heat, mount discretely on one another from granite foundations to rooftop water towers.

I am climbing up the side of a very tall building. I am already perhaps twelve, thirteen stories up when I see that the old iron ladder I am clenching is rotten and starting to detach from the brick wall. I look up and down. There is nowhere else to go. I have no choice but to continue.

Sensuous detailing within the skin of a dwelling has always been an emblem of security in my life, making comprehensible even the grandest spaces to my senses. I think the security of detail stems from the period of early childhood, when the child, beginning to distinguish itself from "mother," relies on the acquisition of increased physical capacities to bring the external world into grasp and focus. Houses that I remember with texture and detail in their structure—window, floor, door, walls—feel safe to me; inhabited by smells, sounds, textures, and detail, they mitigate the anxiety of the outside world and hone my focus and insight, giving me a sense of comfort.

I am sitting on a horse-hair pillow covered in green velvet, inside the window. I can smell the dusty scent of the old velvet and feel the coolness of the small-paned leaded window on my cheek. I study the soft joints of the solder. We slept in an old bed that sank in the middle and whose headboard was filled with ancient National Geographic's that we used to pore over after our parents said goodnight (oh spears and large dangling breasts!) There are two old pump organs in the room with foot

I am constructed of the various dwellings I have lived in over the years; I visit aspects of my ideal house here and there, the amalgamation of all my memories, fantasies, and conscious and unconscious associations.

pedals for air and hundreds of ivory knobs promising exotic sounds and combinations... tympanum, flute, voice... at the foot of the bed is an old tallboy; in the drawers are thousands of treasures: poker chips, golf tees, polished stones.

In counterpoint to the safety of detail and things experienced as near are the dream spaces of terror and fright that are claustrophobic: spaces diminishing abnormally or spiraling endlessly, creating a sense of distance and emptiness, endlessness, unreachableness—an unfriendly confusion of inside and outside.

The back bedroom is the only room in the apartment except the kitchen that is directly connected to the back stair and thus to the basement sixteen stories below. A large heavy metal door with two locks, a bolt, and a chain divides this dark room from the back hall. The wind whistles through the shaft, and we hear strange noises at all hours.

Like the storyteller's hypnotic suggestion to enter the space of his story at more and more intimate scales until the voice seems to come from within, we daily recreate within our dwellings the intimate internal landscape of our fantasies, the spaces of our primal needs and fears. Consciously and unconsciously, we assign meaning to every surface, every cavity, visible and invisible until certain types of spaces become associated with specific feelings and begin to form pockets or sites for the contents of our inner lives. From within these pockets we may occasionally glimpse our hopes and desires or sense our fears and anxieties.

The surrealist writer Alfred Jarry sought to break down the barrier between art and life, between states of sleeping and waking so as to render life continuous. He "deliberately allowed himself to be completely subsumed by his own legend."[9] His dwelling became the concrete expression of the reduction of his physical self as he had been at a young age, and his eventual expansion into legend. This description of one of Jarry's last dwellings was written by Guillaume Apollinaire.

"I climbed up to where Jarry lived—actually on the third floor and a half. The ceilings of the building had appeared wastefully high to the owner and he had doubled the number of stories by cutting them in half horizontally. This building, which is still standing, had therefore about fifteen floors; but since it rose no higher than the other buildings in the quarter, it amounted to merely the reduction of a skyscraper.

"It turned out that Jarry's place was filled with reductions. This half-floor room was the reduction of an apartment in which its occupant was quite comfortable standing up. But being taller than he, I had to stay in a stoop. The bed was the reduction of a bed; that is to say, a mere pallet. Jarry said that low beds were coming back into fashion. The writing table was the reduction of a table, for Jarry wrote flat on his stomach on the floor. The furniture was the reduction of furniture—there was only the bed. On the wall hung the reduction of a picture. It was a portrait of Jarry (by Rousseau) most of which he had burned away, leaving only the head, which resembled a certain lithograph I know of Balzac. The library was the reduction of a library, and that is saying a lot for it. It was composed of a cheap edition of Rabelais and two or three volumes of the Bibliothèque Rose. On the mantel stood a large stone phallus, a gift from Felicen Rops. Jarry kept this member, which was considerably larger than life size, always covered with a violet skullcap of velvet, ever since the day the exotic monolith had frightened a certain literary lady who was all out of breath from climbing three and a half floors and at a loss how to act in this unfurnished cell.

"Is that a cast?" the lady asked.

"No," said Jarry. "It's a reduction...."

"The ceiling of the room was so low that the top of even Jarry's head brushed against it as he walked about, and he collected the flaky plaster like a severe case of dandruff. It was said that the only food that could be eaten conveniently in the place was flounder."[10]

I imagine I am constructed of the various dwellings I have lived in over the years; I visit aspects of my ideal house here and there, the amalgamation of all my memories, fantasies, and conscious and unconscious associations. Their interiors hold me and record different stages of my emergence as a person. To remember, to describe, to daydream about these spaces is one way I have of feeling whole, of grasping parts of myself that might otherwise be lost. The dwelling is a trust of my known and unknown selves.

I realize that this house that I have been living in has a series of rooms of which I have been unaware. I am climbing the stairs to an attic I have never visited. The stairwell grows brighter until I enter a very high space filled with light, celestial—it is like being inside a crystal.

The dream puts the dreamer into its own order.

My Urban History
Paranoia Informing Place Making

John Chase

Fear? I own a good chunk of it. After a childhood overshadowed by the family specter of suicide and depression, fifteen years of friends lost to AIDS, five years of tough economic times due to the great real-estate and architecture bust of the nineties, after the riots, the quakes, and the fires, living in Los Angeles means fear of economic and personal survival. If the post-World War II suburban environment promised anything, it promised order, safety, and the instant scrutiny and removal of anyone and anything that appeared to disrupt serenity and security or challenge possession of turf. The house in tranquil suburban South Pasadena in which I grew up made the already protected environment seem stiller—and calmer, more protected—than it really was. The gentle raining of the sprinklers on the dichondra lawn filtered through the drawn drapes and folded into the hum of the dishwasher and the air conditioner.

My destiny was set within my family. That was where I learned to walk in and out of other people's minds. My mother suffered a nervous breakdown when I was nineteen, in 1972. She became wildly manic depressive. My memories include locked wards, electroshock, stomach pump, and long letters with writing that circled around the page and onto both sides of the envelope. After each suicide attempt, the paramedics cleared out bottle after bottle of pharmaceuticals in her bathroom. I knew it was my job to visit with mom, to walk through the open door to Motel Hell and rescue her. By the time she died I had trouble knowing when I was in the motel and when I was not. Sometimes I worried that I never could leave—if she could not get out why should I be able to escape? (I knew she wanted me to keep staying where she was, and to take me with her.) If a lifeguard could float a drowning person in the water, then surely I should have been able to have floated her to safety. I saw that it was possible for my mother to go crazy, get sick, and go straight to hell while still alive—and then die. I will never again assume that anything is going to turn out all right.

Ever since then, and especially since one of my two closest friends, Roger, died, all bets are off. Given my knowledge of the mental abyss that can be created inside, I do not necessarily expect there to be safety even in what seems to be the safest of places.

In 1996, after Southern California imaginations have been fed a TV news diet of Charles Manson and O. J. Simpson, and of media blurred shootings of all descriptions, there is always that *Blue Velvet* sense that even in the most impossibly serene Los Angeles neighborhood the underlying order could be violated or is less stable than meets the eye. In 1980 my sister Laura and I lived in a tiny house with battered metal awnings and leggy poinsettias on McCollum Street in Silverlake. At $500 a month it was the calmest neighborhood we could afford within commuting distance of Laura's classes at UCLA. It was a quiet neighborhood but the day we moved in there were police helicopters and warnings of a bloodied man running through back yards along the street. This was followed by numerous break-ins up and down the street, including Laura's car and our basement.

One day I came upon a car full of heavily narcotized teenagers, their car stopped dead in the middle of the road. Both car doors were open. The vehicle was silhouetted against the mist-diffused glow of the streetlight like a giant bat. The labor of breaking and entering was so demanding that the zombied-out teens had to take a breather in the middle of the road. The police picked them up, still immobilized in the center of McCollum Street, without any problem.

Still later, there were the McCollum Street firebomb incidents. The first one was a good sized blast at the house down the block (fig. 1). It set off a host of car alarms, and broke windows up and down the street. Inside the house was an invalid wheeling around a portable IV rack. He had to be helped out of the building, while flames flashed up to the second story. I still do not know what provoked the blast. It was festive in a way that only other's people's disasters can be. The only other thing that ever brought the neighborhood together was the feckless woman who never got her car alarm fixed, until one night she was surrounded by a virtual lynch mob of angry McCollum Street residents threatening to convert her beeping vehicle into a heap of spare parts.

My stay on McCollum Street was the first time it had really occurred to me that one's own house and the lot it sat on were like a little territory, that there were allies and adversaries on all sides. Across the street were allies, the elderly couple from Lithuania who gave us epidendrum orchids, she so large she took the long flight of concrete stairs to her front porch by hauling first one side and then another side, he narrow as a stick. Next door to us in the back house was the smiling and hospitable middle-aged shoe salesman with his young wife and new baby from Peru. Across the street and catty-corner to us were gay neighbors with whom I flirted. Again, all friends.

1. Blow-up on McCollum Street

Cozy neighborhood, McCollum Street, especially when I was living with my sister. It always made me feel better to have her right there with me. But even on McCollum Street it does not take much to create an enemy. Our lot had trees on it, an unprepossessing melange of avocado, palm, and volunteer weed ash. Some people hate plants. The elderly neighbors next door certainly did. The woman would cut any foliage that hung over their side of the fence and hurl it over on our yard. I would find wilted and swiftly decomposing piles of severed vegetation and become deeply insulted. Having physical material deposited in your domain always seems to me to be an act of aggression. Once I got mad and threw the stuff back over the fence, hard enough to crack one of their windows. I felt really guilty about that because she was old and frail. I could not believe I had actually damaged someone else's property. The next people to live in the little house after my sister and I were a nice lesbian couple. They made great friends with this woman, despite the fact that they grew an even greater jungle in the backyard than I had.

Laura moved to London to marry, work, and raise her children. I doubt I will ever feel entirely secure again since I know that the best company, and the best friend I could ever have, a completing part of my consciousness and sensibility, is thousands of miles away. I do not expect to be able to fly back and forth to see her. Meanwhile I bought and fixed up and sold two houses with my friend Roger during the real-estate boom of the eighties. My goal was to be able to buy a little house on my own.

Plants were also a big problem the next time I lived in Silverlake, in a house I bought on Francine Avenue, five houses above Sunset, during the last gasp of the real-estate boom of the eighties. I bought the Francine house under the optimistic assumption that things would always get better, that is, that any return of investment would be justified due to a continued rise in what were in reality already grossly inflated real-estate prices. The previous tenants of the house had been a punk rock band with a pet ferret and a set of warrants out for their arrest. When I bought the house the last signs of an old gay neighborhood and the party times of the seventies and the eighties were receding under the onslaught of AIDS. I probably cleared out a gallon bucket's worth of little brown bottles from the front yard, bottles that had been filled with Amyl Nitrate inhalant and used as aphrodisiacs. It made me wonder if there used to be more bushes in the front yard.

The popularity of that neighborhood as a home to immigrants from around the world was increasing. On one side of my house on Francine was Reynaldo, a red-headed Cuban-born costume designer and his Vietnamese lover Max. On the other side was the slummy broken down set of buildings that Max owned as part of a real-estate syndicate. It had started out as a single family house. In the early 1960s, the woman who had raised her family in that house, Mrs. Anderson, built a duplex in the back, legally, and then bootlegged the front house into four gruesomely cramped apartments. Her son, who was a gun nut, never said a word to anyone, and lived upstairs in the old main house with his equally silent lover. Both men worked in the same gun shop. The unit below the gun guys' unit was bad luck, too small, and therefore difficult to keep rented. Another gay couple lived there, at least one of whom was dying of AIDS and addicted to street drugs. Their fighting, including the one on the sidewalk in front of my house the day escrow closed, terrified the neighboring families and brought in the police. The units were only separated by a locked door, a door that shook each time a body was repeatedly slammed against it during a fight.

In the back duplex was the singing fat lady, Ramona. Day and night she warbled the words to "New York New York" into her Mister Microphone home karaoke unit. I had to go to the other side of my house to lose the base. She only

2. The sapote grove on Francine Avenue

left the house to walk her tiny streaked and stained poodle and attend acting auditions. (I do not suppose there was much call for someone with that many facial warts.) The bone of contention between Ramona and me was the sapote trees that hung over her driveway (fig. 2). Sapote are unique trees that manage to dump hundreds of pounds of fruit on the ground over a period of only a few weeks. The yellow-green fruit begins to rot as soon as it is separated from the branch and splatters when it hits the ground. The sickly vegetative stench is both unseemly and repugnant, sort of like lawn clippings mixed with Sweet N' Low. I have a certain affection for sapotes. At Francine the sapote grove flourished exuberantly in the absence of any encouragement or cultivation on my part. I viewed the trees as my part in the noble effort to create a simultaneously drought-resistant and sustainable landscape. Damned if that Ramona did not just hurl anything that hit her driveway back over the chain-link fence. I hurled it back if I found splotches on the side of my house. But at least the Great Sapote War was a species of honest combat, in which the weapons enjoined were relatively harmless.

The Great Battle of Francine was far more serious. It involved lawyers. Behind my house were two fences, and in between the fences was a thicket of golden bamboo festooned with rotting diapers, tin cans, and telephone books. The detritus had been tossed over the fences in long-lost moments of extreme slovenliness. The bamboo was growing over the water heater that I had moved out of the old laundry room in order to convert that room into a study. In my role of guardian of the public good, I decided that this potential trash hazard to the water heater should be removed. Fortunately I had the property surveyed. (At that point I still had the illusion that I was going to build on it.) The survey showed a fence on my property, a fence on the neighbor's property line, and bamboo in between. I demolished my fence and trimmed the bamboo. The next thing I knew—while trying to compose myself after a difficult and troubling day, reclining on the piece of furniture I owned that came closest to resembling a real couch, a process server dropped a subpoena in my lap. It informed me that I had trespassed on my neighbor's property. According to this document, I had uprooted and cut down his bamboo and lowered his property value sixty thousand dollars. What was really going on, it turned out, was that my neighbor owned the oldest gay sex club in Silverlake. He did not want the privacy of his backyard, and the splendor of his hot tub and his Miller Lite stained-glass porch light, devalued by prying eyes. The really weird thing about this was that when it came to court he had his own survey that pretty much exactly matched my survey. That crazy SOB knew the bamboo was on my property all along. The judge came out to see the fence, took one look, and dismissed the case on the spot.

Some time after that I decided to give up on Francine. The sapote-slinging lady's place had three times as many people living in it as it had when I first moved in. It had also acquired a flotilla of giant pickup trucks one-quarter-inch narrower than the driveway, trucks that had to be repositioned at all hours of the day and night. The city had down-zoned my property (there was no warning when I went to the planning counter, and no notice in the mail since the city took forever to update its property records.) No more multiple units. Now that I would not be building new units, the flaws of the original house looked all the more lethal. The foundation had the appearance of having been made out of flour and water by a child. The expansive soil shrank in the dry season, growing dust-bowl gashes wide enough to trip over. The ninety-year-old shingles curled and cupped like corn flakes. They were barely able to hold the scales of paint on them. Every week a few more slipped out and fell to the ground.

I was tired of the daily tide of trash that washed over the front yard. One day it was carburetor parts and half-eaten McDonald's Happy Meals, the next day spaghetti of broken cassette tapes and dismembered Barbie dolls. At night I had to slow my car down to enter my driveway so that the sea of male teenagers hanging out in the middle of Francine Street could part. The local businesses I liked, such as the Argentinean deli, the anarchist bookstore, and the good used-clothing store, had all disappeared, to be replaced by ninety-nine-cent stores and video rental parlors. I was mad at Max next door for milking Mrs. Anderson's old property for every dollar it was worth and leaving it in a squalid condition with a rutted dirt front yard strewn with cars and trash. When one of the tenants fired his gun into the sky at 2:00 in the morning, that was it for Francine.

I left. Thanks to the great Southern California real estate bust of the nineties the house was now worth tens of thousands of dollars less than the mortgage. It was a debt with no equity. I gave the house back to the bank. It was an even deal as far I was concerned. I left the house restored, and had fixed much of the damage inflicted on its original 1906 cottage charm. When the bank auctioned it off it ended up selling for $75,000 less than I paid for it.

I was leaving a gay neighborhood behind that no longer seemed safe for gay people. I did not want to be ghettoized by living around people who were all exactly like me. Nor did I want to wind up as a token presence in someone else's turf. The gay subcultural presence in my neighborhood was weakening to the point where it no longer felt like a meaningful presence. It had helped me feel connected to, and yet protected from, the world. This perception would have been different for someone else. But it was real for me.

Sea Change

The equity I had worked to gain by fixing up houses and selling them with my friend Roger had already vanished. My father had died three years before, leaving me enough money to get a mortgage on Roger's house. Now Roger was dying. The sale of his house needed to happen while he was still alive to use the money. Furthermore, my graduate school classmates were opening up their own office space on the west side of town, near Venice. Sharing workspace with them, their dogs, and their kid would be like being part of a family. It would come closest to making up for the loss of my sister overseas. I bought Roger's house and took out a new mortgage just before the bank foreclosed.

Four hundred sixteen Milton Avenue was Roger's house and it was not Roger's house. He never lived there, because he could never afford to. The tenant-gouging rent he charged was always more than the modest rent-controlled tab for his own one-room beach-front apartment. The house is located in Venice near two local landmarks: the Jonathan Borofsky clown with its four o'clock shadow and tutu, and the giant Claes Oldenburg binoculars that are part of Frank Gehry's Chiat/Day/Mojo Headquarters Building. Milton is the first walk street, south of Rose and west of Main. The house is 1913 vintage, remodeled in the 1950s. It looks like a beat-up, stuccoed-over Irving Gill (with a flat, Buster Keaton straw-hat-like cornice on it) that has fallen on hard times.

The proposed additions to 416 Milton including a double-height art gallery and a little tea drinking loft were always unaffordable to Roger. There was something about the existing building and the program that suggested a massy, blocky civic virtue-laden World War I Department of Water and Power vocabulary. At 416 Milton the small scale of the building domesticated the genre and made it friendly.

The Pagoda Must be Built

There were three basic areas of endeavor connected with my stewardship of 416 Milton. The first consisted of facilities management and property management, putting in the physical improvements that make the building less likely to collapse in an earthquake, catch fire, or leak. The second was balancing what cash I had with the need to spend it to make improvements that would create income-generating units (416 is zoned for three units) so that I could get some income to help out with the $1563-a-month mortgage payments. The third was making all of these improvements in such a way that it reflected my aesthetic preferences and became an example of my work.

Instead of the home/gallery, I made a Pagoda and a Pirate Cave at 416 Milton. Roger knew about the Pagoda before he died. He got the idea right away. The idea of the Pagoda is not, and I repeat not, "Oh Roger has some Chinese blood running in his veins so I will replicate a Chinese building and there will be some kind of one-to-one correspondence between structure and culture." *Au contraire.* Roger grew up around wealthy Caucasian kids. It was easy for him to feel different from everyone else. Roger's dissatisfaction crystallized around not being Caucasian and straight. He had baby blue colored contact lenses for ethnicity blurring and shock value long before anyone else wore colored contacts.

In the 1960s Asian kids who drove Porsches to class at USC were unlikely to have many peers. Roger's boyfriends were never Asian, never black, rarely Latino. By the time I knew him they were always younger than Roger. The boyfriends were

3. Today's version of the Pagoda now under construction

always an attempt for Roger to gain a surrogate identity, to attain by association the primal innocence that one could attribute to someone younger and less well educated. Roger usually described these guys to me as though he were talking about a new puppy: "Look how smart they are; they know almost all the letters of the alphabet, and they can usually tie their shoes without assistance." The problem is that while you can be fascinated by your cocker spaniel, you can never actually be your cocker spaniel. The vicarious identities were a source of pleasure, but were never entirely satisfied.

So why the Pagoda metaphor? Two reasons. One is that Roger had an innate fascination for serious references to aspects of Chinese culture such as herbal medicine, acupuncture, and the uses of honor in family politics. Seeing cultural references played with was also an enormous source of pleasure for him. It simultaneously put him back in touch with certain aspects of his upbringing and liberated him from stereotypes about them.

The Pagoda is no more Chinese, no more Polynesian, no more Japanese than I am. It is about the celebration of American mythologizing of other cultures. These cultures are often viewed by Americans as being less pragmatic, more free, more expressive, or more integrated as a total culture than the United States itself. The Tiki apartment houses of the 1960s are examples of this fictionalizing. The Pagoda is a resort invented because I needed to go there, not because it actually existed and needed to be recorded. It had to be big and tall so that it became the most important thing in the house. The Pagoda dominates and establishes a hierarchy of scale.

The formal point of the Pagoda is that the use of an intricate, frenetic, or passionate density of polychrome ornament and partial spatial enclosures is a strong enough gesture to make a place. The Pagoda is supposed to be tricked out with enough brightly colored, ready-made, non-architectural items—such as nylon climbing rope, strands strung with plastic kitchen sponges, and beach balls—that it becomes altarlike. The Pagoda is a pleasure barge, a treasury of attractive things that were readily available. A hubcap and exposed colored light bulbs exist there both as decorative elements in themselves, and as artifacts of everyday life. Many of the items were inexpensive and usually consumed in a different way from their intended use, so that this altar celebrates the potential of all objects, everyday or not, to both affirm their normal identity and to embody a larger world, (as can any moment in everyday existence). The power of the objects themselves—the power of loading something up with objects—transforms them into a votive offering to the great, many-headed God of color/light/form (fig. 3).

How to Live? Tenant Space Versus Friend Space

When I decided to buy 416 Milton I made the decision in a completely illogical and intuitive manner. Roger was dying, he needed the money, the real-estate market was bad, and by the time a realtor sold the house, Roger would have been dead. The house was where it was, and Roger was in no condition to try to fix it. Once I lived in the house and began to take it apart, I realized just how shaky a beach shack it actually was.

I am still very puzzled that Roger died. His death was the only time I have ever seen someone stop living in front of me. Roger had AIDS and throat cancer. His throat had closed off to the point where he had to eat through a stomach tube. When it closed completely he died, turning red, tendons straining, trying to stay alive for just one more second. The home health-care worker and I had been dumping morphine sulfate down his feeding tube at fifteen-minute intervals. We had to stop because his stomach was already full of morphine. The smell of the morphine and the dark green, cedar-scented Rigaud candles that Roger burned saturated the room. The cloying miasma settled into Roger's possessions so that the smell went with them when I took those possessions to my house. I had that saccharine-sweet scent in my nostrils for months.

The neighborhood around 416 Milton is an old sand dune. There are three blocks between Pacific and Main that are a little higher than the rest of the neighborhood because the sand happened to have been blown into a dune here at the time the neighborhood was developed. The eighty-year-old dune reeds are still visible under my neighbor Sylvia's house. Part of my house has no foundation at all—just a board and then sand below it. Because the Venice bus terminal is two blocks away the house is always vibrating—little shocks that feel exactly like Northridge earthquake aftershocks. It is not a pleasant sensation, and there are still moments when I wonder if having my bed shake every night is something with which I can live.

When I opened the walls at 416 Milton I found out that the termites had not left nearly as much of the house intact as I thought. Shoring up the house cost money, and at the same time business dried up at my office. I decided it was time to split up the top floor again, in order to try and reduce the bite that the mortgage took out of my wallet each month.

The strategy I pursued was to cut up and then pack the existing space down to the inch. One of my biggest anxieties about what I have done to the house is that I will have spent all my money on things other than making more space. In other words, I will have spent money without thereby increasing the resale value of the house. I got a certain compulsive pleasure out of fitting more human beings into Milton without increasing the footprint of enclosed space probably as a product of leftover 1970s environmentalist thinking (all human activity was bad in the 1970s because you were not supposed to leave any marks on the planet, and, inevitably, all human activity does to some degree).

I certainly could never have afforded the gallery I designed for Roger, and, anyway, it was something I designed for Roger, not for myself. The house sits at one end of the lot against an alley. Roger's gallery would have taken up much of the yard space. I wanted to keep the space outside because the sun shines on it, the wind blows over it, and you can smell the tar and seaweed of the beach in it. And for one hour every night a lull in the bus schedule at 3:30 A.M. means that you actually hear ocean waves crashing on the shore. While it is bigger than a pocket handkerchief it is still only a thirty-by-one-hundred-foot lot; the lot is just barely big enough to wander around in. I had a great fear that if I built on the open lot I would not have enough space to put all my possessions outside, something that is very important to me. Most of what I own is a *memento mori* of either my deceased parents or of Roger, and formerly belonged to them. It is always difficult to determine how much of someone you can or ought to keep alive within your mind and around your house.

Cave-In Ahoy

The first plan to rearrange the space at 416 Milton, the Pirate Cave concept, came into being after Roger died. I had been trying unsuccessfully to live in the tiny front unit upstairs. When I bought the building it was essentially a one-bedroom flat—a flat that had been divided into a bachelor and a single apartment in the mid-1950s—over a two-car garage. The single was actually a livable apartment, and had all the choicest rooms, while the bachelor was hellish. When Roger owned the place our friend Dominic managed the building. Potential tenants came to look at the bachelor, liked it, moved in, and then realized it was impossible to actually live there. The kitchen was too small to put a table in, and the bedroom had no closet. Ultimately it was too darn small. It felt like the kind of place where a compulsive gambler who had wrecked his marriage, lost his job, and was eking out a living on disability and panhandling would live.

Consequently I decided to revive the abandoned basement floor so that I could have the top floor to myself. I call the basement a "cave" because it is notched into the sand dune, behind a double set of walls, pierced by just enough windows to make it habitable. The cave bed is even more protected, tucked away in the most sequestered location with the least headroom, the only really private and secure location in all of 416 Milton.

The pirate metaphor, part aesthetic and part *modus operandi*, came from expediency, from accepting whatever kooky conditions I found. The talisman for the Pirate Cave is a roughly fashioned mirror that I found hanging in the abandoned bathroom in the basement. Its silvering is blistered and at each corner is an arrow/ace of spades design formed in wrought iron.

The Pirate Cave tactic was to use cheap materials and ready-made cabinetry—then obliterate them with ornament. But it was not materials that became the real expense, it was actually the labor. So while it was my intention to do things cheaply, by the time I was through getting the Medium Density Fiberboard panels sawed up to make the ornament I could have made other choices. Not to mention the fact that making those curves in the MDF really tears up saw blades. Placing sawed ornament onto plain surfaces was a way of creating ornament that literally had some toothy sawed edges. Flames came into the design because the concept of "cave" implies hell.

4. The primal Pirate Cave mirror and flames dancing on the p.c. cabinetry

5. The Milton mandala

The other inspiration was finding Roger's old skateboard wheels in the basement. Any contemporary Venice pirate would own a skateboard, and Roger loved all things skateboardian. In Venice I always think it is the gangs, the homeless people, and the oceanfront walk crowd of beach revelers who set the aesthetic and fashion mood of the place (fig. 4). So jamming skateboard wheels onto melamine board doors as handles became the MO.

416 Milton is supposed to be heaven and hell, mausoleum and resort, heavy and light. I like to draw flames because of their satisfying combination of curves and spikes. Flames are generally employed in popular culture, particularly hot-rod culture. They are not found in architectural culture because of their dramatic and literal quality (fig. 5).

The overall ornamental parti for the house is based on the shapes I doodle. The unmediated subconscious mind should get a chance to have some say-so in how things look. There are certain shapes and certain motifs that run through my doodling. My friend Travis has shown me examples of schizophrenic art, where the drawings done by patients who have deteriorated to the fifty percent gone stage look most like my doodles. I am hoping the resemblance is coincidental, rather than profound. Basically the doodle shapes are Rorschach blots, tea leaves, chicken entrails, starting points for divination. They are spirit guides, capable of multiple interpretation.

In creating the Pirate Cave I was concerned that I was making a place to live that was so small that no one would be able to live in it. I did not want to make something that could not be used. But as the outlines of the place became visible, I found that a lot of people liked and understood the cave, including people I would not necessarily have expected to, such as Dominic's realtor cohorts, his cleaning woman, and the cable TV installer. I could have rented it out many times over. As the project progressed the Cave became more and more a specific "custom" place in which there were designated locations for things. It became less generic and flexible. I stopped hedging my bets. I became more confident about building in things such as benches that precluded moveable furniture. I allowed the space to become one space with partially articulated subspaces by removing internal windows and doors and creating new openings between spaces. I stopped worrying that the bedroom was oppressively small, and came to accept it as cozy.

Dominic became the resident and consummate denizen of the Pirate Cave. When his wife/childhood sweetheart kicked him out of their marriage, their mortgage payments on the house that they owned in Hollywood became just another part of their marital debt. Like my house on Francine, their house was also upside-down, worth less than the mortgage. Dominic went bankrupt and dumped his house. Before his judgment became final, the Cave was his secret hidey-hole, his whereabouts unknown to creditors. In the Cave Dominic lived out his new identity as beach-side bohemian bachelor.

Dominic is a connoisseur of refinements and details. He helped assemble furniture I designed. The place is furnished with just the right artifacts and is always kept in the immaculate order that truly small living places demand. Dominic believes that the Pirate Cave maintains just the ideal lifestyle balance between his professional identity as a realtor and his personal identity as a man with a taste for eccentricity.

Once I got comfortable with the shapes in the basement I wanted to go beyond them, to turn up the heat on the flames and make them reappear in the upper story. I felt the most successful element in the Pirate Cave was the wardrobe because the whole thing was painted, and therefore saturated with color (unlike the kitchen cabinetry, which was partially white melamine), and its ornament was big. So before I ran out of dough, I designed a whole set of itchy, crawly, scared-cat, claws-out chinoiserie made of sawed MDF for my own unit, ornament that relates to flames but is not actually flames. I still do not know when or if this is going to be realized.

6. My neighbor Norman's house and the alley seen through my bedroom window

As business continued to be flat and Pirate Cave costs mounted, I decided to split up the top-floor unit again. In this version I divided the floor into two units. I got the living room, while the new unit got what was now the only kitchen. I had ripped out what passed for a kitchen in the front unit. This kitchen had once been an exterior porch, and its stucco walls were so lumpy that we stripped them and finished them with tongue-and-groove pine with a built-in desk and bookshelves to make a little study, one that was supposed to be *gemütlichkeit* enough to make me want to sit in it and write. As far as I know personal economics may dictate that this is a lifetime arrangement. For the time being I will do without a kitchen. Creating another kitchen would cost too much money and make this place into an illegal triplex. Legally Richmond, my new tenant and consort of my friend Amanda, and I are roommates sharing a kitchen. A microwave, a little fridge, paper plates and plastic forks will have to act as my kitchen for the time being. The new arrangement also meant giving up the big bathroom with the tub, because that goes with the other top-floor unit.

The last big change was a new raised bed, made of steel trusses, that allowed me to store all of the stuff that used to be in the rooms I gave up. The corner of the room where my bed is has two unusually large, long, wooden sliding windows (usually windows this size from the fifties would have had metal frames). The top of the mattress just meets the window sill height. So now I am more united with my neighborhood, via a panoramic view, than ever before. I now survey both the cute walk street cottages and the Berlin-Wall-like backside of the tenement next door, with its piebald paint, through bolts, stern "no parking" signs, and buzzing security lights aimed at the eye level of my bed. And obviously I have to be more careful about lowering the window blinds. Lounging in bed I can be clearly seen from the corner of Rose and Main as well as from my walk street (fig. 6).

The up side is that the ever-reliable Richmond became the tenant in the back. Richmond will help me finish the Pagoda. Actually the very things that make the triplex pleasant for me to live in with friends are the very things that would make it intolerable if I had strangers living here as tenants. Sharing the garage and the yard with friends is totally different than encountering people you barely know there. Noises that would be disquieting or annoying seem comforting if you know who is making them. Since I have never been and do not expect to be in any kind of long-term romantic relationship with someone, I am interested in creating a sense of community for myself that is based on propinquity and companionship. I am tired of the primacy placed on relationships as a definer and validation of self, both within and outside of the gay community. I think the most profound human communication and awareness is not always necessarily based on sex or romantic love.

Venice the Menace

With Richmond next door and Dominic below, I feel like I am part of a crew, a posse, and feel psychologically stronger in the neighborhood, as if this colony of acquaintances is a little constituency in its own right. Given the volatility of the neighborhood, there is comfort in numbers.

The beach at Venice gives displaced people a place to live with more dignity and grace than in many other neighborhoods in Los Angeles. There is a huge alternative economy in Venice, more so than in most other places in Southern California, based on pawing through trash and selling the bottles and cans to recyclers, and fencing any items of possible value on the beach. Day and night the rumble of rolling shopping carts and the jingle-jangle of tin cans can be heard in

Rose Court Alley, located between my building and La Vie en Rose, which I call "Secondhand Rose." La Vie en Rose is a two-story, covered-parking, vintage seventies building in a schlock Mediterranean style. It has a great view across Rose Court into Richmond's kitchen and bedroom. The rent, too high at $675 for a single with big balcony, keeps the tenant turnover equally high. The average occupancy lasts for about three months, before tenants wake up and realize they can get a better deal elsewhere.

The drawing card for foragers of La Vie en Rose and the old brick hotel next door (which I call Tenement 911) is their trash containers. La Vie has trash cans while Tenement 911 has a dumpster. The dumpster was the foraging receptacle of choice for Alleyites since dumpsters seem to hold more promise of larger and varied treasures than do mere trash cans. On the other hand La Vie has the advantage of a roof over its trash cans in the form of covered, head-in parking. As far as the Alleyites are concerned, this parking area is a choice spot to take a leak, hang out, argue, drink, do drugs, change clothes, and sleep at night. The longest-term nighttime denizen of the garage was a broken-looking women with long dark hair who swept up after herself every morning. If I needed a reminder that not everyone has access to shelter who needs or wants it, all I had to do was to listen to her hacking tubercular cough. La Vie management (consisting of an elderly woman and her elderly Dalmatian, along with the personnel of the black-market washing repair service that the landlord runs out of the basement) leaves the homeless alone, unless the homeless hang out there on an extended basis during the day. For a time a homeless man was living in one of the leftover storage spaces under the stairs at my house. I had no idea I was sharing the house with him until I opened the access door so that I could place some boxes in storage there. For about a year another homeless man, a mean drunk who accosted passersby and swore at them, lived in a derelict house that sits at the corner of Little Main Street and Rose Court, on the other side of my neighbor's driveway.

When Roger first bought this house in 1989, Tenement 911 was a drug supermarket. There was not a street drug invented that you could not buy there. He never seemed to pay any attention to the building. If he did he certainly never told me about it. Consequently, when I bought 416 Milton, I had no idea of what kind of hellhole was next door.

In the 1920s Tenement 911 was a seaside hotel where tourists would stay while visiting the beach. It harks back to the era when parts of Los Angeles, such as Sierra Madre and Laurel Canyon, were seasonal resorts; when it was harder to get around, the resorts close to town were actually destinations. The ground floor of the old hotel (its three stories on Pacific and two and one-half stories facing me) housed small stores. At one of Dominic's barbecues I met Gordon, a former vice cop, who claimed that in the 1960s Milton used to have the highest crime rate of any street in Venice. People shot and killed each other in Tenement 911. In 1965 Gordon himself shot and killed two drug dealers further down on Milton, at a coffee shop that was a notorious drug-dealing center (the druggies shot first, according to Gordon). Tenement 911 has been cleaned up a lot since its low point a few years ago, but it will never be an entirely normal place to live. The seismic retrofitting has a certain *Road Warrior* cachet. Beams, posts, and through-bolts crash wildly through walls and windows. The ground-floor spaces on Pacific are vacant, but not entirely enclosed, There are long open gaps in the storefronts, narrow enough to keep people out, but wide enough to see the shadowy, littered spaces within.

The building appears to have received its last coat of paint at the same time mine did, at some point during the Eisenhower presidency. Neighborhood scuttlebutt has it that the former owner of my house and the owner of Tenement 911 (who has owned 911 since 1928) went in together on the rancid margarine yellow that both buildings are painted. The bathrooms at 911 are down the hall, and the rent is cheap ($325 to $375). It has tended to attract two categories of people: those who have decided to check into this building as a way of checking out of society (they then go on to loose their job and any social mooring to the rest of the world they once possessed) and those who are total loners (I have never once seen the loners with a friend or relative). I would say about one-third of the tenants maintain a conventional level of connection to the world, in terms of activity and social interaction.

Following is a list of some of the psychotic tenants next door, chez 911:

Tenant 1 went to Santa Monica Place, stabbed an old lady, took her purse, and came back to this apartment, where he was arrested.

Tenant 2 habitually pranced around naked while doing his laundry in the laundry room. He deliberately, not accidentally, set fire to his apartment twice before being arrested for arson.

Tenant 3 is the hairiest professional female impersonator I have ever seen. He tried (unsuccessfully) to commit hit-and-run auto collision after bouncing off my concrete retaining wall, and exhibited a confused demeanor suggesting the use of controlled substances.

Tenant 4 is a short biker with full body tattoos and long hair. He dealt drugs out of the corner pay phone at Rose and Main. Tattoo Louie used to ask me for spare change for the phone, no matter how many times I told him "no." He was whisked off by his doting mom and dad so that heartless policemen would not be able to make good on their arrest warrant for him. Louie had a penchant for short hookers with short hair. They came and went at all hours of the day and night. The metal security door on the alley clanged shut continuously (clearly audible in my bedroom), marking the arrival and departure of Louie's guests.

Tenant 5, the infamous Ed, a former plumber's helper who lost his job and used his bicycle basket to collect cans, which he cashed in for drugs and booze. (Fashion tip prompted by Ed—men in their fifties should think twice before shaving down to a Mohawk, unless they really have a strong desire to look like a plucked chicken.) Ed would collar perfect strangers wheeling their shopping carts down the alley and invite these new pals up to his room to "party" with him. Since there is no intercom and no doorbell buzzer at Tenement 911, Ed's pals would stand in the parking lot and yell for him, and would sometimes camp out there until Ed materialized. Getting Ed to show his face was often an extended process, requiring repeated shouted requests over a lengthy period time. The relationship between the alley denizens and Ed emphasized just how blurred the lines were between the housed and the homeless in Venice. Membership in one or other of those two groups was not necessarily permanent, nor did it prevent acquaintances with members of the other group.

Ed would chain his bike and those of his friends through the chain link fence that Roger put up so that the handlebars stuck six inches into the walkway at the border of my property. This and the trash that spilled out of Ed's basket and blew under the fence onto my lawn made me mad. One day when I was in a bad mood, because of other reasons, I snapped. I walked next door, grabbed the bike, and shook it as hard as I could so that all of the crushed cans fell out. I shouted up at his window "Do not chain your goddamn bike through the fence!" What really made me mad was that he had clipped a hole, the size of a cantaloupe, through the chain link in order to put the chain through. Chain link is a sore point with me. The Francine Avenue house had a chain link fence. It eventually fell over because the neighborhood kids played on it so much and the neighbors' cars ran into it so often. Little things like my fence being at an angle threaten me at moments when I am feeling that it is already hard enough to keep it all together.

Doggone Neighbors

"People in this world are prone to be selfish and unsympathetic; they do not know how to love and respect one another; they argue and quarrel over trifling affairs only to their own harm and suffering, and life becomes but a dreary round of unhappiness."[1] *The Teaching of Buddha* was a source of some bitterness to Roger, since his brother Lance gave the book to him. Roger always felt that Lance denied him his fair share of the family fortune. The origin of the book made him even madder because it was the kind of Buddha book that is left in hotel rooms along with the Gideon Bible. As far as Roger was concerned "real" presents (and most especially death-bed presents) came in powder blue bags from Tiffany's, not in the form of travelers' leftover freebies.

I think of this quote when I think of the dog. Oh my god the trouble that innocent half shepherd/half golden retriever puppy triggered. Many of my friends get mad when I say this and claim that I should have handled it differently, that I am using the "Incident" as a slimy excuse to jettison my responsibility as a dog parent. They think the fact that Catch-Up the dog ate my mother's one silver bud vase and the passenger side door panel in my Nissan Sentra has something to do with his eventual relocation (fig. 7). I think there would been no Incident to handle if there been no dog. At the same time I feel very guilty about giving away the dog, and very angry that I cannot have a dog in this neighborhood. Being able to have a dog made me feel that much more at home, and that much more protected. I know Catch-Up loves me.

Catch-Up rarely barked. What he did do was whine, or, as my neighbor has described it, "yodel." He slept with me, went to work with me, and generally, as his trainer at Petville Obedience School put it, was a "high-contact" dog. Catch-Up was not used to being left alone. When he was left alone he did not like it. The one time I experimented with leaving Catch-Up in the yard, Dominic, the tenant in the Cave, had just moved in. Dominic went for his Saturday morning wake-up coffee. When he came back he was surrounded by a small mob of neighbors who felt that the dog should be whisked away by the Society for the Prevention of Cruelty to Animals for ever being left alone. After that, if I had to leave Catch-Up alone I locked him up inside. I shut the windows so that his pleading cries would not permeate the neighborhood in the same way. He sounded as though he were watching his mother and father being flayed alive and then fed into a meat grinder. It was heart rending.

But locking him inside behind closed windows turned out not to be good enough. It came to a head two weeks ago. Usually every Sunday night I go over to my office mates' house for what we call Family Night Dinner. This Sunday Dominic was having a barbecue. Some of his guests had canceled, he had extra food, and I wanted to show my office mates my cozy, newly improved surroundings. So Dominic and I had Family Night at our place. We barbecued. Dominic has this whole monster host and monster machismo thing going that generally involves serving lots of meat and plenty of booze, and always involves protestations of undying affection for the assembled throng. The fact that he was recently

above
7. Catch-Up, bless his heart

right
8. Armed-and-dangerous bunny statue purchased at Standards Brands Paint watches Norman's potentially lethal assault on the barbecuing Dominic

booted out of his marriage by his childhood sweetheart has done nothing to tone down these predilections. Dominic supervised the billowing clouds of smoke, we drank, we talked. As I left to drive my office pals home Dominic was sitting contentedly, smoking his favorite Cuban cigar with his friend Renzo, a stylish Italian scenic designer. Dominic likes to go out on the town with Renzo trolling for dames. Dominic realizes that this is not going to be the way he is going to find true love. However Renzo is so good at using his killer profile and *savoir faire* to attract women that Dominic cannot resist going along for the ride.

I put Catch-Up upstairs behind closed doors. When I came back all hell had broken loose. Somebody, I could not figure out who, was yelling at Dominic through the chain link fence at the side yard of the house and making unsuccessful attempts to climb over the fence. The aggressor was in the yard of the house next door, where the perfectly gentle and unthreatening Marian and her family lived. Marian grew up in her house and remembers when the house that used to sit in front of my house, on my lot, burnt to the ground forty years ago. The guy in Marian's yard had gone crazy; he was yelling and threatening the dog, me, and Dominic with everything up to and including murder. He turned out to be Marian's brother Norman, whom I had hardly ever seen outside. At that point I was mad: my honor and my manhood were under attack, not to mention my pet-care standards. I rushed to the fence, grabbed the wire hard (hard enough to press pink and yellow welts into the palms of my hands), shoved my face up against the mesh, and screamed (loud enough to strip my vocal cords) that I got the point and would take care of the situation.

Just then I realized that Norman had a knife (fig. 8). (It turned out to be an old army souvenir made of a special dense hardwood from Panama). I was so angry and had so much adrenaline surging through my veins that I was ready to have him stick me with the knife just so that he could be arrested. But I did not. Instead I made the better decision to go inside and calm down. Apparently Norman was a cranky former volleyball champion turned cocaine dealer who could not handle stress (but could cause it). He was fifty-five and prematurely fragile, due to a recent triple by-pass operation.

Meanwhile Dominic had gone in and slipped his forty-caliber Sig Sauer semi-automatic loaded with illegal Black Talon bullets into his belt (apparently Black Talons are illegal because fragments of them cut the doctors' hands when they are working on people who have been shot—or so Dominic says). I did not find the gun or the illegal bullets funny and I have asked Dominic, so far without success, to get rid of them. The right thing for Dominic to do would have been for him to go inside when Norman first came out with the knife, and then call 911, rather than return the hostility and egg Norman on. I was worried that the combination of Dominic drinking too much, shouting barbecue bonhomie, and this kind of play-acting bravado (that he actually took seriously, instead of just keeping on a joke level) was going to cause trouble in the neighborhood. I cannot always get through to Dominic that he is a very funny, engaging, and capable individual who is respected just for himself and that he does not need to challenge or best combatants in order to prove his self-worth.

Eventually Dominic went into his outlaw-pal mode familiar to him from the years when he managed a chain of seamy bars in the Valley with his partner, Boris, before Boris quit to go into the meat-packing business. One afternoon at one of their bars, the Scotch Mist in Panorama City, a patron got up, walked out, robbed a bank across the street, walked back, and sat down again. He was having whiskey shots with beer chasers when he was arrested. If you knew the Mist it really would not come as any surprise. Dominic's angle of attack with Norman was, "You and me against the world—just us fellow aggrieved and swashbuckling outlaws." As soon as I saw that passions had cooled, I came back out with my great-uncle Josiah's sword-in-a-cane so that Norman and I could compare and contrast our souvenir weapons.

The day after the Incident both Dominic and I were traumatized. I took Catch-Up straight to work in the morning. After work I dropped him off with my friend Gustavo, who knows and likes the dog. Within a week Gustavo had Catch-Up settled with a family on a half acre in Hacienda Heights, a family with a husky puppy the same age as Catch-Up. And while Catch-Up himself may be gone, there is still plenty of evidence of him, from the holes in the yard to the flea I just picked off my hand.

Now that there was no Catch-Up, everything was copacetic. The next week, at half past five in the morning, I could not sleep. The iron security door of the house next door opened. Norman stepped out, wearing boxer shorts. He stood in the alley waiting for someone. Shortly thereafter, a guy Norman's age or older appeared. He was skinny, drably dressed, with a beaten-down manner. He immediately handed Norman something tiny and white. It looked like the little pieces of rock cocaine on episodes of "Cops." So I thought maybe that was why Norman was acting so whacked out. He was not only a former drug dealer in the past but a crack-head in the present. Norman and his pal had a long argument at top volume (top volume on Norman's side, at least, while his friend maintained a low William Burroughs mumble). The argument seemed to involve how long this guy could keep sleeping in Norman's battered VW bus in the driveway. Norman alternately threatened to throw his pal out on the spot and warned him that he had to be out of there in two days.

During the following week it dawned on me that Norman the whack-attacker was becoming friends with Prince Val. Val was moving out of Tenement 911 into the house on the corner. That house had been kept vacant by its owners ever since I can remember, for mysterious reasons. At about the same time, I found out that Norman also knew Rainbow, the burned-out flower child who seemed pretty scrambled herself. Rainbow was always hailing me to inform me of various neighborhood evil doings, conspiracies, and misdeeds, usually in versions that sounded somewhat dubious if not entirely invented. I had no idea until after the Incident that she was a sometime confidante of the whacked one. There are times that it is clear to me that life on Milton is aggravating my native paranoia.

Family Life on Milton

I have not mentioned the "normal" neighbors, including the Catch-Up fans, since, by and large, we have not interacted with each other. The exception is my friend Sylvia, who lives across the street with her husband and baby. I have known her for almost twenty years, went to architecture school with her, and relish my conversations with her because of her highly analytic mind. When I look out my window, the idea of baby Mike in his crib soothes me. I think of him lying there, blissfully free of adult cares, such as mortgage payments.

But in all fairness to Sylvia and to placing her domestic life on the pedestal of coziness and cuteness, she would be out of this neighborhood in a flash if she thought she could sell her house for anything close to what she and her husband paid for it. The neighborhood makes her crazy. It started with the history of her cottage. The previous owner was a wealthy gay guy who resolved his conflict with the neighbors by firebombing them. The entire neighborhood was evacuated while the Swat team stormed the cottage to capture the mad bomber. When Sylvia was restoring the cottage the neighbors who had been firebombed panicked when they saw gypsum board dust on the sidewalk. They called the hazardous materials police, claiming that Sylvia was showering the neighborhood with deadly asbestos dust. A thousand dollars and one haz-mat hit team later Sylvia was cleared of any toxic waste skullduggery. And while I have had my dog problems Sylvia has had her own cat conundrum. When she expressed concern about marauding cats bothering her elderly feline, she instantly won hysterical accusations of cat poisoning from high-strung neighbors.

At the moment Sylvia is trying hard to remain calm—the house next door to her (not the fire-bombed house but the other one) has been given back to the bank since the mortgage debt was $250,000 more than it was worth. A changing group of single males, mostly young, white, and stinking drunk, have been crawling in and out of the windows for the past three weeks, filling the front yard with trash, and peeing outside in liberal enough quantities so that you can smell it walking by on Milton. On Sunday night I walked around the corner of the house, coming from the alley, just as Sylvia was running into Dominic's open door with her baby, screaming at the top of her lungs. One of the derelicts next door had walked into her living room.

In one sense Sylvia's encounter was perfectly predictable. This neighborhood is close to social services for homeless people and the tolerant milieu of the beach boardwalk. It is plainly turf where the dispossessed belong, and sooner or later everybody has some kind of dealings with everybody else. The city is the lab in which we conquer the fear of the unknown and the uncontrolled, and it is essential that the city belong to different groups, which makes a degree of conflict and tension inevitable. In *The Uses of Disorder*, Richard Sennett compared a mature and civilized urban environment to the process of personal growth that occurs during adolescence.

> Experiencing the friction of differences and conflict makes men personally aware of the milieu around their own lives; the need is for men to recognize conflicts, not to try to purify them away in a solidarity myth, in order to survive. A social forum that encourages the move into adulthood thus first depends on making sure there is no

escape from situations of confrontation and conflict. The city can provide a unique meeting ground for these encounters.[2]

The virtues of urban disorder notwithstanding, Sylvia was less than thrilled about having her living room turn into an agora of conflict and a classroom in cultural differences.

There is a sense in which the continual and direct participation in the urban arena goes against beliefs that are deeply held by most Southern Californians. For at least fifty years after the real-estate boom of 1887, many immigrants came to Southern California from rural and small-town environments. They were suspicious of cities. Even today in Southern California the more space you have in between you and other people, the better your living environment is perceived to be. The more control you have over who passes through your immediate environment, the more responsible you are perceived to be in providing for your family. The value placed on household autonomy and control is so great that this hatred of density and propinquity has impelled greater Los Angeles to reach beyond the San Gabriel Mountains out into the series of desert valleys that stretches towards the Arizona border.

A week after the Intruder incident, I was standing outside in my yard, going over the plans for the Pagoda ornamentation program with Richmond when I heard someone scream, "You are scaring me." A short, preppie-looking youth in a fraternity T-shirt bolted out of the front door of the abandoned house and scooted across the parking lot of Tenement 911 with three cops in hot pursuit. They let him go with a warning.

Density, diversity, and propinquity are valued in the culture of urban design and architecture. At the same time individual Americans often focus on what provides the most convenience and amenity for themselves. For example, for many commuters three hours on the freeway is not too long if they believe that the commute places them beyond the dangers of the city. At all costs they want to avoid Sylvia's experience of smelling urine from the backyard of a repossessed house, and seeing strangers crawl in and out of boarded-up windows next door.

The irony of Venice the Menace is that the menace, in good urban fashion, is bound up with promise. I may hate living among a shifting community of strangers and a cacophony of sirens, car alarms, and conversations shouted at midnight in an alley, but that propinquity is also what makes it possible for me to be near so many things I love. From the Milton house I can walk to the beach, to the thriving boardwalk with its amazingly diverse crowd, or to the conspicuous consumption of Main Street. The comforts of recreation and commerce are available to me. On all sides, skaters, cyclists, joggers, bodybuilders, shoppers, strollers, and members of the neighborhood synagogue flood by. For creative inspiration, the buildings the Borofsky clown and the Oldenburg binoculars are attached to (but not the clown or the binoculars themselves) are visible from my windows. There is even an ocean view, the size of a book of matches, visible from one corner of Richmond's bedroom.

The liveliness and eccentricity of this place, a place that is many different peoples' turf, was why I wanted to live here. I wanted to build something that was celebratory, that did not say "house" in the usual modern or period vocabularies, but something that expressed my particularly unconscious aesthetic mind set in terms of love of ornament, horror of vacuums, and the piling up of individually attractive pieces collectively to make something larger.

The irony is that I came to Venice because I thought this was the one place where I could get away with such building. Old-hippies-never-die-they-just-end-up-in Venice, old-time Beatnik Venice where there was cheesecloth over the windows of the abandoned stores on the boardwalk, concealing the drunken poets within, and a coffeehouse with a bathtub on the floor (Dominic's father remembers Venice this way from a visit in 1955), Jim Morrison's Venice, Charles Bukowski's Venice, cover of 1980 *Domus* magazine filled with Venice architects Venice. Well, there is no place that can ever please everyone or with which everyone is going to be happy. I called attention to myself by building something in a neighborhood where no one has built much for a while. I introduced a pet into a community of dogless apartment dwellers. In a yard visible to hundred of eyes I hang out and wander around, and talk to my gay and straight friends, so that all aspects of my identity are on display, including being gay. All of these things make me stand out and eat away at the degree of domestic privacy and ability to act autonomously that I might otherwise have. I remember beach and artist—I forget homeless, hurting, and packed to the gills, urban warren of too tiny apartments and too few parking spaces.

As a result of my interaction with the neighborhood my feelings have changed in two respects. First I found that I need as much privacy as I can get by means of landscape. I regret this. I like being able to look at and talk to people walking by on the walk street that fronts the southern edge of my house. I have generally always enjoyed ignoring the fact that my house has no backyard whatsoever. I use my yard just as though it were a conventionally enclosed suburban backyard. But in fact it is exposed to the walk street on one side and has only a veil of chain link fence between it and the parking lot of Tenement 911. I feel obliged to plant out my surroundings with timber bamboo because it makes me and anything I do that is goofy less visible, and therefore less likely to be a target of any

I think that I have been so strongly affected by paying attention to the aspects of the neighborhood that threaten me that I have poisoned my soul, and I now need to make peace with my surroundings.

conflict that will interfere with my ability to feel comfortable and make a home here. The rest of the landscaping is yet to be figured out—Dominic is supposed to get his own private space formed by a fence of plywood surfboards and a hedge of cannas and bananas, so that he can keep his blinds open and barbecue in private splendor. The remainder of the space is also supposed to be divided up, not necessarily by hedges or fences, but divided nonetheless into other programmed spaces for specific needs such as the tool shed zone (since Dominic's unit used to act as the tool shed), shaded area for the summer, flower garden, and place for watching TV outside.

Second I think that I have been so strongly affected by paying attention to the aspects of the neighborhood that threaten me that I have poisoned my soul, and I now need to make peace with my surroundings. There is no real danger to my person, only to my personality. Neighborhood conflict is merely an at-home object lesson in the uncontrollability of the larger universe.

Part of me wishes I never had left the perfectly protected world of South Pasadena, and another part thinks that is all I would have needed for the waters to close over me. Right now it is very clear that even while I marvel at how inspiring and how upsetting this spot on the planet can be, it is exactly where I need to be.

Disclaimer

Yes, names and some details in this article have been changed so that I can write about friends and neighbors while still maintaining their privacy. I did not change Roger's name, because although he would not necessarily have been thrilled to pieces with everything I said, I think he would have liked the posthumous attention.

Housing for the Homeless, by the Homeless, and of the Homeless

Michael Dear and Jurgen von Mahs

Los Angeles's Skid Row (officially called Central City East) lies in the midst of sleek postmodern office towers, glitzy retail complexes, a teeming Latino shopping district, and close by City Hall itself. As a physical environment, Skid Row is a landscape of despair, hard-edged and inhospitable. Its locales are infamous: the Nickel (Fifth Street) is a place to buy drugs, while Thieves' Corner is a spot for fencing stolen goods. The sidewalks are almost devoid of trees or other landscaping. They are deeply stained and dirty, and in some areas are lined with old trash cans used as fire pits. Parking lots are barren expanses surrounded by cyclone fencing or razor wire. Many buildings are in disrepair. Symbols of despair and deprivation—used needles and syringes, cocaine pipes, liquor bottles, castoff clothing, and cardboard-box shelters—are everywhere.

Between 1969 and 1981, almost forty percent of Skid Row's single room occupancy (SRO) housing was demolished. Despite this destruction, Skid Row and its environs still contain L.A.'s largest concentration of SRO units—about 100 hotels with over 8,900 rooms housing approximately 11,000 people.[1] Most are owned by absentee landlords, and conventional lenders hesitate to finance them. During most of the 1980s, a city moratorium on demolition and a policy on hotel preservation and rehabilitation (created by the City of Los Angeles's Community Redevelopment Agency, or CRA) were in place. As a consequence, over one-third of Skid Row's SRO inventory was purchased by nonprofit organizations for rehabilitation and rental at subsidized rates.

In addition to hotels, there are about 1,000 low-rent apartments and nine missions and emergency shelters with a total of 2,000 beds. More than thirty social service agencies—including day-care centers, food and clothing outlets, a legal-aid center, employment and day-labor centers, substance-abuse agencies, and mental-health agencies—provided services to almost 8,700 individuals in 1986.[2] Two small parks, once meeting places for drug dealers and users, were redesigned and landscaped in 1986 and 1994; they are now intensively managed by the local SRO Housing Corporation.

The hotels and social service agencies are a prominent part of the local economy. Over $50 million per year flows into the area from public sources. In addition, Skid Row is a vital business and industrial district. The area is home to most of the region's fish-processing plants, a rapidly growing wholesale trade in imported toys and electronics, and garment wholesaling and manufacturing. The Skid Row community thus includes a significant daytime population of workers in human services and in the manufacturing and commercial sectors. Approximately 17,000 people worked in the area in 1980, mostly in manufacturing industries as operators, fabricators, and laborers.[3] Some 1,000 workers were employed by local service organizations, and more operated the SRO hotels.[4]

There are two principal residential groups on Skid Row. The first consists of homed residents, numbering over 5,000 in 1990. They include low-skill workers in downtown industries, retired people, the disabled, unemployed, and artists living and working in the district's low-cost loft spaces. A second resident group is the homeless, numbering between 4,000 and 8,000 in 1992.

The Faces of Homelessness

According to an extensive survey by Farr, Koegel, and Burnam (hereafter FKB),[5] L.A.'s Skid Row homeless people are predominantly male (as high as ninety-four percent) and relatively youthful. Their median age is thirty-five years, and their mean age is thirty-eight years. Thirty-nine percent are African American, twenty-five percent are Latino, and twenty-eight percent are white. The homeless population is largely single and relatively well-educated when compared to other Skid Row residents.[6] Veterans constitute about one-third of the homeless.[7] The percentage of homeless families and women (often with children) is on the rise; estimates of the female homeless population residing on Skid Row range from six percent[8] to twenty-three percent.[9]

The homeless population is extremely poor and has largely been abandoned by the welfare state. Almost half the FKB sample reported earnings of under $1,000 in the previous year, and eighty percent of these earned less than $500—despite the fact that a third had worked for monetary compensation within the last month and two-thirds had done so within the last six months. Many people were isolated from the regular wage-labor market, even though most of those interviewed had held steady jobs in the past.[10] Despite their manifest economic marginality, only sixteen percent of the total sample was currently receiving any type of public-assistance payment such as General Relief.

One of the most striking characteristics of this group of homeless people was the prevalence of psychiatric disorders among them. No less than two-thirds of the FKB sample reported some kind of chronic disorder: thirty-four percent were chronic substance abusers, sixteen percent were experiencing chronic mental illness, and twelve percent reported chronic substance abuse plus mental illness.[11] Rates of substance abuse and schizophrenia were higher among those who had been repeatedly homeless over extended periods of time. The patterns of alcohol abuse were especially interesting, given the traditional association between Skid Row and alcoholism. Almost two-thirds of the people in the sample met the criteria for alcoholism sometime during their lives, and forty-one percent were currently diagnosed as alcoholic.[12] Some thirty-nine percent of the homeless alcoholics also had experienced periods of drug dependence, which lend weight to perceptions that drug problems are significantly on the rise among Skid Row homeless people.[13] Drug abuse was more prevalent among the younger residents, while older adults were more likely to abuse alcohol.[14]

Homeless people also suffered from a range of debilitating general health problems, especially AIDS and those related to the violence of everyday life on Skid Row.[15] Over seventy percent of the FKB sample reported having had a health problem, an accident, or an injury within the previous six months. Almost half those interviewed had sought medical care for a health problem during that time period; another one-quarter reported not receiving care despite the fact that their problem warranted attention. Only sixteen percent of the homeless people had health insurance, so care was obtained largely from hospital emergency rooms that accepted indigent patients or from free clinics, usually associated with missions and soup kitchens.[16]

Community, Containment, and Control

Homed and homeless residents, employers, and workers together constitute an urban community on Skid Row.[17] Social networks link homed and homeless residents, connect residents to service providers and the business sector, and tie service providers to the business community. These networks are important for everyone's welfare. To survive, many homeless people rely on reciprocity and sharing among peers. They also depend on the area's human services and the employment provided by local businesses. These are not simple one-way relationships of dependency, however; service providers need homeless people to rationalize their existence and expansion, and many businesses rely on residents as consumers or as casual laborers. The service-provider community is itself heavily interconnected and interdependent, even though many agencies differ in philosophy and compete with each other for resources. Providers rely on one another to coordinate and deliver services to clients as well as to join their advocacy efforts on behalf of consumer groups.

Despite this interconnectedness, the everyday life of the homeless community on Skid Row is characterized by fear, surveillance, and confinement. Skid Row crime rates are five times higher than the city average. Mugging of drunks (known as "jackrolling") used to be the most serious crime, but at present the district is notorious as a regional "drugstore," and narcotics-related crimes are widespread. For the female homeless population, rape and assault are frequent occurrences.[18] Homelessness means being on the edge of victim and victimizer. Many activities that are normal and legitimate in private homes are illegal in public, including drinking a beer, sleeping, or simply using a rest room. (Most public toilets in the area have been deliberately removed by the city.) Many people cluster together in informal street encampments, but as soon as a single nail is used for their construction, they can be removed by police. Surveillance and control are omnipresent: police vehicles, emanating from a nearby police fortress with windowless walls and fortified security entrances, cruise the streets; sprinklers outside many buildings douse sidewalks periodically to prevent loitering and curbside encampments; "bum-proof" convex benches prevent homeless people from sleeping on them; and video cameras are ubiquitous.

It is difficult for homeless people to escape this landscape of despair. Very few cities elsewhere in Southern California offer services for homeless people; indeed, more and more municipalities are enacting ordinances to restrict or criminalize their behaviors, such as panhandling or sleeping in parks.[19] And in L.A.'s downtown, the CRA has for many years pursued an official policy of containment, intended to move homeless people and the services designed to assist them deeper into the heart of Skid Row and away from business and commercial areas.

A Proposal for a Self-governing Outdoor Living Facility

In 1991, the Community Redevelopment Agency of the City of Los Angeles retained a broadly based consultancy team to devise a new strategic plan for downtown Los Angeles. The firm of Wolch/Dear was commissioned to prepare the homelessness and social services component of that plan—a focus that represented a striking departure from conventional planning practice. Among the most commonly voiced objectives for the Skid Row district were reducing the number of homeless people; cutting down the number of people living on sidewalks; diminishing the levels of illness, disability, and substance abuse in the street population; creating a healthy, viable community and better business environment; and securing cleaner, safer streets.

One of the largest perceived problems in the neighborhood was the presence of street encampments of homeless people. Such encampments, often consisting of scores of people, had been a feature of the downtown landscape for almost a decade. Many sporadic efforts, ranging from lightning police and sanitation department "sweeps" to the provision of formal and informal off-street alternatives, had been made to clear them away. It was clear that homeless people themselves did not like the ephemeral, exposed, and often dangerous environment of the encampments, but that, in the absence of an acceptable alternative, they appreciated them for their relative security and sense of community. Many people suggested that they would be willing to move their encampments off the sidewalks to less prominent sites if suitable spaces could be found where they could rebuild their communities.

As part of their advice to the CRA, Wolch/Dear recommended that on a one-year demonstration basis, a "self-governing outdoor living facility" (or SOLF) should be established on a small lot within the Skid Row district.[20] The facility was envisioned as an open space with a variety of amenities specifically intended for homeless people. The SOLF would enable them to get off the street and, hence, avoid potential conflicts with other community members or with the police. For this demonstration to be successful, the consultants advised that every effort be made to move an established community of homeless people into the SOLF. In this way, interpersonal and intergroup conflicts could be avoided, and established rules of conduct and self-policing applied. The SOLF was not intended as a solution to homelessness, nor to street living. However, until the scale of homelessness could be brought under control, Wolch/Dear suggested that the SOLF could offer one way of humanely removing the homeless from the sidewalks by providing them with a safe alternative, while at the same time offering an avenue whereby people could be hooked up with effective helping agencies.

The following design specifications were suggested for the SOLF:
•The lot size would be approximately 50 by 150 feet.
•The SOLF periphery would consist of a landscaped green belt; it would be fenced except where buildings already formed the property line.
•Only the street facade would be gated to allow security and control of access and egress.
•The facility would consist primarily of hard space and would be equipped with central patios fitted with concrete tables and cooking pits.
•A sleeping arbor, consisting of a number of discrete living-space "pads" of crushed granite would be positioned in the most secure part of the park.
•Generous amounts of shade would be provided either from trees or awnings.
•The following minimum utilities were recommended for the facility: portable self-cleaning toilets, showers and laundry unit, storage lockers, seating, water fountains, and trash containers.

Informal street encampment of homeless people, Towne Street, Los Angeles

Off-street encampment for homeless people established by the city of Los Angeles

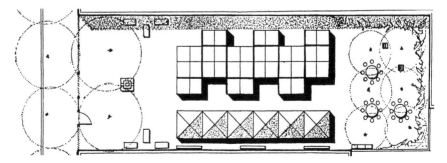

Schemetic plan of a self-governing outdoor living facility (SOLF)

Programmatic guidelines for the SOLF were:

•SOLF capacity would be 25–40 people.

•The facility would be self-governing, with minimal externally imposed rules (such as no violence).

•Outreach and referral assistance would be regularly available to help people make the transition out of the SOLF to permanent housing.

•Job-training programs would be made available to residents, with assistance provided in overcoming barriers to reentry into the work force.

•Day labor opportunities associated with the SOLF itself as well as with the surrounding neighborhood (such as neighborhood clean-up crews and security) would be created.

•The facility would have a legitimate mailing address and mail delivery service.

•Security and surveillance opportunities would be facilitated if the site were surrounded on three sides by existing structures (such as SRO hotels). This would not only secure the boundaries, but also provide opportunities for oversight.

•Where SOLF boundaries were "soft" (as at the street entrance), no fencing, vegetation, or other landscaping would interfere with clear sight lines into and out of the park.

•Any cluster of structures within the facility would not interfere with clear sight lines into and out of the SOLF.

And finally, Wolch/Dear offered the following guidelines for establishing and operating the SOLF:

•The facility would be primarily conceptualized as a relocation effort. An existing encampment of homeless people would be identified for relocation, and meetings held with members to discover their willingness to move, their particular needs, etc.

•Meetings would also be held with prospective neighbors to introduce SOLF members, discuss SOLF rules, and identify areas of possible conflict and collaboration (such as food giveaways from restaurants at the end of the day and permitting SOLF members to use neighbors' trash disposal facilities).

•SOLF members would participate in the physical preparation of the facility (for example, in construction of facilities and planting).

•On the date set for the relocation, all encampment members would be assisted in the move to their new surroundings.

•Following the establishment of the SOLF, outreach workers would regularly contact members and connect those seeking specific benefits or services with appropriate providers. For instance, outreach workers could assist in locating rehabilitation programs, job training, and day labor opportunities.

•Outreach workers (from nearby SRO hotels, for instance) would visit the facility to explain their housing services to members and assist them in making a transition out of the park when they were ready to do so.

•Periodic meetings would be held with neighbors and outreach workers to air problems and resolve them.

•New members would be permitted only so long as there was space available and only when camp organizers approved their admission. A log would be maintained to monitor new registrants and departures from the facility.

•After a suitable period of operation, an evaluation of the project would be undertaken to make recommendations about continuing the project and the feasibility and desirability of other SOLFs in the region.

•A designated public agency would be responsible for the establishment and oversight of the SOLF's operation.

The SOLF proposal never made it into the final downtown strategic plan. It was too controversial. Opposition from potential neighbors was voiced; in addition, many service providers worried about liability and about giving the impression that SOLFs could be sanctioned as the solution to homelessness. However, in the deepest of ironies, and totally independent of our efforts, a few weeks later, Ted Hayes announced the opening of his Justiceville "dome village"—a SOLF by another name.

The Genesis I Project

This is the first truly original thing that we have for the homeless in fifty years.
—Carlton Norris, ARCO Foundation, on Genesis I

In 1985, Ted Hayes, a homeless activist, founded "Justiceville/Homeless USA" (JHUSA) as a nonprofit organization. JHUSA established a series of self-governed, unofficial encampments for homeless people in many different parts of downtown Los Angeles. All of them were subsequently dismantled by city officials who claimed that they did not conform to fire and zoning regulations.

In 1986, Hayes first envisioned domelike structures as transitional living facilities for homeless people. By 1993, he had gained enough financial support to launch his idea. With a $250,000 corporate grant from the ARCO Foundation and the assistance of downtown property owner/developer David Adams, a suitable one and one-half acre location adjacent to a freeway that marked the western edge of downtown L.A. was identified. With support from the mayor's office and the city council, it took only three weeks to get the necessary permits and to arrange a $2,500 per month lease for the property. Shortly after, eighteen Plexiglas domes were erected on the site.

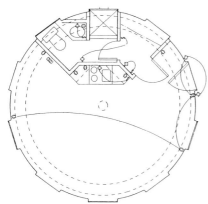

above: General view of Genesis I, the "dome village"
left: Floor plan of two-person dome unit

The domes—known as "omni-spheres"—are lightweight, easy to erect, water- and earthquake-proof structures, each costing at that time $6,500. Twelve domes were designed to accommodate two persons each (in separate rooms), providing shelter for twenty-four individuals. The domes include access for the disabled. Three domes were linked to form an office/community room/kitchen complex; two others contain shower/toilet/laundry facilities. The domes were designed by engineer Craig Chamberlain after the prototypical geodesic structures of Buckminster Fuller. Advisors in the conceptual process were designer Nick Edwards, architect Nadar Khalili, and Jamie Schneider, grandson of Buckminster Fuller. The shells are constructed from bolted curved panels of nontoxic polyester fiberglass and sit on concrete footings. They are twenty feet in diameter and twelve feet high, and they can be erected by two people in two hours. Lighting is powered by solar panels.[21]

In September 1993, the Genesis I Transitional Community (the village's official name) opened and became the new home for eighteen male and six female residents, the majority of whom came from an encampment that previously existed at the site. Since its inception, Genesis I has been highly successful, except for one incident in which a reporter was abducted and raped by two village residents. The village has managed to overcome serious financial difficulties, and recently received a $161,461 federal grant, which will help to cover operating costs in the years ahead.

Concept and Governance

The best form of governance is self-government.
—Ted Hayes, Justiceville founder

JHUSA's Exodus Genesis Incentive Plan (EGIP) aims to establish a series of self-governing dome villages to assist chronically homeless people. In this sense, Genesis I is a pilot project to test the viability of the village, its residents, and the underlying concept. If Genesis I is successful and can attract additional funding, EGIP envisions the construction of a number of additional specialized villages, providing shelter and assistance to the elderly homeless, homeless people with AIDS, and homeless troubled youth.

Genesis I intends not only to provide residents with shelter, but also to stabilize their lives and to link them with social service agencies. It has developed an extensive network of referral contacts with service providers and organizations, including medical clinics, outreach programs, and drug and alcohol counseling agencies. Ultimately, Genesis I aims to give residents an opportunity to return to mainstream society. Along the way it also intends to help residents develop organizational skills and regain self-reliance and self-esteem. Residents are required to do daily chores, maintain personal appearance and that of the property, hold rotational twenty-four-hour security watches, and participate in village governance.

A strong philosophy of "tribal social democracy" permeates the social organization of Genesis I. This emphasis is deliberately related to the nature of homeless society, in which people tend to be less susceptible to conventional forms of leadership and rules. The levels of leadership begin with the General Community, comprised of all the village residents who attend the Council of Peace sessions—regularly scheduled meetings to discuss community matters. The next level is the Council of Justice, a smaller version of the General Community; any resident may be a member. This smaller group convenes for the purpose of more focused debate over issues that the General Community feels is too problematic for a large group to decide. The final level of governance is the Servant Director (currently Ted Hayes), who is the ultimate decision maker, having veto power over any issue before the General Community or Council of Peace. As a consequence of these arrangements, there are significant levels of resident participation in all aspects of village governance, outreach, and self-empowerment strategies.

Another important objective of Genesis I is that residents will develop sufficient organizational skills to take on managerial positions in future dome villages. Office management, public relations, and supervising/directing staff are envisioned as possible future occupations for Genesis I "graduates." Other career opportunities for residents are planned through the Justiceville Occupational Business Services (JOBS), which currently has three operational branches: Project Clean Environment, designed to clean and maintain the local neighborhood; Project Trashbusters, contracted to clean specific areas in other neighborhoods; and Cottage Industries, an arts and crafts sector, producing jewelry, T-shirts, stickers, and badges. Other village activities include weekly Community Council meetings, multicultural education, site-improvement efforts (such as tree planting, recycling, and gardening), and hosting cultural meetings with the local Korean and Jewish communities.

In sum, the dome village is envisaged as the first step in a transition to affordable housing and independent living. However, Ted Hayes also acknowledges one potential disadvantage of the concept and physical realization of Genesis:

> I'm concerned that people will become more excited about the shell, the structure, the dome itself, rather than the contents of the dome—the homeless people. Because these are cheap and quick to build, there might be a tendency to build massive numbers of domes and force or lure homeless people into this kind of living condition, which I would consider low-class welfare housing projects.

Village Residents' Reactions
Each day I learn a little more and help the community work better.
—Genesis I resident

Since the Genesis I and SOLF concepts were so close in conception, we were naturally very keen to monitor events at the dome village. The residents welcomed us into their homes and made this report possible.[22] By the time of our survey

(February through May of 1994), a total of thirty people had lived at Genesis I. During this period, eleven people had vacated the village, and seventeen adults were currently in residence, plus two children. Thirteen adults were interviewed to ascertain their status and progress since taking up residence at Genesis I.

The Genesis I population was largely composed of long-term homeless people, and was predominantly male and African American (seventy-seven percent). The median age of females was 34.5 years; of males, 44.2 years. The reasons given for becoming homeless were mainly related to family, medical, and legal problems. Almost one-quarter of the residents identified money-related problems as their principal personal difficulty; a further twelve percent mentioned the need for a job. Other significant personal difficulties related to health problems, difficulties in traveling around, substance abuse, and family problems. About one-half of the residents were currently in touch with formal service providers in the region, mostly medical facilities, but also social service agencies and police. Residents were virtually unanimous that the village was a great help with their personal problems. Mostly they valued the sense of community—being able to live and work as a valued member of a stable group. There were very few dislikes regarding the village, mostly complaints about co-residents and some inconveniences of village life (such as lack of privacy).

Residents identified a wide variety of personal objectives. In the short term, exactly half the personal goals identified were related to the village, its duties and governance, and the prospect of establishing a new village. Other emphases included the importance of helping other homeless people, particularly in light of residents' own familiarity with the problems of homelessness. "I want to help homeless people, because I know what keeps them up and what takes them down," confided one resident, a father of two children. Such concerns also found expression in residents' long-term goals, but there was also evidence of a more personal introspection (for instance, relating to self-realization or educational/career goals). In all cases, residents relied very heavily on the village to help them achieve their goals.

Even though the village had only been operating for three months, most residents claimed that many positive changes had already occurred in their lives, and that they had made progress with their personal goals. People's lives had changed for the better primarily because a new stability had been achieved, and because self-respect had been regained. Eleven people had graduated from Genesis I since its inception. Just over half of these graduates voluntarily left the village after their lives had been stabilized: six individuals had secured permanent accommodations; two also had acquired jobs; and three had reestablished contact with their partners. Three people had their residency terminated by the consensus of village residents. The remaining two members of the community were arrested on kidnapping and rape/assault charges.

Two months after our first interviews, nine out of the original thirteen respondents were reinterviewed. They reported that two-thirds of their personal problems had either been resolved or shown improvement; and progress had been made with over eighty percent of their short- and long-term goals. All but one of the residents reported that their lives had greatly improved since they took up residence at Genesis I.

Neighborhood Response

People stop by all the time because they see or hear something about the village. The residents enjoy it. They like meeting people and showing off their work. The residents take pride in the village; it makes them feel good.
—Ronda Flanzbaum, Genesis I staffer

As part of the Genesis I development strategy, Ted Hayes had insisted on a strong community outreach effort. We explored the broader neighborhood reception of the dome village, focusing on two groups; neighbors and key local informants. Of fifty-five respondents in the surrounding neighborhood who knew about the village, two-thirds recalled their first information about Genesis I as positive. Opinions regarding the village's presence in the neighborhood were generally highly favorable. Over three-quarters of the respondents expressed varying degrees of support for the project, mostly because they felt the project was good for the homeless. Only two people were hostile to the village.

Respondents were asked to identify specific effects that the village had on the surrounding neighborhood. Eighty-two percent claimed there were no negative effects, while five people identified negative impacts. These included the rape/assault incident, the village's potential to act as a magnet for more homeless people, and the perception that residents provided a negative example. On the other hand, seventy-nine percent of the neighbors identified positive neighborhood effects from the village, most especially the fact that the village kept people off the street and had generally improved neighborhood amenity.

We also talked with five key informants who represented local business, police, and social service provider interests. All five individuals had had previous contact with the village, and were supportive of its objectives. Genesis I was regarded as a positive force in the neighborhood, having especially impacted the general levels of cleanliness in local streets. In addition, workers who used parking lots adjacent to Genesis I reported feeling much safer in the neighborhood since the village opened. Other supporters related how CALTRANS, the state high-way agency, had been pressured to clean up the freeway offramps after village residents had successfully tidied up the rest of the neighborhood. A representative from a neighboring hotel stated that the village constituted a "one hundred percent improvement of the area," and continued, "it's the best thing that's happened to this side of town in years."

Making Space for Homeless People

[The village] shows homeless that they can live for free. Homeless people are a bunch of losers who need to get a fucking job like anybody else.
—Genesis I neighbor

Not everyone believes in Genesis I, or in homeless people's abilities for self-improvement. Others critique the potential to see the domes as a cheap solution for the dilemma of affordable housing. Yet the Genesis I/SOLF concept has worked. It has taken homeless people off the street, rebuilt their lives, and returned some of them to the mainstream. The omni-sphere concept was a public relations masterpiece resulting in unprecedented levels of community support, and providing a stream of volunteer assistance in excess of the village's needs. Many volunteers, known as "peace workers," actively help to maintain the infrastructure of the village. Other supporters donate food and clothing. The Genesis I project has shown how important self-determination is to the successful exit from the condition of homelessness. The project is truly a demonstration of architecture by, for, and of the homeless. When such spaces are created, the issue of fear is demonstrably reduced.

Addressing Fear through Community Empowerment

Lois M. Takahashi

Orange County, California has long been associated with theme parks (exemplified by Disneyland), high-tech economic development, relative affluence, and, most recently, municipal bankruptcy. However, amidst the landscape of gated, often visibly homogeneous, and planned suburban communities, there are neighborhoods where families and households live in daily fear of violence. In these neighborhoods, located primarily in the cities of Santa Ana and Anaheim, predominantly low-income, Latino residents must cope with illicit drug dealing, gang activity, and drive-by shootings.

To address the fear among residents in these communities, the Congregation-Based Organization of Orange County (CBOOC)[1] uses strategies for building leadership and empowerment. Empowerment and neighborhood organizing are not new strategies, particularly with respect to low-income minority neighborhoods. What is unique about CBOOC is its work through congregations of various denominations to build leadership for improving local quality of life and reducing resident fear. This essay will discuss, from the point of view of CBOOC organizers, the ways in which individual leadership can be developed within a faith-based multidenominational organization, and how such work potentially serves to change the built environment and its concomitant social relations. CBOOC is striving to change the neighborhoods of Santa Ana and Anaheim from places of fear to communities of vitality.

Background

I first learned about CBOOC when Julie, a sociology professor who, like me, taught at the University of California-Irvine (UCI), asked if I would be interested in developing a partnership between UCI faculty and a local community group. Julie was very interested in creating a bridge between university faculty and the Latino community in northern Orange County. She had been attending CBOOC meetings and had established a friendly and trusting relationship with Diane (the executive director of CBOOC at the time). Since I was and continue to be interested in the processes of mobilizing, particularly among minority residents, I was very enthusiastic about the idea. A little over a year ago, Julie and I set up a meeting between Diane and UCI faculty members, students, and administration representatives to discuss possible areas in which we could work together. At that first meeting, there was a great degree of skepticism on the part of many faculty members mainly, I think, because of the association of CBOOC with the Catholic church (although, as CBOOC often points out, there are multiple denominations represented in their organization).

Over the past year, Julie and I continued to organize meetings between CBOOC and the UCI faculty, students, and administration representatives. During the same time period, I met informally with Diane to talk about CBOOC's ongoing projects, and to determine whether there were opportunities for students to work as interns, to discern whether there were possible joint projects to develop, and to learn more about Diane and the organization. About four months ago, Diane moved to another congregation-based organization in southern California, and Bob stepped in to head CBOOC. Bob has a very different style of social interaction than Diane, and Julie and I have had some difficulties in communicating with him. Our efforts to develop a partnership between UCI and CBOOC is somewhat at a lull, but Julie and I are continuing to interact with Bob and Tim (another CBOOC organizer) on our individual research projects.[2]

Social Relations and Life in Orange County

Whenever I am asked about the location of Orange County, my response is usually that Orange County is the home of Disneyland. Orange County, in contrast to its more visible neighbor Los Angeles, has long been identified with suburban affluence.[3] Most people are less familiar with Orange County's diverse population, the conflict among its urban, suburban, and rural interests, and the fear that permeates the lives of many local residents. Fear in particular is not usually associated with life in Orange County, especially given the fact that many of its cities rank among the safest in the nation. However, residents in many neighborhoods, particularly in the northern portion of the county, experience fear associated with urban decline, increasing rates of poverty, and gang violence.

Orange County has felt the impacts of welfare reorganization, economic restructuring, and demographic change that have influenced urban patterns across Southern California.[4] Ongoing reorganization of social programs, for example, has been promoted at all levels of government through strategies of privatization, cutbacks in programs and funding, and changes in eligibility requirements.[5] Such strategies at the federal level have meant a shifting of program and funding responsibilities to the state and local levels.[6] The state and municipalities, however, have often been fiscally unable or politically unwilling to recreate the safety net. Transfers to lower tiers of governance has thus meant that local health-care and other human services are now provided through an often chaotic system of private, non-profit, and informal sector sources. The reorganization of the Medi-Cal benefits system, for instance, has shifted responsibility for indigent medical care from the state to the county level, and has resulted in a privatized system of hospital contracts for services.[7]

To make matters worse in Orange County, its recent bankruptcy has generated a drastic reorganization of county services and employment, along with substantial social service cutbacks. A residue of uncertainty and fear are widespread concerning public services (such as police, fire, and transportation), public K–12 education, and the availability of social and medical services. In addition, the ongoing demographic changes being experienced throughout Southern California have incited public backlash against immigrants, particularly those who are undocumented. For example, Proposition 187, passed recently by California voters, would deny public and social services to undocumented immigrants. In the city of Santa Ana, planners are lobbying to decrease residential density standards in order to prevent the spread of contagious illness and fires. Opponents argue that such standards are specifically directed against Latino households.

In this context of growing need and diminishing resources, CBOOC is working to fill the gap by developing leadership among neighborhood residents and establishing relationships with institutions and individuals designing and implementing public policy in Orange County.

CBOOC: A New Wave of Local Mobilization

Using empowerment to address urban problems is not a new strategy. The advocacy planning tradition, for example, was one of the mainstays of planning practice during the 1960s and 1970s. Such strategies usually involved providing information and technical assistance to neighborhood groups in an effort to increase access to political power and improve quality of life.[8] Church-based organizing has also been used over the past few decades in the United States and Latin America as the basis for urban social movements, in particular the civil rights movement of the 1960s.[9] The tradition of Christian political theology, termed "liberation theology," has used Marxist notions to motivate grassroots organizing for social change, especially in Latin America. Liberation theology takes as its foundation the three-component framework of impoverished conditions, awareness concerning the structural causes of poverty and oppression ("conscientization"), and commitment to change.[10]

What is unique about the mobilization taking place in the cities of Santa Ana and Anaheim is the organizational shift from neighborhoods to already existing religious congregations.[11] Church organizations have long been involved in providing charity and social services, but community organizations based in congregations appear somewhat distinct because of their emphases on multidenominational cooperation, community and structural change, and leadership building. In the case of CBOOC, their four-step process includes assessment, research, mobilization, and reflection.[12] In the assessment process, the professional organizers engage in "one-on-ones" with congregation members to establish relationships and to determine specific issues for later action. The research component calls on leaders and organizers to develop research questions and to obtain information concerning these questions. Following the research component, mobilization takes place, usually in the form of public meetings, termed "actions." Finally, following an action, the organizers and congregation participants engage in an evaluation of the action. Such evaluation includes the performance of leaders, the turnout of the wider community, and the question of tracking stated commitments.

CBOOC works to improve local quality of life through established religious congregations in twelve cities.[13] There are fifteen congregations that participate in CBOOC, spanning class, race, and ethnic differences. The congregations are drawn from Catholic, Methodist, and Presbyterian churches. Many of CBOOC's most active congregations are located in the largely Latino cities of Santa Ana and Anaheim. In its mission statement, CBOOC describes itself as "an interfaith, multicultural organization which unites families to improve the quality of life in our communities."[14] CBOOC has identified several broad areas as being important priorities for action: neighborhood safety, education (especially K–12 and adult education opportunities), employment (both job development and job training), health care (especially access to services, specifically for increasing treatment for substance abusers), housing (especially creating low- and moderate-income housing), and recreation (including after-school programs for children and safe, well-maintained public parks).

CBOOC formally convened in 1992 after religious leaders and an already existing neighborhood organization had been merging their organizing efforts through an Orange County sponsoring committee since 1985, when CBOOC began receiving corporate, religious, and congregational financial sponsorship. Among the corporations and foundations that have supported it are ARCO, the Beatrice Foundation, Chevron, Disney, Home Savings of California, The James Irvine Foundation, McDonnell Douglas, Mervyn's, Pacific Mutual, Rockwell, TRW, and

Western Digital. CBOOC has also received sponsorship from large religious organizations, such as the Campaign for Human Development, Episcopal Diocese of Los Angeles, Jewish Federation of Orange County, Presbyterian Church, United Church of Christ, and United Methodist Voluntary Service.

CBOOC works within a national organizations network, NNO, the National Network for Organizing, founded in 1972 and based in the San Francisco Bay Area.[15] As a member of this network, CBOOC members have access to annual leadership training (through yearly retreats), recruitment and training of professional organizers serving as staff, and consultation and technical assistance. The NNO network currently consists of approximately 350 congregation-based units in eight states and forty-five cities.

The Potential for Empowerment in Orange County

There are three primary components to CBOOC organizing methods, strategies, and goals in the congregations in Santa Ana and Anaheim: targeting "winnable issues" over more broad-based concerns or problems, using the developmental model of empowerment to develop leadership, and forging linkages with other neighborhood-based organizations.

Targeting "Winnable Issues"

Although one of the goals that CBOOC seeks is structural change, the methods it uses do not focus directly on resolving large structural problems. For example, rather than work directly to alter the existing distribution of resources or to eradicate poverty, the organization instead attempts to build leadership and establish relationships between oppositional groups or individuals. CBOOC organizers argue that large structural issues present distractions to the professional organizers, as opposed to what they see as "winnable issues." CBOOC's executive director, Bob, described the essence of congregational organizing:

> When we look at the theological aspect of organizing, it's that it relates to the person. We do this on a value base, and that value base relates to the idea that my child can't go outside and that child deserves to. Spiritual would be that. Social would be the idea of the democratic side of the distribution of resources. And what we find is that's where a lot of the distractions are.

For CBOOC organizers, the difference between "concerns" and "issues" is that concerns are not winnable and issues are. Issues are determined after speaking with individuals and families and conducting research involving speaking to city departments, apartment owners, and others who might contribute to resolving problems. As Bob commented,

> What makes [the issue] winnable is very concrete solutions.... So what makes it
> winnable is if we can get the chief of police to say, "I'll have a cop that sits down with
> you once a month"—that's a winnable issue. Reduce crime—that's not really
> winnable because you can judge it but you don't know what it means. It's just an
> abstract known. It's the person or the thing or the structure that you can see and
> taste that's going to make it win.

The idea of "winnable issues" is drawn from the Saul Alinsky tradition of neighborhood-based organizing. Other Alinsky-style strategies include being invited
into a community (here, a congregation), seeking out "partial leaders" (those who
represent significant components of community life) and building them into
broader based leaders, developing a list of winnable issues (rather than philosophical "problems" that cannot be resolved, at least in the short term), and eval-
uating the organization's success or failure in its activities.[16]

Winnable issues are vital for CBOOC for at least two reasons. First, without a
continuing stream of victories, participants might become frustrated, disillu-
sioned, or lose interest and discontinue their work with the organization. Because
of the many resource constraints (such as lack of time and material resources)
that prevent interested congregation members from participating, winning issues
becomes a vital component of mobilization. This is linked to the second reason
for CBOOC's pursuit of winnable issues: a continuing stream of victories provides
evidence of the organization's effectiveness to participants and outside organizations. The evidence of CBOOC effectiveness lends legitimacy to the organization's
methods and projects.

But while Alinsky-style strategies provide many of the methods used by
CBOOC to pursue projects and goals, the developmental model of empowerment is
the primary basis through which individual leadership is nurtured.[17] The basic
distinction that CBOOC organizers make between neighborhood-based organizing
and congregation based organizing is that the former originates with identifiable
issues and often has difficulty sustaining long-term participation by members
while the latter begins with *relationships* among individuals, groups, and institutions. As Bob suggests about a parish-based model of organizing,

> The easiest way to [describe] it is what gets you into action. If I talk to you about city
> resources—I go into a neighborhood and there's a gang here or there's no police
> response. OK, the neighborhood is under siege by drug dealers—like Shalimar. What
> gets me to the point of rage over that issue is [not] only related to the city not
> responding to the needs of the community or the fact that money is being spent on
> a highway instead of being in our community.... Is it the fact that our daughter can't
> do anything? She's trapped. She's under siege.... If we can focus our people on

Shalimar Street to say Christine Espinoza doesn't sleep at night; she's too scared to sleep; she sleeps at school because she can only sleep when she falls asleep and it's destroying her—that's the human dignity question. That in essence is the difference between church-based organizing and neighborhood organizing. Church-based always starts with the person—values, morals—a moral standard for our community.

CBOOC thus tends to operate from a combination of a developmental model of empowerment, which functions as the general guideline for creating the potentials for leadership, and an Alinsky-style set of strategies, which enables organizers and CBOOC leaders to pursue and accomplish stated goals. In the developmental model, empowerment is defined largely through leadership building. Leadership building is seen as enhancing the capacity of organizational participants through training and action to access structures of power and, in so doing, improving the quality of their lives.

Developing of Leadership

Within CBOOC, many of the potentials for empowering members, building leadership, and reducing resident fear lie in the institutional structure of the organization. Residents who participate in CBOOC are viewed as comprising three interlinked circles (fig. 1). The definition of these circles remains relatively fluid, with organizers constantly working to move individuals from the outer circles to the inner circle. The inner circle is viewed by CBOOC organizers less as an exclusive group of elite leaders and more as the current set of individuals taking responsibility for organizing other congregation members, obtaining information through research, and speaking at actions. Movement in and out of circles is often constrained by family responsibilities (such as caring for children and elderly parents) and time limits brought on by employment. The organizers are constantly trying to motivate congregation participants to become more involved in CBOOC activities, but they balance this challenge with the current constraints and desires of the individual. According to Tim, a CBOOC organizer,

> People have all kinds of stuff going on. And I try to find out where people are at and how much we can challenge them to move towards the middle [core group of leaders].

The inner circle is comprised of the core "leaders" with which the professional organizers (the staff of CBOOC) develop the most intensive relationships. These inner circles range from five to ten individuals for each congregation. One of the CBOOC organizers is responsible for six churches in Santa Ana, comprising an aggregate core leadership group of between thirty and sixty individuals, who have attended NNO training sessions, have taken a role in an action, and have played prominent roles during community meetings.

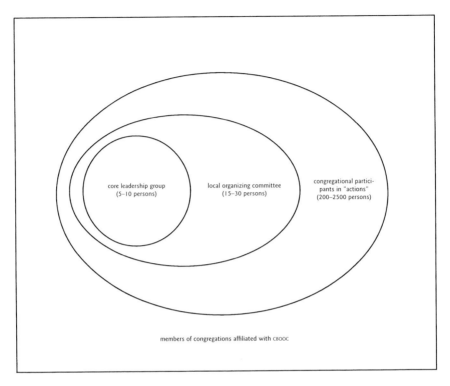

core leadership group
(5–10 persons)

local organizing committee
(15–30 persons)

congregational partici-
pants in "actions"
(200–2500 persons)

members of congregations affiliated with CBOOC

1. Organization of CBOOC participants

The next circle of individuals is defined as the local organizing committee (LOC) and consists of between fifteen and thirty individuals for each congregation. Since the LOC meetings are publicly announced, usually at church meetings and at masses, the LOC groups consist of an extended group of individuals representing both the parish and the general community. Individuals who attend LOC meetings may have attended an action or may have interests in the specific issue being discussed. Often the attendees at the LOC meetings represent the constituencies of the core leadership. That is, each leader may bring four or five individuals who are identified as being constituents by the CBOOC organizers.

The third and outermost circle consists of the large numbers of residents who attend "actions" in the community. CBOOC often draws on this large circle for attendance at major events (such as meetings with the mayor of Santa Ana, representatives of the local school board, or police officers). Attendance at events organized by CBOOC congregations have ranged from 200 to 2500 at various actions between 1986 and 1992.

The primary strategy used for leadership development is the "one-to-one" meeting with congregation members. "One-to-ones" usually take place at the resident's home (after work) or in other locations convenient for congregation members (such as restaurants during the work day). In these one-to-one meetings, the organizers develop lists of issues, engage in informal leadership training, and provide evaluations of participant behavior during actions. The organizers meet with core leaders two or three times a month in "one-to-one" discussions. According to Tim,

> That's where the real development takes place. That's where the teaching, I guess, or the mentoring really takes place. [It's] having that time to sit down and talk with the folks. I'll meet with those folks on a more intense level.

The content of one-to-one discussions vary, but they often consist of three basic factors: accountability, practicality/relevancy, and imagination/challenge. Accountability, according to CBOOC organizers, concerns the leaders' accountability to CBOOC (for example, the leaders' constituents' attendance at actions and meetings) and to their constituents (such as the constituents' knowledge about CBOOC activities and CBOOC's addressing of their problems or concerns). As Tim explains,

> I always ask them, Are you talking to them [the four or five folks in their constituency]? Do they know what's happening around and what's going on?

Practicality and relevancy often influence the types of issues being informally discussed among residents and CBOOC participants. Such issues define the current state of affairs, and indicate to the professional organizers the context of existing knowledge, perceptions, and potential activities. Practicality and relevancy also serve as criteria to indicate to CBOOC organizers the concerns that might constitute winnable issues given the perceptions of leaders and congregation members.

Finally, imagination is invoked to challenge the existing assumptions and goals of congregation members in an effort to promote long-term and broader perspectives (beyond the individual or household) concerning change. As an example, Tim described a one-to-one with a leader who had been very frustrated by an action. During this action, several issues that she deemed very important were not addressed, but she did not speak during the meeting. During the informal evaluation that took place after the action, CBOOC participants discussed the action and the woman expressed her deep frustration over the meeting's progress. Tim describes his follow-up one-to-one with her,

> She was a really good person. She's done a lot of work with us. And so, I had a one-to-one with her, and I started talking with her, and I had no idea where this was going.... I had no idea what was going to happen, and she was very upset and very frustrated.... And I went in and started talking to her and I said, "Well, how'd you

feel about the meeting?" and all this stuff. But within the first five minutes of the conversation, we were talking about what it meant to be a leader. And how she didn't see herself as a leader in the community. And I said, "Why, what do you think a leader does?" And she goes, "Well," and then she started going into the times she had assumed leadership roles within her own family, "I did this for my family, and after I did it, excuse my language, but all hell broke loose. I couldn't please everybody. Somebody got mad at me, and my sister-in-law wrote me out of her will . . ." All this stuff started coming out, of what was happening in her own family when she would speak up about what she wanted. She would be punished for it. About, I don't know, it was probably 45 minutes to an hour there, we talked through it. So what does that mean, what happened to that situation? . . . And then, what I try to do is bring it back to the organizing. Now look at where you are at now at the LOC committee. Then it was, I think, easier for her to say, "Oh, OK, now I see that the reason I got so mad at the meeting was because all this other stuff was influencing me. If I ever, if I spoke up at home about something I wanted to see happen with the family, I'd get in trouble. So, at St. Mary's, I'm not going to speak up either. Because I'm going to get in trouble." Then we talked about the environment of organizing and how that's what makes us strong. . . . I mean it was that kind of conversation which I think was a tremendous learning for her.

As this statement indicates, much of the leadership building activity that occurs in the one-to-one meetings consists of psychological or individual empowerment. However, rather than focus on improving coping skills and competence building, CBOOC organizers tend to view this process as an "internal revolution." As Tim continues to explain about this particular one-to-one experience,

And that's for me the central fundamental element of organizing is that power is in a relationship and that was borne out with me sitting down with this leader. . . . So there was a certain amount of power, if you will, in having that relationship already there, that I was able to do something. . . . But there's this other [principle of organizing], which is sort of a fringe one, which I think is important in the aspect of leadership development—which is, the first revolution is internal. When people have to come to terms with their own fears. With their own questions. With their own concerns on a very personal individual basis.

Creating the Context for Promoting Mobilization
Besides individual leadership through one-to-one meetings, the potential for mobilization may be greatly enhanced by changes in the context of issues. In the case of CBOOC, such changes have meant not only the attainment of monetary, political, and other resources, but also the building of relationships with local

political and human service agencies and groups, the NNO network, and the church. A relationship is defined by Bob as "someone knows who I am and knows how to respond to us." Thus, relationships may be friendly and cooperative, or they may be more confrontational, depending on the circumstances involved. Bob gives an example of a relatively tense relationship,

> Shalimar Street is a good example. The mayor is incredibly angry with us. He used to have a very constructive relationship with us, but now he's in there. He came up with his own solutions. He closed down the street. He brought in "no parking" signs everywhere and all this stuff. The community doesn't like it and there's a lot of anger on both sides. What we've tried to do is sit down and stick to the issue and get beyond the anger. Clearly, he's really upset with us, but he will respond to us.

While CBOOC's primary missions are to develop relationships with residents and power structures and to build leadership for congregation participants, it has also been increasingly active in cooperating with other organizations. Part of this increasing role may be a consequence of Orange County's municipal bankruptcy and the ongoing recession. In the past, CBOOC has not actively sought out cooperative activities with other organizations. Bob explained the reasons for this minimal role of cooperative activities and why circumstances have changed.

> We traditionally allied ourselves very little.... The idea that we're only responsible for our people and the possibility of co-optation and being sidetracked by the muck of everybody else. So what we do is we've defined the need in our community. We constantly go back to our community and as we look for solutions to the problems we've defined as an issue, our traditional road to the city is blocked by bankruptcy, lack of funds, or just doesn't address the concern like we need it addressed. We've begun to look at other allies and that's where the Catholic Charities and Cambodian Family [two local service organizations] and other folks like the Orange County Fire Association have come into play. We've had some trouble in that their vision is different than our vision and they'll try to pull us into that vision and we simply have to make it very clear.... We can work in a quid pro quo if it's beneficial.

Work has been ongoing with the Orange County Bar Association (OCBA), for example, to develop an internship program for inner-city youth in Santa Ana. Forty youth from Santa Ana have already participated, and the OCBA is planning to expand this program every year. Also in the preliminary stages is the development of family support centers in conjunction with Catholic Charities, named Project Adelante. At present, Project Adelante has activities set up in three churches, encompassing adult literacy, citizenship courses, and parenting classes. Although CBOOC is based in congregational organizing and it is increasingly working collaboratively with groups such as Catholic Charities, the organizers believe that CBOOC is minimally influenced by the varying church hierarchies. As Bob argues,

> They have an understanding that they cannot delegate what we do. We go in—unless we have the blessing of the pastor, we will not organize. But the pastor always understands that the issues we work on come from the community....The pastor of this church is...the president of Planned Parenthood, and St. Joseph, our other church, has protesters out here every Sunday. Yet these two churches worked together last year on a $500,000 program for kids in this neighborhood. They are able to separate it.

Discussion

My experience with CBOOC left me with very positive and somewhat tentative impressions about congregation-based organizing in Orange County. My positive impressions come from the significant steps that CBOOC organizers have taken to mobilize low-income, minority, and largely non-English-speaking residents in neighborhoods in Santa Ana and Anaheim. CBOOC organizers have been very effective in encouraging large groups of residents to attend "actions" and in eliciting tangible and intangible responses from policy makers. Tangible responses include opening a police substation in a neighborhood in Santa Ana. Intangible responses include increased access to politicians and bureaucrats.

The success of CBOOC in organizing congregation members has been due in large part to the three components of congregation-based organizing, which were followed consistently by CBOOC organizers. First, the focus on winnable issues means that issues and solutions remain concrete to be viable. For example, when organizers speak to the LOCs in the congregations, they continually challenge the participants to define improved quality of life not as broad goals, such as eradicating gangs, but rather as concrete issues that can be addressed through an action, such as developing "homework centers" for youth. By defining quality of life as concrete issues and mobilizing large numbers of residents to attend actions, CBOOC forces city officials and departments to respond to their demands. Second, the CBOOC organizers describe the development of leadership in terms of improving psychological health ("internal revolutions") and creating and strengthening community ties (emphasizing building relationships). Thus, leadership more than merely trains and builds the competence of individuals, it also involves creating relationships between CBOOC leaders and various individuals and entities. Many of these relationships had hitherto been nonexistent (for example, relationships between CBOOC leaders and other congregation members, politicians and bureaucrats, and larger institutions). Finally, the cooperation between CBOOC and other service agencies represents recent efforts to expand the context for organizing and

By defining quality of life as concrete issues and mobilizing large numbers of residents to attend actions, the Congregation-Based Organization of Orange County forces city officials to respond to their demands.

for enabling mobilization. This relatively new direction for CBOOC was brought about in part by the changing fiscal environment in Orange County, and indicates a potential for wider organizational coordination across the county.

I was also struck by the prolonged and intense participation brought about by CBOOC's shift from neighborhood-based to congregation-based organizing. Prior to its formal convention in 1992, CBOOC had engaged in more traditional neighborhood-based organizing, which focused more on issues than on building relationships and leaders. Perhaps one of the most distinctive facets of congregation-based organizing is the clarity with which it defines the community, the issues, and resident needs. While much research on group participation and empowerment laments the lack of a clear definition of community, in congregation-based organizing, the community is relatively clear—the congregation of the various churches involved. The clear spatial definition of community influences the potential for participation by congregation members. According to the CBOOC organizers, the greatest participation occurs where there is spatial concentration of congregation members, such as that in Anaheim and Santa Ana in Latino congregations of Catholic churches (although not all CBOOC members are either Latino or Catholic). In terms of community fear and community vitality, short-term issues for CBOOC are also relatively clear: neighborhood safety, education, employment, and access to health-care services. These issues are drawn from CBOOC leaders and congregation members through one-to-ones and LOC meetings. Thus, community needs are being defined and redefined on an ongoing basis by members of the congregation-based organization, but they remain relatively clear because of CBOOC strategies and methods.

Not all of my impressions of CBOOC were entirely favorable, however. One misgiving I had about this growing form of grassroots mobilizing was the somewhat questionable linkage between social change and organized religion. CBOOC shifted from neighborhood-based to congregation-based organizing primarily because of the access to a well-defined group of individuals who had long-term connections to a long-standing social institution, that is, the church. Working in congregations provides organizers with a ready social network of individuals who look to church leadership for moral and spiritual guidance. Organizing through such institutions provides a cohesive and potentially large group of individuals in terms of grassroots mobilization. As Bob suggested,

> You have the greater parish, the greater neighborhood willing to support that [deteriorating] area. In fact, that . . . somehow determines that Shalimar Street is somehow important for them to work on. It comes from the idea of the value of the church which says we are responsible for our whole community. So if Shalimar is dying, the whole parish is dying. I was initially surprised at how true that was—how people actually bought that, that they were able to say that, no, I'm not here simply because I have to be. But it's important for me to see that Shalimar Street can survive and thrive. It's unfair for them to be in this condition and so you get the support of the whole parish and that's what gives us a more powerful structure. If it's just a neighborhood fighting, it usually doesn't win. The city will come in and they'll say, "OK, let's start a neighborhood watch" and the people will say, "OK, that'll work." And that never works.

But the power relations within organized religion also temper the nature of empowerment sought by CBOOC. The distinct hierarchy involved in organized religion embeds existing race, gender, and other social relations into the CBOOC definition of empowerment. Thus, the types of empowerment that CBOOC pursues are not only constrained by existing power relations in the cities of Santa Ana and Anaheim, but also by the churches whose congregations are involved in organizing activities. When I asked about these potential problems, CBOOC organizers often responded that they address such issues as they arise within the neighborhoods within which they work, realizing that there are always the potentials for co-optation and oppressive relationships. Bob explained this inherent tension in congregation-based organizing by saying,

> All this crap up here [indicates a higher level of discussion] about abortion, euthanasia, moneys, Protestants hating Catholics . . . all that stuff. The only reason organizing works is because it sticks to the value base in the church and not the institution and what the value drives is human dignity and the fact that we are responsible to do something for our fellow man. That's it.

I think that most of my discomfort came from the integral roles that faith, religious beliefs, and the church play in CBOOC organizing. Questions posed by UCI faculty members, students, and staff during meetings with CBOOC organizers also tended to focus on the potentially disempowering relationship between religious institutions and CBOOC organizing efforts. From my discussions with CBOOC organizers, this question is one that they must explain periodically to non-congregation members. As Tim explains,

> One thing we do is, we start our meetings with a prayer. We weren't going to give that up [referring to a meeting with a Buddhist-based service organization]. [So we had] them start with a prayer too. So, once we'd have a Catholic prayer and then the closing prayer would be from the Buddhist monk. So it was a neat ecumenical atmosphere. People were all different kinds of faith. But the thing is that something keeps us going, and that's our faith.

While I still have reservations about the potentials for empowerment within the institution of churches, what is clear is that CBOOC organizers and congregation members are working together to resolve many issues that have often gone unaddressed. For those congregation members living in low-income communities in Santa Ana and Anaheim, CBOOC provides a proactive means of overcoming the daily fear that they experience. As a model for reducing community fear and improving neighborhood quality of life, congregation-based organizing represents a growing phenomenon that will provide important lessons concerning grassroots organizing and empowerment both for policy makers and residents.

Hetero-Architecture for the Heteropolis
The Los Angeles School

Charles Jencks

With the gap between rich and poor increasing since the 1980s, even more with the cultural gaps between immigrant groups being exacerbated by mass migration, Americans have finally had to confront the conflict built into pluralism. In Los Angeles forty-four percent of the adult population was born outside the country, while in Miami the figure has reached a staggering seventy percent.

For these reasons, and twelve years of divisive Reaganism, the country is undergoing its first real bout of "wallification." The great American tradition—counter to so much of the rest of the world—has been the absence of fences between properties. From in-town residences as a streetscape of front doors and open porches to suburb as open, flowing parkland, the tradition has continued. Contrast this openness and accessibility to the Pompeian house, the Chinese courtyard residence, or the Jerusalem apartment—all archetypes of defense, estrangement, "keep out"—and the message is clear. In the former the American Dream presumes neighborliness and a tacit understanding of boundaries, while in the latter the older civilizations presume conflict, difference, and a contradiction between public and private realms.

As Los Angeles "comes of age," it has to confront the contradiction inherent in its open-door policy. For one hundred years it has carried forward the American agenda proclaimed on the Statue of Liberty—give us "your tired, your poor, your huddled masses yearning to breathe free"—and thrived on the policy. One ethnic group after another defined itself in this open space. Many lifestyle clusters and interest groups and ten million individuals came to the city to assert their particularity and difference from the rest.

But at a certain moment this self-definition by difference reaches a fracturing point, and the population defines itself by what it is against. And then the virtues of pluralism become corresponding vices, out-groups to be feared, sub-cultures to be stereotyped: Koreans or gays, Salvadorans or feminists, Hispanics or hippies, Anglos or policemen, blacks or politicians, Iranians or lawyers, Jews or students, Vietnamese or Republicans, Chinese or free-thinkers, and so on. I have purposely alternated some of the vilified out-groups first to show how incommensurable they are, and second to show they may end up including everybody. Each positive category may turn into a negative epithet of paranoia. The fear of multiculturalism is that the upward mobility of any one group will entail the downward mobility of another; positive discrimination may mean that qualified whites will loose jobs because of the color of their skin.

Defensible Architecture

By the late 1970s Los Angeles architects Charles Moore and Frank Gehry were inventing their different versions of a "cheapskate aesthetic" to respond to the reality of street life. Their dumb stucco walls and chain link fencing were turned into ambiguous signs of inventive beauty and "keep out." By the late 1980s deconstructionism had swept across the schools of architecture and there were many shades of alienation, heavy-metal expressionism, and fortress design to call on, varying from "dirty realism" and "post-holocaust design" to "dead-tech" (that is, high-tech after the bomb). At that time enough representations of alienation had been discussed, designed, and built to understand, well before the L.A. riots, what a riot realism would be. The Shatto Recreation Center near downtown Los Angeles was constructed like a World War II Quonset hut from highly defensible galvanized steel rolled in the shape of a ground-hugging parabola that would deflect any explosion. Front and back windowless walls were protected by textured brick to defy graffiti. These walls, climbing up in fragmented, growing shapes, were at once the image of computer-generated fractals and the semblance of a crumbling ruin.

Also in the late 1980s, many architects, from Aldo Rossi to SITE, had proffered similar strategies for what could be called "neo-ruinism." Their work varied from the burnt-out, haunted "house of the dead" to the peeling fractured archaeological site. These were not pretty ruins, not eighteenth-century follies in the garden. Rather they were the beginnings of a professional shift, the first time architects could look into the dark of division, conflict, and decay and represent some unwelcome truths.

Among those truths facing heterogeneous Los Angeles was the necessity of supplying "defensible space." In 1972 Oscar Newman wrote a book of that name, attacking modern architecture for not supplying clearly defined and clearly owned territory.[1] Instead of the abstract green and open space of Le Corbusier and the housing estate, he proposed a more privatized architecture of walls, "keep out" signs, security cameras, security men, and private property. Many vandalized housing estates in Britain and "the projects" in America were redesigned along these guidelines, thereby effectively reducing crime at these points (though critics said the defensible architecture merely pushed crime elsewhere).

In 1985 Frank Gehry altered a library in Hollywood, which had suffered constant vandalism including arson, with twenty-foot walls and grand sliding entrance gates—all of which said "fortress" to the L.A. writer Mike Davis, who condemned both the building and the trend.[2] "Stealth houses," he called the genre as a whole, especially those buildings that dissimulated their luxurious interiors with "proletarian or gangster facades."

Brian Murphy built several houses in Los Angeles that took defensive architecture to an even greater extreme. The Dixon House, which had been broken into five times before Murphy's treatment, exaggerated the exterior as an alienated ruin—with faux graffiti, walled-up windows, and raw plywood and tar paper—while the inside became a luxurious, skylit house. For ten years the structure has been "burglar-proof."[3] Murphy's house for Dennis Hopper carries the schizophrenia even further with a windowless steel wall and "ironic" white picket fence on the exterior of a warm domestic interior (see photograph on page 51).

In such doubly coded buildings Americans face, for the first time since they built structures to defend against the Native Americans, a contradiction that has a venerable tradition in Europe, going back to the work of Filippo Brunelleschi and Inigo Jones. The latter proposed a sober, understated exterior that would not attract envy but would still allow an interior to "fly out licentiously." Anthony Vidler gave these trends a two-hundred-year pedigree in *The Architectural Uncanny*, summarizing the antecedents of urban anomie with the theories of Walter Pater, Martin Heidegger, György von Lukacs, Sigmund Freud and the more up-to-date deconstructionism of Jacques Lacan, Jacques Derrida, and Jean Baudrillard.[4] According to Vidler, "transcendental homelessness," "rootlessness," and "spatial estrangement" were the social facts and values represented in this architecture, which holds a mirror up to reality.

But the shift in architectural discourse, previously given to ideal imagery, should not be underrated. Before this shift there had never been an architecture of positive alienation. It is true that just after the First World War a few German expressionists tried to fashion a new style of building to represent the recent catastrophes and even the wild sexual longings of the poets and painters of the moment, but a dada architecture never took hold. And the new brutalism in Britain, 1960–65, which in some respects tried to turn rough urban reality into a new poetics of building, soon became a *genre de vie* for university campuses and concert halls, more the equivalent of designer blue jeans than real blue overalls worn by the working class. That class did not take to brutalist housing estates; to them they symbolized the all too real brutalism of social deprivation. Deconstructivist architects partly continue the brutalist version of the "sophisticates' tough," as ivory-tower Derrideans dispense frenzied cacophony to the masses, *de haut en bas*. Oh, the irony of the avant-garde trying to be "real," meeting head on those mired in reality looking for ideal images!

The L.A. School

While a representational eclecticism was camping up mini-malls all over L.A. with gables and colorful peaked hats *à la* Aldo Rossi, the fractious L.A. School—consisting of Frank Gehry, Morphosis (Thom Mayne and Michael Rotondi), Eric Owen Moss, and Frank Israel—turned more ascetic, difficult, and tortured in response. Dead-tech designs depicting ecological catastrophe signified a new, sophisticated attitude towards modernism coming out of the Southern California Institute of Architecture (SCI-Arc), the avant-garde school of architecture that Michael Rotondi took over in the 1980s. Whereas modernists had faith in industrial progress, signified by the white sobriety of the International Style, the postmodernists of SCI-Arc had a bittersweet attitude towards technology. They knew it brought pollution and knew that progress in one place was paid for by regress in another, but nevertheless still loved industrial culture enough to remain committed to the modernist impulse of dramatizing technology.

The L.A. style—with its calculated informality that I would call "en-formality"—is rough and ascetic. Though these qualities predominate, along with the heavy metal contraptions, behind them is another mood altogether, an ambiguous mixture of aggression and hedonism, sadism and restraint, functionalism and uselessness, self-promotion and withdrawal. En-formality is more than a style and approach to design. It is a basic attitude towards the world, of living with uncertainty, celebrating flux, and capturing the possibilities latent within the banal. It is hardly as simple or straightforward as it appears, and it has appeared in so many buildings, not to mention restaurants, that we can really speak of a new convention, a shared aesthetic and attitude.

Despite everything, the architecture is friendly at heart, outgoing, open, and accepting. This "hetero-architecture" accepts the different voices that create a city, suppresses none of them, and makes from their interaction some kind of greater dialogue. A central focus of hetero-architecture is the ability to absorb many voices into a discourse without worrying too much about consistency or overall unity. That such an approach should reach consciousness with Frank Gehry, and then self-consciousness with subsequent members of the L.A. School, shows a maturity rare in an era of quick change. The information world usually dissolves move-

"Hetero-architecture" accepts the different voices that create a city, suppresses none of them, and makes from their interaction some kind of greater dialogue.

ments of shared sensibility as soon as they are formed in a blitz of media attention, but here a common attitude has managed to develop, perhaps because of the background culture of Los Angeles. It too mixes a sunny gregariousness and an openness to new experience with a tough streetwise realism.

Aside from en-formality the L.A. School has made one other contribution to the architectural world: the workplace as urban village. This often amounts to an office as a small city turned inside-out. Postmodern architects in other cities have contributed to this new paradigm. There is Anton Alberts and Van Hunt's neo-expressionist NMB Bank in Amsterdam, Albrecht Jourdan Muller and Berghof Landes's hanging gardens of the Landeszentral Bank in Frankfurt, and Hiroshi Hara's office village in Tokyo, but these are all new buildings on a bulldozed site. The Los Angeles architects have developed instead the art of converting large warehouses into internalized streets and squares. Part of the reason is pragmatic: these externally disguised, informal types turn their back on the real, hostile street for security reasons, and they retrofit an old structure because it is cheap.

They are like a geode with a rough, weather-beaten facade and a *luxe* interior, but the luxury is something else. The stained concrete is polished just so; the sheet metal is carefully chosen to be both aggressive like the real street and artfully twisted and over-detailed with a thousand bolts and unnecessary structural members that say "this is the real craftsmanship of a postindustrial society, not the Disneyland version." The message? The raw and uncooked are more nutritious than the pseudo-reality of Universal Studio's CityWalk (see photograph on page 29).

The art of en-formality is a high art for office work, in many ways much more suitable than the totally new building. An office, where most of the labor force in the First World will spend most of its time, must be more than a one-dimensional factory for work—much more. It must incorporate other building types, such as the home and the place of relaxed entertainment. This is especially true during the electronic revolution where many people find it more attractive and functional to telecommute. Already Los Angeles has more office-at-home space than other cities. Whereas most metropolitan areas have twenty square feet of office space per person—New York has twenty-eight—the electronic cottages of L.A. have reduced in-town office space to fifteen. The place of work must become ambiguous, domestic, and heterogeneous to survive.

Cabrillo Marine Museum, San Pedro, 1979
Frank Gehry

Chiat/Day/Mojo Headquarters, Venice, 1991
Frank Gehry with Claes Oldenburg and Coosje
van Bruggen

Shatto Recreation Center, Los Angeles, 1991–92
Steven Erlich

Bright and Associates Offices, Venice, 1988–90
Frank Israel

Hetero-Architecture for Heteropolis

The Russian critic Mikhail Bakhtin, applies the term "dialogic" to describe the double nature of words that entail two different attitudes at the same time: that of the speaker and that of the listener about to become a speaker.[5] The dialogue is thus equally determined by at least two different codes, by words shared by addresser and addressee. And if this is true, then it is fundamentally open and oriented towards a future world, for no one can determine the outcome of a true dialogue, which might go in any direction.

Similarly, if Los Angeles now contains more group differences than any other city, it will have to learn both greater tolerance *and* greater respect for boundaries. Architecturally it will have to learn the lessons of Gehry's aesthetic and en-formality: how to turn unpleasant necessities such as chain link fence into amusing and ambiguous signs of welcome/keep out, beauty/defensible space. Semiotically it will have to come to terms with an important social truth: as the Korean immigrant said when asked about his new-found identity, "I'll always be a hyphenated-American." Precisely. This expresses a real insight. The fate and possibility of a pluralist culture that celebrates heterogeneity is to turn *everyone* into a hyphenated American.

Gehry and the rest of the L.A. School, particularly in their warehouse conversions for the workplace, combine many texts, many voices. Dialogues between the formal and informal, the present and past, the industrial and vernacular, violence and safety, and the animal and mechanical. There is even an understated, half suppressed, dialogue between the utilitarian and the spiritual; Israel, Moss, and Gehry, time and again, design a conference room, in a formal shape, juxtapose it with exposed beams and mechanical ducts, and then give it an ethereal skylight that turns it into a small chapel.

The opposite of hetero-architecture is not homo- but mono-architecture, that is, building that is reduced, exclusive, over-integrated, perfected, and sealed off from life and change. Mies van der Rohe's architecture, minimalism, most classicisms, and most corporate and academic building are monological and limited by definition and legal contract. After the drawings are made, the bids are sealed, the specifications are written, it is a deterministic affair. Any nagging ambiguities and changes are to be disputed in court. With the L.A. School, particularly Gehry and Moss, it is often not clear when, or even if, the building is ever finished. How can you sue an architect when the building makes a virtue of accidents, mistakes, and improvisations?

It is this improvisational, "heteroglottic" nature that is so characteristic of Los Angeles as a whole and the L.A. style in particular, a mode that, because of globalizing forces, can be found in several cities around the world. Just as the office-village has become a prototype to be shared, so perhaps will the peculiar Los Angeles workplace, with its mixture of categories, functions, and voices. If America must reinvent more adequate attitudes to work in the nineties and reestablish a public realm, then convivial models can be found here.

Nevertheless, architecture, even when pluralistic, is never enough. It is no answer to the lack of effective political pluralism, which can be created only by civic institutions, respect for cultural traditions, and concerted willpower. Architecture can accomplish much by accepting and celebrating heterogeneity, but it is no substitute for better politics, economic opportunities, and community cohesion. This is quite obvious from the high crime rate, the conflict between ethnic groups and classes, and the prevailing fear indicated by the omnipresence of security devices.

Clearly a single public building cannot bring a heterogeneous culture together any more than it can heal the wounds of a riot. It is vain to ask art or architecture to make up for political, economic, or social inadequacy. Yet it still makes sense to ask a public building to symbolize a credible public realm, to set a relevant direction and act as if its meaning could be universalized for society at a given time and place. For Los Angeles and for the rest of America this means a particularly heterogeneous culture where no one architectural language—traditional, classical, Anglo-Saxon or Hispanic—is dominant or uncontested. Demographers predict the country will be more than fifty percent non-white by the year 2050—as it was for the first fifteen thousand years of its occupation by Homo sapiens. It is probably the case, because of political turmoil and mass migrations, that most world cities will have many of the ethnic problems, and advantages, that Los Angeles experiences today. So in an important sense the "heteropolis" of L.A. is the archetypal global city of the future.

Given this increasing pluralism, Gehry's architecture, and hetero-architecture in general, are intelligent responses for a heteropolis. They are sufficiently abstract not to legitimize *any* subculture: Anglo, colonial, or whatever remains the dominant visual language of America. Yet they do delegitimize modernism, which promotes abstraction as an official style. (Modernists still remain a leading professional tribe within the American Institute of Architects.)

But hetero-architecture is also representational and metaphorical in all sorts of ways that make contact with the public at large, and in this sense it challenges the modernist dominance as well. Truly postmodern, its doubly coded discourse inscribes *and* subverts social meaning at the same time to define a "poetics of postmodernism," as Linda Hutcheon (and I) has pointed out for some time.[6] Its agenda is to transcend or contest divisions in taste in order to overcome institutional and linguistic barriers that fracture contemporary culture. The poetics of postmodernism are radically eclectic, inclusive of any discourse that is locally relevant and of modernism itself.

This approach is particularly relevant to heterogeneous America as a whole, as it tries to reinvent a new public self-image. *E pluribus unum,* "out of many, one," is no longer quite adequate, since this unity has all too often meant the values and tastes of the dominant culture or, even worse, a faceless corporatism. The "melting pot" as a metaphor is no longer accepted. The "boiling pot," its antithesis, also misses what immigrants and their host country want: neither the bland homogeneity of "middle America," nor the fractious disjunctions of separate ethnic ghettoes. Other images and models, such as a "mosaic" or "kaleidoscope" of subcultures, come closer to reality, in which immigrants assimilate in some ways—economically, legally, technically—and still remain culturally distinct. Culture—the peculiar values, customs, ideas, and religious practices that are always historical—is, in the end, what makes life worth living. In this sense all those who have something to contribute are already what the Korean man said he would always be, a "hyphen-ated-American," a hybrid of the local and universal, the past and present.

If this is true—and I realize some people would prefer to call themselves "American-Americans"—then it would propose social unity and *at the same time* entail a sensitivity to difference. It would represent unity *and* dissent, *unum* et *plura* (the one *and* the many). The debate on multiculturalism has foundered because one side of this dialogue is always promoted at the expense of the other: classical Western civilization versus ethnic culture, assimilation versus resistance. The antinomies are too well known to need rehashing. We understand the arguments and are tired of the caricatures, such as "political correctness."

Immigrants keep coming to America. Its culture is vital, not only because of this long-standing argument but also because it can be transcended to produce invention. The task of creativity is to make conflict lead not to destruction, but to an entirely other situation that none of the contestants had imagined. Poised between fracture and a new culture, Los Angeles seems like the rest of America writ small; it is on the verge of either splitting up or of making something strange and exciting that no one has seen before.

The long-term goal of the heteropolis, its defining goal, is not only to sustain itself as a viable economic and ecological entity, but to further a slow, peaceful interweaving of world views. Such intermixtures can only take place when there is a true dialogue between cultures—neither coercion nor domination of one by another, but a sustained relationship of talking and listening, which is sometimes painful, sometimes enjoyable.

Unless one emphasizes the pleasure and creativity basic to the hybrid culture, the whole project of a heteropolis, and a city like Los Angeles, becomes insupportably heavy, just another set of moral and economic problems to be solved—or from which to run away. The pleasures of a heteropolis are reward enough for facing the difficulties. The hetero-architecture of Los Angeles reminds us of a truth that has been obscured by all the ethnic strife that dominates the news today, that difference can be transformed from a pretext for conflict into an opportunity for pleasurable creativity—the invention of something beautiful or striking, something unknown. And that transformation is supremely sensible, sensuous, and enjoyable.

This essay is excerpted from Heteropolis: Los Angeles, the Riots and the Strange Beauty of Hetero-Architecture *(London: Academy Editions, 1993). Reprinted with permission from Academy Editions.*

Soc. Culture; Singapore:

David Turnbull

In Singapore possession of a firearm is punishable by life imprisonment. In 1994 a young American, Michael Fay, received four strokes of a cane plus four months in prison for vandalism, despite a plea for clemency from President Clinton. In 1995 Nick Leeson, a Barings Bank futures trader charged with fraud by Singapore's Commercial Affairs Department, resisted extradition for trial from his detention center in Frankfurt to Singapore because he feared the latter's tough approach to crime.

In a recent interview Singaporean architect and urban theorist Tay Keng Soon stated, "I think what people are starting to realize is that this is the most advanced city-state in human civilization, this is the twenty-first-century city and if they don't like what they see then they'd better do something about it fast: because this is the future of urban living and a host of countries are lining up to learn how to copy what they've done here."[1] For Tay Keng Soon, Singapore is the Manhattan of Asia without the social problems, a city that "integrates ethics, societal values, and cultural proclivities through a clear collective vision that works."[2]

Gangster Town

Just eat it, okay? The people at the next table are staring.

So what if they stare, Liz, Shiau Chi-eh.

They may make trouble. They're the kind who carry bearing scrapers and won't think twice about using them.

Over a bowl of prawn mee, which they don't even sell? Don't be crazy, Liz. This is Singapore you know. Not some gangster town.[3]

Since achieving independence in 1965 Singapore has been described as an economic miracle, as the most successful of the "tiger economies," an economic dragon. Singapore has established itself as a model city-state of the future despite its limited natural resources, inadequate water supply, and small land area. To achieve this Singapore's leadership has been ruthlessly unsentimental and pragmatic. Its attitude toward the landscape is abstract, aggressive, utilitarian, and exploitative. Nothing is left to chance.

The Singapore government installed a comprehensive erasure and replacement policy to address both urgent postcolonial issues and to provide the infrastructure necessary to encourage foreign investment. In a twenty-year period the number of housing units has increased fourfold, and shops, offices, and hotels tenfold. The slum and squatter population has been reduced from 783,000 in 1970 to 28,000 in 1990. The number of new housing units built over the same period increased from 189,600 to 735,900. Over 2,000 kilometers of roads, highways, and expressways have been constructed; ten percent of the land area (6,000 hectares) has been reclaimed from the sea.

The Official Guide[4] promotes Singapore as a "super-city." This island of just over 640 square kilometers in surface area has the world's second busiest port after Rotterdam, and its airport is consistently voted as one of the world's best. It is one of the world's major oil refining centers, a major supplier of electronic components, and a leader in shipbuilding and repairing. It is also an increasingly important communications and financial center for Asia. It is a global city, strategically, economically, and culturally. Around six million visitors a year visit Singapore. It is one of the few countries in the world to receive more tourists than its resident population. Over five million trees and shrubs have been planted and nearly 1,800 hectares of parks, gardens and recreation spaces have been created, forming a garden city.

Metacity

In 1962 Yona Friedman predicted that the entire world population would be agglomerated into 1000 big cities.[5] Also in the early 1960s Constantinos A. Doxiadis envisaged an "ecumenopolis"[6] consisting of groups of major cities linked to each other (by air traffic and electronic communications) more firmly than to the surrounding districts of the countries in which they are located. A global elite, crossing national boundaries daily, would be the ultimate form of civilization. According to metabolist theory set out by Kisho Kurokawa in 1967, each of these cities would be a "metapolis," an urban unit for ecumenopolitans built in "super-architecture": "A Metapolis will be a junction point of mobile information. It will also be the place from which directives are issued."[7] Singapore *is* the apotheosis of Metabolism.

The architect and urbanist Rem Koolhaas sees Singapore as a "petri dish," an urban laboratory where experimental social and architectural organisms are grown.[8] He finds Singapore as evidence of the city as a "pure ecology of the contemporary" as "pure intention." Singapore's "songlines"—the erasure of its past, its unswerving belief in the most extreme urban renewal policies, its high-speed roads, and the advanced condition of its electronic communications systems—make this small island an exemplar.

Singapore, a city of three million, like Le Corbusier's Ville Contemporaine (1922), has become a paradigmatic metapolis, which is particularly extraordinary in that it has no national hinterland on which to rely. It is all city. There are no other districts. Instead, it has to remain completely open to global markets, information, and resources. It is intensely vulnerable and persistently runs the risk of total collapse.

Shopping

On Orchard Road, the Fifth Avenue of Southeast Asia, wide sidewalks teem with apparently contented shoppers. Large multiuse buildings up to thirty stories (120 meters) in height line the street. Ngee Ann City, Asia's biggest shopping center which includes the Takashimaya Department Store, is clad in shining red granite. It is only one of countless buildings that combine shopping and entertainment with offices, parking and service areas, and hotels or residential uses in one mutilevel structure. Every available square meter is occupied; unsupervised, interstitial spaces are minimized. In Ngee Ann City nightclubs are entered through parking lots on the eighth floor in the gap between the shopping zone and office suites, while luxury restaurants on the fifth floor are entered through shops. Different zones fold into each other in commercially profitable, codependent relationships. Transnational companies—SEGA, Hi-TEC, Armani, Gaultier, Boss, DKNY—rub shoulders with local traders—Mims, Blum, China Silk House. Emporia are placed next to clinics. Electronic equipment stores, jewelry stores, leather goods outlets, antique shops, tailor shops, and tour operations are distributed without any apparent hierarchy. Department stores and the smallest retail outlets are bundled together around multistory atria, "city rooms," in the relentless pursuit of a critical mass established by the black art of the property consultant.

This compression is at once extreme and provocative and yet paradoxically conservative. The occupants of former street-front shop houses, markets, motor workshops, coffee shops, and hawker stalls built between 1900 and the 1950s, shops that were torn down in the first wave of urban renewal, were relocated in the earliest shopping centers. As the traditional street pattern was violently displaced, folded, compressed, and replaced, the heterogeneity of the street—its energy—was captured, contained, and accelerated.

In Singapore as elsewhere in Asia shopping is the primary civic activity; shopping centers are the primary location for social interaction. Their names include Plaza Singapura, Orchard Plaza, Orchard Point, Peranakan Place, Cuppage

Views of Orchard Road

Plaza, Centrepoint, Paragon, Promenade, Tong Building, Lucky Plaza, Tangs, Far East Plaza, Shaw Centre, International Building, Orchard Towers, Delfi Orchard, Tanglin Shopping Centre, Forum Galleria, Singapore Hilton, Far East Shopping Centre, Liat Towers, Lane Crawford, Wisma Atria, Ngee Ann City, Mandarin Singapore, and Specialists Shopping Centre. Outside the centers, areas are carefully demarcated for eating Asian food *al fresco* in front of and inside carefully reconstructed three-story shop houses. Cuppage Terrace and Emerald Hill re-present remnants of a colonial past in streets running at right angles to the main shopping street and framed by larger, more recent development. Häagen-Dazs ice cream and TCBY frozen yogurt stalls serve the main shopping sidewalks. Burger King, KFC, and McDonald's occupy the lower ground-floor areas under the entrances to the shopping centers at regular intervals along Orchard Road. The hawkers who would have supplied fast food on the streets in the past have been brought inside, corralled, and cleaned up to compete with their global counterparts, providing "local" flavor and a "festive" ambiance.

Speed

Singapore's Urban Redevelopment Authority (URA) was established in 1974 as part of the Ministry of National Development (MND) to "plan, facilitate, and regulate the physical development of Singapore into a tropical city of excellence." URA declared Orchard Road a "dynamic activity corridor" with a planned "total pedestrian network."[9] Each building is complete as an entity and competes with the others for the attention that will be the key to its commercial success. Density and building height are subject to a variable rule that allows increases over the fixed plot ratio for any area if the site is within a 200-meter radius of a mass rapid transit (MRT) station or if the site is more than 10,000 square meters in area. But there is no grid, no consistent pattern of blocks. Singapore has abdicated from any obligation to the city as a stable form; it is rather a loose agglomeration of self-

Views of Singapore from the series *The Bodiless Dragon* by Lucas Jordogne

absorbed bodies provisionally anchored in proximity to each other in an amorphous but nevertheless highly regulated sea. Constantly shifting, changing rapidly, the overarching spatial metaphors are those of fluidity and flux. Any idea that this accumulation acquires meaning as a centered hierarchical organization is rigorously dismantled. Radically polycentric, ruthlessly opportunistic, this fabric resists cohesion.

The arrangement also appears to be very livable. The sidewalks feel safe. Only in the early hours of the morning is there any frisson of danger as prostitutes work the sidewalks around Orchard Towers and the Scotts Road intersection. The buildings are generally connected at the ground level, and the typologies of connection are conventional: the arcade, the gallery, the covered way, the promenade. However, the planner's vocabulary of linkage and action, "city corridors" and "city rooms," is persuasive evidence of the persistence of Metabolist ambitions on Singapore's urban renewal policies. The aim was the acceleration of the metabolism of the city, and apart from a minor economic recession in 1985, Singapore has shown few signs that it will slow down.

Agility and flexibility are the keywords. Singapore expects the worst, and so constantly subjects itself to change in order to anticipate and prevent this from happening. Singaporeans imagine themselves as being in a state of perpetual crisis, solving one problem in order to anticipate the next. Social administration in Singapore is informed by the *idea* of speed, the urge to redefine and adapt to situations quickly. Singaporeans are obsessed with fighting complacency and being the best. Their history is articulated in relation to the future, not the past.

Scraping the Ground

After race riots during the fifties and early sixties, dismantling the ethnically exclusive kampung settlements became part of Singapore's program of planned social change and development. The declared agenda of Singapore's public housing program was the eradication of disease and crime through the elimination of slums and squatter settlements and the creation of a new artificial residential landscape. The rhetoric was familiar. The production of low-cost public housing and a more hygienic residential environment would ensure a more productive labor force, greater prosperity, and a higher standard of living. Failure could not be an issue.

From 1965–79 the Housing and Development Board (HDB) planned housing estates following practices established in postwar Europe, as neighborhood arrangements of slab blocks and towers set in landscaped parks, organized around neighborhood centers. The aim of the neighborhood concept was that residents from old and established environments would retain their Asian, community-oriented relationships when resettled in the new vertically organized housing estates. HDB estates were planned with a variety of apartment sizes to mix different classes. Lower-income groups would be encouraged to aspire to and achieve upward mobility—to keep up with their neighbors. Controlling ethnic mixing was seen as a way of ensuring racial harmony. The government even passed a rule in 1988 to prevent the proliferation of any one ethnic group in a block or an estate. The logic of modernization demands interracial solidarity.

In 1979 Singapore adopted a *precinct* concept, which places a strong emphasis on the definition of boundaries. By forming neighborhoods around a "community focal point," HDB encouraged an emotional attachment to place and a shared sense of identity. Housing policy continues to evolve.

These ideas have been part of discussions on social housing in Europe and the United States and are generally regarded as failed experiments. Their aims and ambitions are somehow embarrassing. But in Singapore the aims are unambiguously stated and their implementation has been unrelenting.

Amnesia

Flor Contemplacion was one of the 100,000 maids imported from the Philippines, Indonesia, and Burma, to sustain a country where 60% of women work. Her controversial hanging for murder focused unwelcome attention on Singapore. The Philippine Government insists that she did not get a fair trial. The Singaporeans were incensed by the furor that turned her into an international symbol for migrant workers.

Flor Contemplacion was hanged on March 16 despite appeals from Amnesty International, the UN, the Commission of Human Rights and the Filipino government. By the time she was cut down from the gallows she was already a martyr in the Philippines. In Singapore, the 62,000 resident Filipino maids hardly dared mention her name. On the Sunday after her execution they gathered, as usual on their once-a month day off, on the grass across from the Lucky Plaza Shopping Mall. Unusually, men from internal security moved among them, their bulky revolvers showing under their jackets. The maids had already been warned through a government announcement in the *Straits Times* that any commemorative gathering for Flor Contemplacion was against the law.[10]

Happy Meals

In 1994 McDonald's launched the Kampung Burger with a tropical fruit relish, marketed to a younger generation that knew almost nothing about the ethnically exclusive kampung settlements that had been almost entirely obliterated. Thus McDonald's deliberately acknowledged, apparently without irony, a nostalgic association with the kampung along with the relationship with nature and each other that the kampungs evoked.

Language

Hokkien, Teochew, Cantonese, Hainanese, Hakka, Foochow, Malay (Sinitic), Baba Malay, Javanese, Boyanese, Tamil (Austronesian), Malaysian, Hindi (Dravidian), Punjabi, Bengali (Indo-Ayran), and English are languages commonly spoken in Singapore.[11] The development of Singapore's language policy started in 1956 when an all-party committee reported that at least two of the following languages—English, Malay, Mandarin, and Tamil—should be the media of instruction for everyone. From 1959 the Peoples Action Party (PAP) officially promoted multilingualism, the equal treatment of the four official languages. An emphasis on English was emerging; in 1963 the Commission of Inquiry into Education endorsed the importance of teaching in English while emphasizing the learning of a second language. To this end the educational system was reorganized in 1968 to streamline learning. But by 1978 there were indications that bilingual education was not producing "effective" bilinguals. A review of the entire education system led to the implementation of the New Education System (NES) in 1980. This program encouraged a wider use of Mandarin (rather than other Chinese dialects) through the Speak Mandarin Campaign. The NES simultaneously promoted the use of English as the principal means of interethnic communication. These steps oriented Singapore towards mainland China, maintained English as a common business language, and diminished Tamil and other southern Indian and Malay dialects.

It was by now becoming clear that an English-language education gave clear advantages in terms of employment and mobility, at the expense of Asian languages

Singapore's material success was achieved by the 1980s, but the government's focus on the development of a highly efficient infrastructure and a fully employed, skilled, and willing workforce had completely eliminated the *soul* of Singapore.

and difficulties communicating between generations. The use of English allowed the rapid absorption of information and technology from the West. This has made Singapore very attractive to foreign investors, but it has also encouraged the absorption of values that conflict with traditional Asian values. The values of the Confucianists, for instance—to regard "cultivating the person," "regulating the family," "governing the state," and "pacifying the world" as the highest ideals of life—are confronted by what can easily be seen as corrosive forces: individualism, materialism, utilitarianism, and decadence. Nevertheless English is emphatically the language of modernization. As the dominant language it is also a powerful and effective instrument for negotiating diversity and difference in the construction of a cross-cultural national identity.

Ghosts

> There appears to be a paradox in our appreciation of our past. On the one hand we treasure the silver gilt "sireh" set by Ta Xing salvaged from grandmother's house before it was thrown out and is now proudly displayed in our own living room. On the other hand we are often ignorant of, and evince little or no interest in, the riots that broke out in the 1950s. The "sireh" set displayed in our living rooms says something about our way of life; while the riots also say something about how we, as a nation, came to be where we are today and not somewhere else.[12]

To support the modernization program the Ministry for Education eliminated history from the curriculum in primary schools. In 1968 history became non-examinable at primary level and from 1972–75 was dropped completely until it became part of a non-examinable subject called Education for Living (EFL), that is, morals. Awareness of the past posed particular problems for Singapore. It was feared that the extraordinary multiracial and multicultural mix of Singapore society created a situation in which the search for, and an understanding of, the past could strengthen ethnic and cultural identities, which would "turn Singapore into a bloody battleground for endless racial and communal conflicts."[13] So in schools, both history and geography, were pushed out to make room for more "useful" studies. (In a context where the perimeter and topography of the island are entirely artificially constructed it is easy to see how geography could be abandoned.) Useful studies were, of course, technical and oriented towards industrial growth. In 1979 EFL was reconfigured as Social Studies in an attempt to revive the study of national history. In the 1980s the Ministry for Education rethought their position, concerned with their "indecent haste" to obliterate their historical heritage and with the evident risk that they may be creating "a sparkling new Singapore with no trace of the past."[14] B. G. Yeo said,

> We went through a phase when we became very Westernized, when we as a result of the colonial experience looked to the West for ideas, for insights, inspirations. But as Asia becomes more developed...there is a sense that, look, we are ourselves drawn from an ancient civilization, ancient cultures, and that we should not lightly discard those. It is part of the maturing process.[15]

Anticipating problems—planned amnesia gives way to selective recall.

Real People

In spring 1995, Calvin Klein launched CK One "a new fragrance for a man or a woman" all over Asia. In Singapore the MRT stations, bus stops, and sidewalks were overwhelmed with images of young models, including the face of CK, supermodel Kate Moss, with androgynous bodies wearing cut-off jeans, Doc Marten's, and tattoos, along with carefully constructed scenes of sexual tension, sexual ambiguity, aggression, and transgression. According to Vogue,[16] CK One is Klein's latest exercise in democracy—crossing boundaries, one perfume regardless of gender, regardless. He calls it his "anti-perfume." The campaign for CK One is the grittiest to date, a sort of cross between Warhol's factory and late-sixties Avedon. Shot by Steven Meisel in stark black and white, it features members of the young Hollywood set, like Sofia Coppola and Donovan Leitch, and dozens of models, including Moss, posing as "real people."

Gardening

Singapore's material success was achieved by the 1980s, but the government's focus on the development of a highly efficient infrastructure and a fully employed, skilled, and willing workforce had completely eliminated the *soul* of Singapore. A dark side to material success was emerging. Despite the themed attractions of Malay Village—a taste of traditional kampung life, Ming village, or Tang Dynasty city—memory and ethnic identity had proved to be more difficult to do without than had been assumed in the early stages of independence. The National Arts Council was formed to manage the reconnection of modern multicultural Singapore with its past while nurturing the "new" arts. Art, heritage, tradition, and memory are now being recultivated with the same developmental rigor that drove the urban planning, housing, and education policies.

The gardening metaphor is pertinent. Digging up, reviving the ghosts and traces of earlier artistic practices is a testimony to their resilience. Yet the planned cultivation of cultural practices is also a source of anxiety in that it suggests that artistic freedom will be controlled. Individual artistic production is encouraged as long as it supports the image that Singapore aims to maintain and project. This tendency is echoed in the government's interest in maintaining a green environment and controlling pollution. The Greening Campaign (1963), Keep Singapore Clean Campaign (1968), Anti-Pollution Unit (1970), Tree Planting Day (1971), and Keep Singapore Pollution Free Campaign (1971), along with the formation of a Ministry of Environment (1972) are all perhaps less a consequence of a firm belief in ecological maintenance than they are about the production of seductive images of the super-city, images of Singapore as a tropical city of excellence. Such images are fundamentally concerned with marketing the island, illustrating the amenities that will encourage clean industries to relocate, and supporting the lifestyle of the specialist staff that maintain Singapore's status as a "junction point of mobile information"—a metapolis. The gardeners remove any weeds.

1.1.1994—Brother Cane

Early in the morning at the 5th Passage Gallery, which occupied a service corridor in Parkway Parade, a large suburban shopping center dominated by Isetan and Yaohan department stores, the Singaporean Artist Josef Ng gave a performance. Immediately after it finished the gallery was raided by the police; the spectators, and there were many, dispersed rapidly. The gallery was closed. Ng and his collaborators were arrested. Ng was charged with committing an obscene act. Iris Tan, the gallery manager, was prosecuted for allowing him to do it. In the following weeks the Singapore government placed a ban on improvisational performing arts.

Singaporean performance artist and academic, Ray Langenbach, recalled the performance Brother Cane in an affidavit for the defense in the case, Department of the Public Prosecutor versus Josef Ng Sing Chor (1994):[17]

15 minutes: Ng, dressed in a long black robe and black briefs, carefully laid out tiles on the floor in a semi-circle. He placed the news cutting, "12 Men Nabbed in Anti-Gay Operation at Tanjung Rhu" from the *Straits Times* on each tile. He then carefully placed a block of tofu on each tile along with a small plastic bag of red dye.

1 minute: Ng crouched behind one tile and read random words from the news cutting.

5 minutes: Ng picked up a child's rotan. Striking the floor with it rhythmically, he performed a dance, swaying and leaping from side to side, and finally ending in a low crouching posture.

3 minutes: Ng approached the tofu blocks, tapping the rotan rhythmically on the floor. He tapped twice next to each block, then struck the bags of red dye and tofu on the third swing.

1 minute: Ng said that he had heard that clipping hair could be a form of silent protest, and walked to the far end of the gallery space. Facing the wall with his back to the audience, he lowered his briefs just below the top of his buttocks and carried out an action that the audience could not see. He returned to the performance space and placed a small amount of hair on the center tile.

1 minute: Ng asked for a cigarette from the audience. He was given one. He lit it. He smoked a few puffs, then, saying "Sometimes silent protest is not enough," he stubbed out the cigarette on his arm. He said "Thank you," and put his robe back on.

Langenbach suggests that this performance could be seen as an instrument of social healing, drawing on the Southeast Asian ritual tradition of Taoist shamanism. "Ng produced a state of catharsis in the audience—through the performance, a social trauma and schism in the community, the transgression, arrest, punishment, and public exposure of the twelve men was ritually remembered and redressed."[18] Drawing together sexuality and ritual, memory and social cohesion, the performance served as a challenge to government policies on both homosexuality and history simultaneously. But Langenbach was not called on to testify.

On 22 January 1994 the Ministry of Information and the Arts and the Home Ministry issued a statement that the government "is concerned that new art forms such as performance art and forum theater—which have no script and encourage spontaneous participation—pose dangers to public order, security, and decency, and much greater difficulty to the licensing authority."[19] B. G. Yeo, Minister of Information and the Arts, stated,

> We do not want artistic license to degenerate into pornography. Of course there is a fine line to be drawn. It is not easy to draw that line, and it requires courage to draw it well. Being too lax can be as bad as being too strict. So what I do is employ committees of wise men and women from a wide cross section of society—old and young, different races, different religions—who have the job of drawing these lines. Civilization is maintained by lines being drawn.[20]

Singapore's tolerance of—and dependence on—the international community has (like its acceptance of the English language) caused it to rethink its priorities.

Scars

> Holland Village: just putting his shopping bags into the car boot when he spotted it—a long deep gash above the rear lights, just under the lid, running all the way from the left-hand side to the right. Disbelievingly he looked at it and rubbed the scratch with his fingers, as if massaging it.[21]

Staring

Singapore's tolerance of—and dependence on—the international community has (like its acceptance of the English language) caused it to rethink its priorities. Increased prosperity has allowed more tourism out of Singapore as well as to it and a corresponding increase in awareness of Western values. Students educated overseas on government scholarships are exposed to attitudes toward the body and gender that differ radically from those that are promoted at home as good Asian values. The government simultaneously applauds the Internet as a means of making Singapore an Intelligent City and worries that it will be a bad influence on its population. Singapore is even more concerned when interaction becomes dependency, such as its dependency on Malaysia and Indonesia for water. The anxiety of influence is bound into the necessity of outside investment and outside involvement for survival in the ecosphere and the global marketplace.

In 1988 Goh Chok Tong, Singapore's Defense Minister, referred to Singapore's relationship with its neighbors as being

> like two strangers "staring" at one another in the face. Each misreads the other's stare. Suspicious thoughts go through their minds, ending up very often in punches. . . . While we must be prepared to "stare" back if necessary, it is more sensible for us to remove the reasons for staring at one another, that is, remove strangeness and promote openness and trust, and build linkages.[22]

Goh Chok Tong is referring to the defense policy of a small city-state, but this staring analogy works equally well looking inward on Singapore as it does looking out. It summarizes a dilemma: the removal of strangeness and the promotion of openness involves the negotiation of risk and security, danger and safety, the relaxation of control and the enforcement of restriction, and learning where to draw the line.

In Singapore the streets are safe. There is virtually no crime and no unemployment. Governmental power is great and affects every aspect of life. Singapore is not a welfare state. Its locally evolved political structure, in which one party operates with little or no opposition through the pursuit of a clearly defined vision, is clearly very different from the "adversarial system" that currently obtains in the West. This has allowed the expression of a complex multicultural setting through intriguing hybrid urban forms; these systems effectively critique the "neo-traditional" arrangements that are becoming more and more common in the West. Experimental configurations that have failed in the West succeed in this setting. Paradoxically, while there are strictly enforced codes of behavior there is an extraordinary freedom in relation to urban development. If, as Tay Keng Soon suggests, Singapore *is* the future of the city-state it should be taken seriously. It cannot be ignored.

Creating Landscapes of Safety

Sharon E. Sutton

My Imaginary Walk, by Chester, fifth grade
One day I was walking through an awful, dirty, stinky, and rundown neighborhood. There was fighting, killing, and shooting going on in the streets. There was yelling and screaming as people were getting shot. Parents were crying that their kids were getting shot. As I was leaving this dangerous neighborhood, I was also shot in the arm. For the days following, I always had gloomy dreams about it.

My Imaginary Walk, by Charles, sixth grade
I woke up Saturday morning and I got dressed, ate breakfast. Then I went outside and I met my friend Jeremiah. When we reached uptown it was the most dirtiest town I have ever seen. People were killing each other and ugly fat women were running and sitting on people. All the stores were dangerous. The people in the stores were shooting everybody. Kids were playing in garbage cans and wicked policemen were taking people to jail for no reason. When I went home someone turned out of an alley corner and shot me. . . . I woke up Saturday morning and it was all a dream.

These two very similar stories describing the horrors of inner-city life were authored by children living in strikingly dissimilar communities. Chester, an impoverished inner-city boy, was most likely elaborating on a real experience that had occurred in his neighborhood—a depressing place filled with burnt-out buildings, overgrown vacant lots, crack houses, and the smokestacks of a city incinerator as well as with the social pathologies that are prevalent in impoverished communities. For days afterward, Chester tells us, he continued to have bad dreams about what he had witnessed. Charles, an affluent suburban boy, most likely imagined the place he described based on media depictions of inner-city violence, since his neighborhood consisted of stately houses on curving roads, protected by layers of lush landscape and computerized security systems.[1] As it happened, this child's experience was only a dream. He woke up, still safe in his comfortable suburban home.

These portrayals of inner-city life recall a number of conversations I have had in recent years while visiting public and private schools in sharply contrasting physical environments and speaking with children about the problems in their communities. I have found that poor children typically discuss things they have experienced first hand. Several friends were killed by stray bullets from a drive-by shooting. The police beat some kid and threw him in jail for a crime he did not commit. Drug pimps threaten them on their way home from school. Threaded through their comments are feelings of contempt for the rich, white folks who have it all. Well-to-do children speak more abstractly, but in an equally unnerving manner. Some are afraid of being robbed, beaten up by gangs, ripped off by welfare cheats, held back by dummies, or passed up by geniuses. Others have heard about kids who commit suicide under the strain of it all. Their comments are laced with self-absorbed descriptions of luxury as they express their need to be protected—to be kept separate—and an association of their worst fears with persons of color. Across income groups, most children do not believe that historically ordinary people have been able to make peaceful changes in the world, instead asserting the need for vigilantes, bulletproof clothing, surveillance equipment, guns, and body guards.

In talking about children's propensity to develop a positive or negative inner character, child psychiatrist Robert Coles wrote, "A child's mind is a window not only to a family's psychology and psychopathology, but to our world at large."[2] As I reflect on the hundreds of children's stories and drawings I have collected over the years, I ask, What is happening in the world at large that teaches both impoverished and well-to-do children to have such contempt for the "other"? How does the culture of schools as well as children's physical surroundings reinforce this need for separateness? With the growing emphasis on multicultural education, are affluent children learning how to better understand persons who are unlike themselves? What are all children learning about violence and the appropriate means of controlling it? How can adults create safe spaces so that young persons can gain a sense of responsibility for and connection with the other? These are the questions I address in this essay.

I begin with the premise that the socialization of children—especially well-to-do children—into fear of the other contributes to their increasing need to be separate, which, in turn, leads the next generation of adults to engage in higher levels of destruction to the physical and social fabric of society to maintain their separateness. To support this premise, I discuss the nature of power as domination and control, which not infrequently takes a vicious form, and the sensationalizing of that type of power in contemporary society. I suggest that the media's

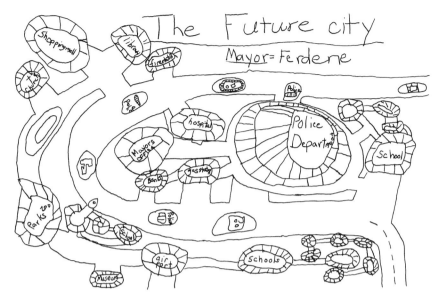

A drawing by an inner-city fifth grader illustrates a future city governed by the police and containing enormous roads that isolate each function

emphasis on the extraordinary diminishes the ordinary human endeavors that are required in a democratic society. I show how the educational process further disempowers children. Finally I suggest how adults might modify their mental map of society so that children's real and imagined places can be ones of nonviolence.

A Culture That Glorifies the Powerful Also Glorifies Violence

We have all experienced the consequences of the uses of power. This began when we were born and continued throughout our childhood. We learned about the power relationships among people including the relative worth of different people—people of different ages, between females and males, people of different races, among people of different levels of wealth and income, and between people of different sexual orientations. Much of our childhood learning occurred in our families but also in school, our neighborhoods, in synagogues, churches, and other organizations.... Most organizations' power structures were hierarchical and consisted of a pyramid of positions or roles in which each level of the pyramid was subject to the direction and control of the level above it—all the way to the top—where there was one position that held the right and power to direct and control all the positions below it in the pyramid.[3]

Although hierarchical power has shaped most institutions, including the family, throughout history, the degree to which power is concentrated in the hands of a few persons has been increasing at an exponential rate since the end of World War I, when large national corporations and banks first began to alter the ability of local communities to be independent and self-governing. Paralleling the development of large-scale economic organizations were "the various 'tracks' to achievement laid out in schools, corporations, government, and the professions."[4] At the turn of the century, about one-third of all working adults were autonomous entrepreneurs (farmers, artisans, professionals); as we approach the next century, the economy is dominated by vast corporate empires, and individual productivity is engineered by major universities and professional associations that have succeeded "in carving out an occupational monopoly restricted to the elite minority who [can] afford college educations and graduate degrees."[5] During the recent Reagan-Bush era of empire building the gap between the powerful and the powerless widened so that by 1989 the top one percent of American Households held about thirty-six percent of the nation's wealth[6] while the bottom ten percent lived in poverty.[7] As the extremes of wealth and poverty intensified, the aberrations of each condition became the focal point of our collective media-dominated consciousness.

Consider today's real-life public heroes of power—corporate magnates like George Bush, Jr. and Charles Keating, Hollywood stars such as Woody Allen and Michael Jackson, politicians like Marion Barry and Robert Packwood, professionals such as Clarence Thomas and Oliver North, sports stars like Mike Tyson and O. J. Simpson. The enormous salaries and consumptive lifestyles of these super heroes (and most of them are *he*roes) are glamorized by the media, even when their behavior is socially unacceptable. Our public villains—ordinary citizens like Ted Bundy, Jeffrey Dahmer, and Wayne Gacy; or Third World scapegoats like Ferdinand Marcos, Manuel Noriega, and Saddam Hussein, whose crimes are so reprehensible that they compete with the super heroes for prime-time television spots—are also larger than life. As a backdrop for these famous and infamous superstars is a constant stream of powerless, nameless teenagers—most of them poor, half of them black—who are the perpetrators and victims of countless assaults and murders.

At the same time that youth observe the sometimes overlapping behavior of real-life heroes and villains showcased by the media against the monotony of ghetto crime, they are exposed to a cornucopia of fictitious violence that exceeds the horrors of real life by a long shot.

Television, our most popular form of entertainment, is arguably the most violent. The old-time formula in which one murder could busy two detectives for an hour has yielded to a high volume, high tech form of violence with kinky overtones.... Prostitution—child and adult, heterosexual and homosexual. Child molestation and kidnapping. Sadomasochism. Fetishism. Devil-worship. Neo-nazi extremism. Rape. All these mingle with the more conventional styles of violence such as international terrorism, drug dealing, and gang warfare to make up a "normal" weeknight fare in an average American home.[8]

Young persons also witness society's heightened control over nature as increasingly powerful technologies become available to alter the planet and its life-sustaining processes, sometimes resulting in advances, other times in catastrophes. Seductive forms of control range from the creation of mammoth regional malls, convention centers, and recreational centers (such as the Georgia World Congress Center and Disney World) to such scientific victories as landing on the moon and transplanting multiple vital organs. Darker forms of exerting control over nature include nuclear disasters at Chernobyl and Three Mile Island, the dumping of thousands of barrels of toxic waste in Africa, and deforestation in Brazil. Whether depicted as the victories or failures of technology, such forceful interventions into the ecosystem are the outcome of the increasing concentration of power in the hands of a few persons, which strips many others of the possibility to develop a self-supporting relationship with the landscape.

With such contradictory and overlapping messages of good and evil, it is small wonder the children with whom I speak feel such a sense of powerlessness in the face of larger-than-life public figures, technological feats, and violence overload. Small wonder they have such a desire to be kept separate from these seemingly uncontrollable aspects of modern life, especially the rampant violence among teenagers. Children learn that our democracy guarantees everyone certain inalienable rights, but they also learn that powerful persons and corporations have much greater legal protections than their nameless peers for what is essentially hurtful behavior against people and nature. They learn that everyone has an equal chance to succeed, but they also learn that prime-time success requires extraordinary physical strength, wealth, social status, or technological wizardry. Thus a culture of violence is spawned in which poor children who live in extremely hazardous conditions seek to imitate the materialistic lifestyles of the rich and famous, often with deadly consequences, while well-to-do children live in fear, not just of the barbarity perpetrated by the other but of losing their superior position.

Messages Communicated Through Children's Immediate Surroundings

Children's school and neighborhood environments reinforce the sense of powerlessness and disconnectedness derived from media-glamorized deviance and the life-threatening potentials of technology. Consider, for example, what children learn by experiencing the segregated settlement patterns that came into being in the United States between 1950 and 1960 as millions of middle-income families vacated urban areas to reside in suburbs.[9] The federal government's subsidies for suburban living and industry's disinvestment in cities constituted a form of ostracism of certain socioeconomic groups. Within suburbia zoning laws maintained even more specific geographic divisions, separating industry and commerce as well as rental properties from same-size single-family housing.

> Homeowners are isolated by design from apartments, shops, public squares, or anything else that might attract people with less money or of a different race. Deed restrictions and community associations see to it that no one will ever bring down the tone of the neighborhood by turning his [sic] living room into a beauty parlor. Success for a [suburban] development lies in freezing for eternity the social and economic class of the original purchasers.[10]

Despite the increasing economic, social, and environmental costs of commuting, despite the abandonment that is occurring in older suburbs as residents flee further into rural areas in pursuit of even greener pastures, despite the proliferation of low-quality subdivisions, and despite the lawlessness that is occurring in suburban and even rural areas, suburbia's image of wholesomeness persists.[11] Unlike the stereotype of deteriorated cities with high concentrations of impoverished persons and persons of color, the perception of the suburbs continues to be that of places filled with "free-standing single-family homes with lawns where everyone is white, middle class, and has children."[12] According to sociologist David M. Hummon,[13] suburbanites tend to characterize themselves and their neighbors as being family-oriented, and they describe their neighborhoods as being clean, quiet, and safe places where children can enjoy freedom of movement and receive a good education. Even though the persons in Hummon's study lived in socioeconomically homogeneous areas, most failed to mention this distinctive characteristic.[14] Race and class segregation seemed to be a given—something they did not need to explain in light of their communities' other features.

Families in search of such suburban housing, driven by the fear of crime, are willing partners in developers' conquest of cheap virgin land, which has destroyed approximately twelve square miles of farmland a day during the last ten years, or a total area equal to that of Vermont, Connecticut, New Jersey, and Delaware combined.[15] In search of safety, many Americans in all types of communities also "are sealing off their homes and neighborhoods with iron gates, razor-ribbon wire, and iron spikes"[16] as lawlessness increases across the nation. What does such spatial separation tell the children who are both literally and figuratively inside or outside these walls of security? What are children learning about who is in control and who reaps the benefits of a democratic society?

Unfortunately this compartmentalized use of the landscape is not an isolated phenomenon in children's lives but rather reflects a broader set of beliefs about human existence that underlies the educational process. Schooling teaches children in subtle, and not so subtle, ways that the individual is much more important than the community—that individuals are more likely to succeed if they distance themselves from others who are different. Children learn early on that boys should line up separately from girls, that fourth graders should be in a different classroom than fifth graders, that intellectually gifted children are set apart from average ones. Every class they take, every grade they receive, every counseling session they have, everything from kindergarten to graduate school confirms to young persons that they must distinguish themselves relative to their peers—that to excel in a particular situation and in later life they must set themselves apart from everyone else. Such individuality is a cornerstone of American society and the freedoms it guarantees.

Children also learn that their success is defined and measured by persons with greater power—teachers, principals, school boards—who exert control over their lives and define their worth as human beings. At one time in the self-governing villages of an earlier era, these authority figures were an integral part of a child's community; in today's socioeconomically homogeneous neighborhoods, this is unlikely. Instead the persons children see on a daily basis are distant representatives of lumbering bureaucracies that are driven by labor unions, textbook publishers, school bus companies, athletic competitions, and the maintenance of grounds and facilities. Political economists Samuel Bowles and Herbert Gintis described the bureaucratization of education in the following manner:

> The once highly personalized authority of the teacher has become a part of the bureaucratic structure of the modern school. Unlike teachers in the chaotic early nineteenth-century district schools, modern teachers exercise less personal power and rely more heavily on regulations promulgated by higher authorities.... The very rules and regulations that add a patina of social authority to his or her commands at the same time rigidly circumscribe the teacher's freedom of action.[17]

The depersonalization of the schooling process reinforces what children learn after school from media-glamorized violence, technological gigantism, and the social isolation that derives from greater mobility, higher divorce rates, smaller households, and isolationist home entertainment, among other contemporary forces.

Children learn through a screen of disassociation that teaches them to stay apart from others who are different, frees them from the need to assume responsibility since higher authorities are in charge, and confirms that credentials, not

If democracy is to flourish, we will have to stop running and face up to the truth, including the sharp differences between the haves and the have-nots and the violence that is occurring between and among them as a result of their extreme circumstances.

character, are the route to mainstream success. A win-lose focus on individual ambition undermines their capacity to see themselves as linked to—and responsible for—other people, places, and events. This screen of disassociation is reinforced by children's observations of the designed environment. Middle-class families create a landscape of separateness, each person trying to be as isolated as possible from others, riding in single-occupant vehicles, striving to possess the biggest house on the largest lot landscaped with the most chemically treated grass, distancing themselves from those who do not have the wherewithal to own such property.

Children's sense of disassociation is also fueled by increasing crime and society's reaction to it. Crime escalated during the latter part of the 1980s—the era when differences between wealth and poverty also sharpened—so that by 1991 cities with a population of over 250,000 experienced 758 acts of violence annually per 100,000 persons.[18] In response gated communities and other defensive mechanisms multiplied, attempting to ensure the safety of those barricaded inside. The number of handguns owned by individuals now exceeds 50 million, with half the households in the nation possessing firearms.[19] Prison construction is soaring as is law enforcement; more black men are incarcerated than enrolled in college. Companies selling low-tech paraphernalia (mace, burglar alarms, attack dogs) and high-tech apparatuses (cellular phones, electronic alarms, video door-bells) report soaring sales. Yet with all these deterrents to crime, the United States firmly holds the lead as the most violent industrialized nation in the world.[20] To paraphrase the Neville Brothers' lyrics in their song, "Sons and Daughters," everyone seems to be running, trying to get away from everybody else. If democracy is to flourish—if we are to engage with each other as equals in managing our communities—we will have to stop running and face up to the truth, including the sharp differences between the haves and the have-nots and the violence that is occurring between and among them as a result of their extreme circumstances.

Landscapes of Safety Require a Nation of Equals

In the 1800s Georg Hegel and Thomas Jefferson expressed opposing views of how a civil society might develop in the United States, as politician Daniel Kemmis pointed out.[21] The urbanist Hegel believed that the nation's open frontier would block the attainment of civic culture because Americans would not have to learn to live with one another in cities. The agrarian Jefferson disagreed, proposing that the frontier would enhance the sense of community because the rigors of farm life would draw families together. Despite their differing views of civilization, both concurred that a collective identity derives from the exchanges that people have in and with their physical surroundings. The dynamic act of inhabitation—living in a place that has limits, becoming bound to others by struggling against practical constraints, developing certain place-related habits and behaviors—leads to shared interests, especially if the place comprises limitations. Proposing that democracy requires persons to work together while meeting high standards of excellence, Kemmis wrote:

> It is these standards of excellence, arising out of the soil itself, bodied forth in certain habituated and deeply shared patterns of behavior—it is these lived standards of excellence that alone give meaning to the concept of "value."... What makes values shared and what makes them politically powerful is that they arise out of the challenge of living well together in hard country.[22]

In the last half century, we have witnessed a dramatic increase in personal freedom, mobility, individual rights, and the reorienting of culture around individual needs. While this loosening of restraints on individuals has had many positive outcomes, it has simultaneously led privileged Americans to loose sight of struggling together in hard country—of being together in a place and manner that has limits. Without such disciplined limitations people have become incapable of addressing the harsh realities of poverty, greed, ignorance, and prejudice that are part of the human condition. How can privileged Americans learn to live without force and fear, not just of violence, but of losing our privileges? How can we create a cultural context that does not require our children to be imprisoned in gated communities? How can we embrace rather than ostracize our impoverished brothers and sisters? What would this landscape of safety look like?

Instead of being submerged in unlimited real-life and fictional violence running neck-to-neck with outrageous materialism, children inhabiting a landscape of safety would be surrounded by examples of powerful persons sharing not just their economic resources but also their social power. Young persons would neither be bombarded by the failings of society's superheroes and villains, nor would they be immersed in the sentiments of such benevolent leaders as Thomas

Jefferson, John F. Kennedy, and John D. Rockefeller, Sr. who espoused ideas about individuals owing a debt of service to society while maintaining their own superior socioeconomic status. Instead children would wake up to daily news of billionaires who had realized the need for a more equitable distribution of the earth's economic, social, and physical resources—billionaires who had donated their excessive earnings to restore the nation's cities—billionaires who had declared that moral fortitude was the most sought-after asset.

In this place of nonviolence, consumption and ostentation would be as frowned upon as illiteracy and impoverishment currently are. Religious leaders would appear on prime-time television, encouraging persons with enormous homes to atone for their sins of consumption by sharing them with homeless persons and orphaned children. Developers who built on virgin land would not only be charged enormous fees to cover the costs of new infrastructure, losses in worker productivity, and disinvestments in older communities, they would be as socially ostracized as the urban poor currently are. Those who redeveloped older neighborhoods would be honored as would the families, institutions, and businesses who chose to inhabit these places; all would be elevated by the media as local heroines and heroes. The owners of failing shopping malls would donate them back to the community to use as greenhouses for growing produce. And every child would know that no politician would be reelected who did not make substantial progress toward turning the federally funded highway system into greenways replete with light rail public transport.

Within this broader milieu of social and environmental responsibility, children would see the power of community spirit in their neighborhoods as strangers gained the courage to take responsibility for themselves and for one another. Ecofeminist Starhawk provided the following suggestions for increasing community spirit:

> We might organize, block by block and neighborhood by neighborhood, to establish "safe corridors" for children and old people. Many areas have instituted successful Neighborhood Watch programs to discourage burglaries. Similar programs could establish street safety. Parents and other interested adults could volunteer to take shifts as "eyes." Training in nonviolent intervention and conflict resolution could be held. "Safe houses" could be identified and marked with stickers on the door or window. Porch lights could be lit when people are home so that a woman being followed or a frightened child would know where to run for help and shelter. Such projects would also build neighborhood networks and solidarity.[23]

As community spirit and solidarity increased, many of the middle-class persons who are moving further into the landscape would return to decaying cities, choosing to walk shoulder-to-shoulder, vulnerable and open, on sidewalks instead of riding enclosed in thousands of pounds of steel and glass on highways. Television networks would help viewers to envision community spirit by replacing broadcasts of body-contact sports, murders, and rapes with quilting bees, block parties, and art festivals. In schools educators would teach children to cooperate rather than compete with their peers for the biggest share of the pie. Learning would be reconceived so that every child was assumed to be as worthy and successful as every other child.

The term "empowerment" is generally used to describe the processes through which disadvantaged persons seek to increase their fair share of resources. The word ought to include, as well, the processes through which privileged persons gain the courage to share their advantages and meet their responsibilities to society and the environment. The struggle for peace and justice must involve the empowerment of privileged persons who have the resources to control other persons' realities. In the opening stories of this essay, Chester could only have gloomy dreams about the violence he witnessed because he lacked control over his circumstances; Charles, instead, was in control and woke up in safety. Privileged persons have a responsibility to use their ability to control the political directions, lifestyles, values, and moral tone of the general public to invent a different mental map of human settlement. If we are to wake up from the gloomy nightmare of violence, we must be willing to participate as equals, walking shoulder-to-shoulder with all the nation's citizens.

Landscapegoat

Richard Ingersoll

Every garden during the present age of accelerated entropy is inherently a sacrifice, a bit of nature preserved and set off from either the gradual movement of
natural growth or the more anxious processes of human development. The suburban front lawn, neatly trimmed, watered, and fertilized, as much as the great
national parks, shielded from the hunter's bullet and the lumber industry's buzz
saw, represent the extremes of a landscape victimization system, which offers
scapegoats for appeasing the unarrestable devastation of the biosphere. The
scapegoat, as analyzed by René Girard, is an essential component in the foundation of civilization, an innocent figure able to absorb the blame for the cycle of
violent conflicts in a vindictive society. Through the sacrifice of a scapegoat
ancient tribal societies created a mythical moment of unity that was preserved in
the rituals of their religious and political institutions.[1] Landscapes designed during the late twentieth century have become the privileged victims of a society
committed to exponential development, set aside to absolve humanity for its
detrimental exploitation of the natural environment. Industrial civilization,
which eviscerates the hills and forests for fuels and materials, swallows up the
fields for urbanization, and exhausts the land with high-yield farming, unconsciously consecrates the innocent garden as a "landscapegoat." Flower beds,
hedges, and fountains, whatever the landscape ingredients may be, serve as ritual
paraphernalia in the act of framing a place that can absorb the guilt of the community whose survival depends upon the exhaustion of nonrenewable natural
resources.

The contemporary garden is thus a paradoxical artifact. While it establishes
a reassuring sense of stability in its immediate vicinity, it also functions as a scapegoat and the antithesis to the reality outside its frame. In downtown Dallas, for
instance, one of the most impressive skyscrapers built during the office construction boom of the 1980s rises sixty stories as a twisted, mirror-clad prism, a gleam-
ing shard in the city's skyline, while at its base is an almost impossibly effulgent
and forgiving garden. The building, originally called Allied Bank Tower and
designed by Henry Cobb of I. M. Pei and Partners, is an inviolable sculptural

object with no reference to human occupation or scale. The landscape beneath, known as Fountain Place, was created by Dan Kiley and is an engaging revel of oblique pathways, planters, waterfalls, and intimate encounters with gurgling water and shimmering vegetation. The four-acre site is flooded by rushing fountains that consume 650,000 gallons of water per day. In the midst of this swirling, man-made delta are 300 bald cypress trees, wading in cylindrical planters.[2] Occupying the flat patio that was meant as a transitional space between the tower and a planned but unbuilt twin is one of the most alluring fountains to be conceived since the days of Pirro Ligorio's fantasies at Villa d'Este. The so-called "Dancing Fountain," a 30 by 30 foot grid of 217 jets of water, squirts in constantly changing configurations, creating the kind of slowly building rhythms and variations of ocean waves hitting the shore. The dramatic contrast of the seamless and mute office container with the gregarious ground level was an intentional trade off, an expiatory gesture by the developers.[3] The sound and mists emanating from the gardens of Fountain Place help not only to mitigate the harsh, hot streetscapes of a city where over half of the downtown blocks are covered by barren parking lots but also compensate for the sublime, unnatural essence of the tower, the apex of run-away development that characterized the 1980s.

J. B. Jackson, the great historian of landscape, suggests that the idea of landscape, despite the autonomy of its natural contents, is always culturally determined. A landscape in other words is more about the mind that frames than about plants, water, and topography.[4] Through the act of creating a frame, nature is separated from the continuum of life and forced to represent itself, acquiescing to industrial society's demand for a sacrifice. Hedges, walls, fences, and lines of trees are the most conventional ways of establishing the physical frame for a garden, but framing can also be socially determined through the less tangible or permanent agents of fear and repression.

In the flatlands of West Oakland, a predominantly African-American community, for instance, there is an evolving tradition of placing plastic bleach bottles, called "dookie bottles," on otherwise immaculate front lawns of single-family houses (fig. 1).[5] The plastic bottles—sometimes filled with water, sometimes upturned on stakes, sometimes in the center of lawns, sometimes at their edges— are intended as prophylactics, deterrents to dog do (whence the name "dookie"). On block after block, at house after house, the bleach bottles are regularly maintained, as redounding as the repetition of the lawns they protect. Neither scientific nor magical explanations of how dookie bottles work are as important as their social significance in a community that is adjacent to poorer neighborhoods afflicted by violent crimes and drug traffic. The bottles, which appear like ritual

The contemporary garden is thus a paradoxical artifact. While it establishes a reassuring sense of stability in its immediate vicinity, it also functions as a scapegoat and the antithesis to the reality outside its frame.

talismans framing a sacrificial space, represent the solidarity, or conformity, between different unrelated families in opposition to the forces of social disintegration found in nearby, troubled neighborhoods. The vigilance against dogs found on all the lawns implies an overall social vigilance as well.

A more public form of sacrifice was recently inaugurated in Manhattan's Lower East Side after two decades of bitter conflicts. The redesign of Tompkins Square (fig. 2), a park that during the 1980s was one of the most visible campgrounds for homeless people, the fulcrum of punk culture, a drug emporium, the site of numerous demonstrations and a bloody police riot, is a good example of a public landscape involved in the victimization system.[6] The New York City Parks Department in 1991 closed Tompkins Square for over three years after repeated attempts to rid it of indigents. The contentious turf was then bulldozed and cleared of all ad hoc structures. Meetings with some local neighborhood groups were held, and a new design emerged that tried to provide for the different categories of inhabitants in the neighborhood: old people, small children, yuppies with dogs and tennis rackets, and loiterers. An enclaving strategy set aside discrete areas for each of these groups, while the path system was redesigned to discourage the idea of no-man's lands or areas for large gatherings like those that had previously occurred at the bandstand. The most persuasive touch of the redesign was the use of the much-loved Victorian style street furniture of Central Park, including cobbled paving, wrought iron benches, and spiked fences, all of which give a comforting, though mostly bogus, sense of historical stability to the place. The boundaries of the park, which used to be permeable in many places, are now protected by spiky fences with only a few gated access points. Within the park higher spiky fences and controlled gates protect the children's play areas. The dog run is also fenced in and even its trees are enclosed by spiky fences. Tompkins Square is physically outlined by the black spikes, but the framing is ingrained in the neighborhood's collective conscious by the presence of police in electric golf carts who regularly circumscribe the grounds, and by the loud speakers that announce closing time. Through the ingratiatingly repressive means of friendly fences and dowdy police buggies, the redesign of Tompkins Square has been completely successful in resolving the struggles that once afflicted the park. The spontaneity, danger, and excitement, as well as the plight of the poor people who once depended on the space as a campground, have been sacrificed to placate the fears of violence, social entropy, and anarchy.

The threat of urban social disruption is a strong factor in attracting ever greater numbers of Americans (by 1990, forty percent of the population) to the edges of cities where they are supposedly safe from poverty, ethnic and sexual diversity, drug dealing, poor schools, and high taxes. These edge settlements for the new majority of urban dwellers could not exist without the automobile, and reliance on the automobile has been the single greatest contribution to the acceleration of entropy. The landscape of the automobile has witnessed some of the most formidable acts of violence to both rural and urban settings. Although it was generated by American consumer culture, the automobile-based landscape, which in scale is the antithesis of the traditional city fabric, is now found everywhere, in developed and lesser developed contexts alike.

One particularly well-conceived automobile-based landscape was part of the projects commissioned for the 1992 Olympics in Barcelona. One of the games' four special districts was Vall d'Hebron, in the western foothills, where the architect Eduard Bru created a grand landscape (fig. 3) of flowing lines and tilted planes that girded a series of playing fields and sports facilities and linked feeder roads to a new section of the Cinturó Freeway loop. The urban fabric of Vall d'Hebron is necessarily looser than in the historic city due to the more varied topography and peripheral location. In this sparsely inhabited area the architect chose mostly to work with inorganic materials, such as asphalt, various shades of Astroturf, Cor-Ten steel planes, light fixtures borrowed from airfields, and large aluminum planters on wheels. Spindly catwalks soar across bald slopes, giving sinuous shape to the voids caused by automobile circulation. At the bottom of the district one drives through a pop propylaea, Claes Oldenburg and Coosje van Bruggen's Olympic Matchbook. The colossal scale and twisted shapes of the sculpture are well matched with the abstract lines in the terraces above. Bru composed a landscape of shifting levels and intersecting planes that is more enjoyable from a speeding car than on foot; it is a place for uninhibited driving and parking. His attempt to integrate as much overtly synthetic material as possible corroborates the hypothesis that gardens, as part of the victimization system, are the most unnatural representations of nature.[7] The violent presence of the automobile, which has caused so much damage to the form of traditionally scaled cities, has in this case been allowed to determine rather than break the frame of the landscape,

1. Dookie bottles, West Oakland, California
ca. 1978

2. Tompkins Square Park, New York
redesigned 1991–93

3. Vall d'Hebron, Barcelona
Edward Bru, 1992

4. Time Landscape, Greenwich Village, New York
Alan Sonfist, 1978

and the choice of an inert palette of recyclable materials brings the sacrifice at Vall d'Hebron into direct contact with the phenomenon that it is trying to appease: accelerated entropy.

That entropy could become the subject of art instead of the subject of denial was eloquently addressed in the writings, photographs, and works of Robert Smithson during the 1960s.[8] Projects such as Smithson's "Spiral Jetty" in the Great Salt Lake (1970) and Michael Heizer's "Double Negative" (1969) in a Nevada canyon are works that were executed in remote places, more visible to the heavens than to man, away from the obvious sources of entropy. Although the interventions are simple, recognizable forms—in one case a spiral shape made of landfill added to the shore of the lake, in the other two straight slots carved into opposing cliffs— they are more importantly actions, created with industrial equipment. While they have minimal representational functions as unnatural marks, they have been inserted into an evolving landscape that does not need maintenance. For the two years that the Spiral Jetty was affected by the tides of the lake, the various colors of red algae in the water played against the caking up of white salt crystals on the

Gardens, as desperate offerings that try to extract one's complicity with accelerated entropy, cushion the fear of the end of nature. But neither gardens nor lack of gardens will end the violence.

rocks. Today the shadow of the work beneath the surface of the water still evokes the sense of entropic consequences, and soon the lake will reach the original level of 1970, allowing the jetty to reemerge. At Double Negative the spillage caused by the bulldozer cuts, the consequences of the two opposing subtractions, creates the shapeless entropic residue of Heizer's work. Unlike the pumping stations and strip mines that exploit the natural resources of the desert areas where these works are located, as landscapes they have no other purpose than to interrupt nature and demonstrate the consequences of the second law of thermodynamics. The emptiness of their settings and the reliance on film as a witness to them implies no immediate boundary but rather a global frame and a problem for the world.

Although all landscapes that have been set aside will tend to revert to a state of homeostasis, their representational role of providing a stable image as an alternative to what exists outside the frame of landscape prevents this from occurring. Inside the frame, artificial techniques—the pruning, the draining, the policing—must be employed to maintain the illusion of permanence. Gardens, as desperate offerings that try to extract one's complicity with accelerated entropy, cushion the fear of the end of nature. But neither gardens nor lack of gardens will end the violence. The landscape victimization mechanism does not prevent the violence to nature; it merely shifts blame. Only if the sacrifice can be recognized as such will the blame return to those who must be accountable. The scapegoat helps to justify violence, but the only way to stop the cycle of shifting blame for the violence is to recognize this victimization function.

Walking the length of Houston Street in Manhattan there are two small gardens, both kept behind fences, that in different ways attempt to break the cycle of violence. The Liz Christy Bowery-Houston Garden between Second Avenue and the Bowery on Houston occupies a plot left vacant by a demolished tenement house. The Time Landscape (fig. 4), on La Guardia Place and Houston, is discretely tucked onto a similarly sized lot on the edge of New York University's Silver Towers faculty housing, one of the more admired modernist attempts to replace the New York block and the tenement type with towers in a park. The first is folksy in style, with craftsman style trellises masking its protective cyclone fence enclosure. The second seems utterly abandoned, surrounded by a perfunctory four-foot-high cyclone fence with no apparent point of entry. Each garden is a conscientious attempt to restore what has been lost during the violence of urbanization.

On the minimal site of the first, initially a squatted piece of land, the Liz Christy community of gardeners, a group known as the Green Guerrillas, has channeled their spare time since 1973 into planting flowers and vegetables of extraordinary variety on sixty raised beds, while fertilizing them with natural compost generated on the site. The entropic processes of nature have been exploited in the maintenance of the garden. After more than two decades it has become an intense display of a renewable landscape, maintained in defiance of New York City's nonrenewable built development.

The Time Landscape, conceived by the artist Alan Sonfist in 1965 but installed in 1978, is a more subtle way of raising consciousness about the extermination of nature.[9] The project attempts an ecological reversion, a landscape that respects the time and spontaneity of nature rather than that of the city. After its initial restoration of soils and planting of indigenous flora such as sassafras, wild roses, red cedars, and apple trees, the only thing that has been maintained in the Time Landscape are the cyclone fences surrounding it. Otherwise the biotic relationships of soils, leaves, seeds, and other actors of nature have been left to behave in autonomy. The site is thick with unkempt grasses, bushes and trees, the fruit is left to rot on the trees in complete abandon, and a lost nature is allowed to evolve in one of the densest, most unnatural cities in the world. The removal of the site from the processes of the city's time is a provocation against the civilizing instinct to make it productive as either a building or an expiatory garden. Untouched by developers or gardeners, the Time Landscape is quite evidently a sacrificial victim set aside in a world dominated by the values of real estate. It is in this recognition of the scapegoat that conscience is born.

Above and following: artwork by Jody Zellen
Urban Decayed, 1995

Cyburbanism as a Way of Life

Fred Dewey

The Exquisite Corpse of the Magic Kingdom

Los Angeles, the trendsetter in so many areas during the interwar and cold war eras, is again becoming a battlesite. As fear proliferates, and as telecommunications increasingly saturate the region, design, architecture, and theory are striving to defend the civic realm. The built environment has always been about the geography of power. Los Angeles, however, suggests something more troubling. It raises the possibility that the geography of power may well be taking aim at the civic aspirations, and future, of architecture and urbanism itself.

It remains hard in Los Angeles, as in other places across the country now, to see how much architecture and community design are affected by a dirty war on the people and their self-government, a war that is now cracking the very foundations of the republic. The efforts of concerned architects in L.A. to revitalize public life through brick, mortar, and greenery are thus entirely inadequate to the task.

In Los Angeles, landscape and power form an iron-tight feedback mechanism of vast proportions, rendering the built world of architecture and electronic circuits a veritable laboratory for the destruction of public space. Los Angeles has achieved this through its privatistic development pattern reliant upon stand-alone houses and subdivision lots, cars, and freeways; its historically antiworker, anti-grass-roots power structure; its predilection for psychology and self; and, most of all, its definition of the imagination in terms of popular culture. Movies, music, television, new forms of electronic entertainment, and the constant proliferation of subcultures are regarded as signs of public imagination. Yet it is equally possible that the region's richness may be a result not of vitality, but of an extraordinary and unprecedented political death.

Surrounded by a tight ring of fraying military bases and contractors, with a police and sheriff's force that treat the citizenry as subhuman, L.A. is segregated into territories whose regulation and separation lack any counter-balancing political entity constituted by its inhabitants. Private enclaves of associated interests and common traits have sprung up in the void where public, political life might otherwise be, producing a geography of probability determining movement in

In a mutation derived from the old American South, segregation in Los Angeles, beginning with innovations in physical territorialization, has advanced into the structure of the mind itself.

ever softer and more savage ways. This landscape exists as much for the destitute and hopeless as for the elevated and powerful, for black, brown, and white, for artists as for businessmen, for one immigrant cluster after another. Community compositions and demographics shift, but the segregation grows ever tighter, more complex, and more fascinating. In Los Angeles, people concern themselves perpetually with how they appear, yet the space in which they can appear remains profoundly social rather than political, bound up in the struggle to secure image, territory, family, and economic caste status.

Separation is hardly new in Los Angeles. What is new is the impossibility that members from separate existences might link, mix, meet, and challenge each other as people have throughout history. In a mutation derived from the old American South, made easier because of the automobile, segregation in Los Angeles, beginning with innovations in physical territorialization, has advanced into the structure of the mind itself. It is not necessary to ban different races, castes, or groups from a particular lunch counter—they simply do not come to the neighborhood. Whereas in the Deep South, African Americans and whites interacted even under the most vicious segregation on a daily basis, their strata inviolable, rigid, and visible, here the distance of a quarter mile can divide an all-Anglo school from one that is ninety percent Spanish-speaking—and the two groups will probably never meet. This novel form of apartheid, hard and powerful in fact yet intricate and intimate in its mechanism, is periodically reaffirmed by overt force; it is asserted, however, far more by landscape and by the affected groups themselves.

A deep segregation by metaphysical and moving enclosure has grown out of this unprecedented merger of technology, architecture, planning, random happenstance, and private development, creating an expansionist, super-religious existence within yet apart from the world. French theorist Luce Irigaray, invoking Spinoza, identified God as "that which provides its own envelope."[1] That is what people want and work so hard for in L.A.: to provide their own envelope, to become God on their own quarter acre.

Emerging during a century brimming with mass fiction and its catastrophes, Los Angeles offers a new sort of organizing motion. The region symbolizes the potential to inhabit and create your own private fiction, individually crafted, physically enhanced, and relentlessly adhered to, however destitute your prospects may be. You can exist undisturbed inside an immaculate dream of possibility, even if you live in roach-infested, untouchable circumstances. People rise and fall, come and go, live and die, existing in their envelope, being kind, suffering, or committing unspeakable brutality, yet it never seems to *matter*. The car over there moves on, and you go home.

Hollywood, of course, assists in manufacturing and enriching this unprecedented interiorization. Those in positions to defend a real imagination that might constitute the political, rather than the social, turn away, enslaved by their need to fit in. Power disappears as a political thing, becoming part backwoods Mississippi sheriff's gang, part Paramount Studios backlot. Its disappearance organizes every aspect of daily life; its tapestry of secret fantasies becomes soft, slippery, and brutal in its cellular self-maintenance and self-interest. "Otherness"—that which might breach the metaphysical envelope and block the teleology of line and circuit, but also that which forms the foundation of politics and solidarity—becomes "awkward." Lives, continuities, and differences in the historical world become less and less real, more and more opaque.

The uncanny, unreal attraction of Los Angeles is that it is a veritable Mecca of such pseudo-private utopias, of places where world and otherness need not impinge, where stasis appears as if it were ceaseless change. Narcissism becomes this zeitgeist's signature, not because of new-age psychologies that stretch to the horizon like desert scrub, but because the public realm, that space of plurality and enduring interaction with the truly different, has been wiped out. Private space is regarded as the only place where anything can endure, the only thing that can secure possibility. It is the only place where the dream is safe. Only there can imagination immaculately renew itself, *in privacy*. This interiorization dates to the early days of Los Angeles. As one diarist summed it up in 1928, the goal was "getting away from the stream of civilization to live in a sphere of beauty and contentment as one's imagination attempts to picture it."[2]

In Los Angeles, the ancient principle of the polis, of an imagination and activity built by widely differing individuals and groups assembled in common spaces, has found little support. The dream has become one of a frictionless refuge where contest and conflict cannot arise. Everything and everyone become a means to some end, from whatever talent you have to the way you adopt an accent and dress, from what you drive to how you build your house or juggle the rent, with whom you associate and when. Friends and acquaintances vanish, never to be seen again, not because they are far away, but because they have sold a script, found a new job, or given up and left.

Containing the Space of Appearance

The problem in Los Angeles, and increasingly elsewhere, is not simply that people do not participate, that they lack a civic sense. The problem is that the places necessary for people to participate, where people might appear to each other as *political* creatures, have been eliminated. Traditional identifications said to be at the core of civil society—PTAs, little leagues, block associations, consumer organizations, community and civic boards—once common in older eastern, midwestern, northwestern, and even northern Californian cities, have not endured. The only "neighborhood" organizations and "activists" that have persisted are tiny, minority caucuses pushing an initiative interest, narrowly interested homeowner groups, and those working as adjuncts of police as "block captains," "watch" groups, or residential police boards. None of these are public in any sense, but instead operate as covers for preset political arrangements.

An African-American block captain I interviewed had been working for some time in South Central L.A. to build neighborliness on her street. Fighting bone-jarring conditions, she would walk at dusk, moving trash bins back to the curb and helping neighbors with their gardens, asking how people were doing and what she could do to help. The street had a feel and look strikingly different from those in every direction only half a block away; it was well maintained and people came out at night to talk across well-kept lawns and driveways. It was an island world, floating. Yet this person, someone who might be regarded with either suspicion or gratitude as a local link to police, found herself in conflict with neighbors the moment she put her family in front of her relationship to the police. As soon as she stood up in community meetings to defend her son against drug dealers and offered evidence of possible police complicity in the drug trade, neighbors' trust of her seemed to disappear, precipitated, as she later learned, by calls originating from the local police station.

In another example, during a recent, notorious public trial, a member of the LAPD, Mark Fuhrman, committed perjury. It was revealed that Fuhrman himself had bragged that he could legitimately manufacture reality because he and his colleagues could tell—where average citizens could not—who is guilty. African Americans and people of color were left to nod their heads knowingly. The public lesson is that in Los Angeles, abidance to law by officials is less important than by citizens; indeed, there are circumstances where totalitarian behavior

Stairway to Elsewhere, 1995

and control of meaning are justified if they advance and protect the interests of the political center and bureaucracies.

Events, now all too famous, reveal the grave consequences of this invisible web moving against the public realm. After the Simi Valley acquittals of the police charged with beating Rodney King, Los Angeles exploded, but hardly in an ethnic and racial protest as was widely reported. Neighborhoods consumed themselves in a generalized rage; people destroyed buildings and businesses *en masse*. Then, like a television show whose audience fell too low, the devastation vanished from the city's official horizon, leaving suspicion to gnaw away at civic life. Even now, years later, the trust that would allow people to conceive and enter common spaces seems unable to take root.

The problem is not merely power within the LAPD but power wherever it exists becoming violence and thereby ceasing to be power. People are reduced to fearing what they cannot hope to counteract. The consequence is a learned helplessness typical of the abused. Common life is circumscribed not by freedom but by periodic cruelty arising in amorphous, slippery, and eternally vague shapes. Restrained by mazes of intimacy, men and women become simultaneously obsequious, manic, aggressive, and numb, unwilling to act publicly upon knowledge of right and wrong, fair and unfair. Prior restraint, undermining any possible constitution of a polis, takes aim first of all at the imagination. While people are suspicious of otherness and politically locked in place, terrified of holding or contesting power and too embarrassed to admit this, information and imagination come almost entirely, if invisibly, from official and bureaucratic sources. Retaining the idea that the world of power is immaculate, corruption free, scientific, and professional becomes more desirable than having to embrace a world of imperfect humans.

Why do messy facts about power never endure in political and public spheres? A policeman parked in his car across from Fuhrman's West L.A. station told a reporter that the LAPD has "their way of dealing with people who talk."[3] This extraordinary statement, printed in a leading paper and one that in another era might have launched a national examination, vanished instantly. This suggests how reality becomes an official fiction, enforced by a brutal, completely invisible regime of silence and complicity. Force is aimed at cohesion of the fiction; without the silent threat of retaliation, a lone official might be tempted to speak up or break ranks.

The day after the Simi Valley acquittal, I felt trapped behind my electronic window of television; I needed to see for myself what was "out there." Breaking curfew for an hour, I drove the deserted Santa Monica Freeway and surface streets through a landscape dotted with towering, half-mile-wide columns of black smoke. My reassurance in reaching the actual world was matched by my awe at the scale of its self-consumption. A sense of omen lingered, as acrid as the thick haze of smoke and flame: a delicate political contract was poised on the edge of catastrophic collapse. I was not alone in sensing this, for not long after the riot, citizen groups arose across the city to discuss taking back power. For my part, I became involved in a grassroots effort to reorient decision making and urban design back to local, self-governing neighborhood assemblies, a very old, indeed founding American tradition. It was my misfortune to discover that Los Angeles residents seemed not only unable to imagine such a civil politics but assembly of any kind. Where in Singapore it is illegal to gather politically in groups of more than three or four, in new-age Los Angeles, laws forbidding assembly and speech are unnecessary. Neighborhoods lack all enduring, empowering sense of place; they cannot imagine themselves as real communities, no less coming together to hash out problems.

Our difficulty was no doubt a result of our small size, our reliance on coffee-cup fundraising, and inexperience. The principle may yet succeed, but will have to overcome the political structure of a region where the evaporation of civic life has become the invisible organizing principle of activity. Gone is any notion of "civitas," that indivisible combination of citizenship and city where those who benefit from the public realm pay back their debt, as revealed by the region's minuscule philanthropic rate, lower in its total contributions than cities with a quarter of Los Angeles's population.

The Machinery of Probability

The virtualization of Los Angeles has been building for over a century. While early and mid-twentieth century social theorists spoke of rootlessness and atomization in cities, of a dangerous flight into the mass of bodies assembled and moving as one, the suburban paradigm refined and separated this and rendered everything the same through a homogeneity of products, space, and rules. Suburbanites became dependent on jobs, telephones, cars, and individual houses, bound by endless repetition of foreign threat and the decline of the inner city. They were drawn by fantasies of an urbanized rural possibility, devoid of the friction of poverty and otherness, first of immigrants and then of African Americans. What had started as utopian environments in the minds of artists and had been realized around cities such as Philadelphia and Boston in the mid-nineteenth century expanded in mass, discount form across the country after World War II.[4] Suburbia, what Lewis Mumford characterized as a "mega-machine," had political effects, diffusing activism and turning liberally minded city people into protective, narrowly focused "suburbanites."

Los Angeles began experimenting with suburban development after World War I as the automobile began to define the way people would, or would not, interact. Freeway bond financing in 1926 was followed by mass acquisition of tract homes purchasable without down payments. Mortgage financing proved extremely lucrative for private interests and politicians steering development, in turn sucking money in from all over the country. This led inexorably to a pre-World War II bust, affecting financial institutions across the country, forcing the creation of federally backed mortgages that in turn sped the rise of a general American suburbanization.[5] Los Angeles's powerful gravitation, according to conventional wisdom asserted through the unworldly realm of cinema, actually ungrounded by such excesses the nature of environments everywhere.

Out of the confluence of cars and suburbia, the foundation for a new, more egalitarian mass "popular" culture of franchising and homogeneity emerged, realized as much through music, film, and television, as fast cars, food, clothes, and housing. It was an order where meaning came from inhabiting uniform pseudo-spaces. This nascent virtuality redefined imagination and space as regularized, produced by others, and inhabited, rather than created through common, civic activity. Los Angeles, like most of suburbia, became a place where open-ended contact with otherness, and people in general, was increasingly neutralized by subordination through the mobile frame of car and television. It was for many, for a while, truly a utopia.

With the revolts and chaos of the 1960s, the old organizing fiction collapsed and the priorities of the political order shifted. A rising underclass and a seemingly unreformable political structure fractured and resegregated the placid, organized world of suburbia along caste-driven lines. Inner suburbia, gradually reduced to Third-World conditions, became a virtual stage set from which to summon and export the drumbeat of the criminal other. Yet because this threat existed at home and not around overt ideology, it allowed the possibility that some might investigate it and come to their own conclusions. Suburbia, it turned out, had the unintended benefit of making such independent verification unlikely. The lessons of inhabiting prefabricated realities left people, desiring definition by place yet lacking public space, with no choice but to accept the fear saturating their homes via mass media. While villains were the dark and the poor, the heroes, enshrined under Harry S Truman, Dwight D. Eisenhower, and especially John F. Kennedy, became professionals, the police, the military, and, most unworldly of all, celebrity personas. Whites had learned to accept and embrace the political

Captured In, 1994

demands of police, police unions and protective leagues, prison guard unions, and the ever-growing and ever-more-invisible national security state. The spoils now went to anyone who could, to quote George Wallace's campaign aide, "promise the moon, and holler 'nigger.' "

To fit this model, the "inner city" of Los Angeles had to be manufactured as a vision out of prosperous suburbs. South Central L.A. is composed of some of the first *suburban* areas to have their economic feet knocked out from under them, the unknown fact of almost every "ghetto" in the region. The problem in Los Angeles is thus hardly the decline of the city, but the decline of suburbia, where not only poor but also middle-class residents, divided into areas that never meet, cannot see the empire has finally turned upon them all.

The Cyburban Condition

The new dilemma of our time is hardly merely that of image and information. It is the drama of how these facilitate the metamorphosis of a tapeworm inside the world itself. In Los Angeles, heavily secured and encased environments can be found a block away from intensely vulnerable areas; sophisticated communications technologies rise amid communities without telephones; trains for edge-city "information-age" riders zip by overcrowded, filthy, and virtually unsubsidized buses for the laboring poor. Rising from the ashes of its own mistakes, and most of all propelled by them, Los Angeles has become a laboratory for the new cyburban order.[6]

While the freeway system was kept clear, by Eisenhower, of private co-optation, the massive force it exacted by means of the automobile is still undermining localism and the stability of place. The profound damage of television as a non-public mechanism for the creation, transportation, and control of public meaning is lamented, but nothing can be solved by referring to such developments as technological. Indeed, we seem congenitally unable to confront their profoundly political nature. Cybernetics makes this particularly clear. Conceived in government labs and research centers during World War II, the cybernetic signal's central trait, its very core, was exclusion of the world. Things had to be shut out in order to achieve a "steering" of matter and effect. From observing the telegraph, telephone, and radio, early cyberneticists deduced the unsurprising concept that "signals" could regulate and control behavior of both things and people. The scientists, rather than seeing in these prior forms sobering lessons for human decision, action, and assembly, saw that the signal "achieved" aims and goals. Anything that interfered with the signal, that might block its command, was seen as noise, resistance, and interference.[7] Inside the signal, you enter the realm not only of total fascination but of mobilized immobilization, mind and body separated and

Cyberspace, for all its novelty, represents the suction of the impeding world away into nothingness. By convincing us to turn away from our own world, cyburbia throws us into an infinite regress.

reconnected by the coordinating, electrical tug of a mindless, chaotic motion that has no place. With cybernetics, as the physical world is made to disappear, command becomes clearer, more absolute, and less visible. In this way, a cybernetic message becomes the only meaning, disappearing every previous, subsequent, and surrounding possibility, which is to say, context. The result would be a total, unambiguous, immediate "now" of control, corroding and neutralizing the world in perfect, masterly sequence, striving against memory, consciousness, and the meaning the world alone can provide.

The cybernetic signal, like the enclave, theme park, and mall, is a materialization of power pursuing a division between inside and outside, enclosing and removing the world from within. Embodying a politics of invisible buffers and exclusions, this artifice becomes only more insidious with the language used to describe it, as people speak casually of the "space" in cyberspace, the "highway" in "information highway," "on ramps," "salons," "virtual communities," and, most chilling of all, from the founder of Microsoft and software billionaire Bill Gates, "the road ahead." Such metaphors do little more than embed deep-seated confusion, sanctifying a broad illusion of space and possibility.

The notion that electronic signals could constitute space, no less an "urban" or "community" space, consolidates a much larger political erasure. Wonderful interactions may indeed occur on the Net, but that is not the point. The issue is what happens in the world in which we still live. Cyberspace, for all its novelty, represents the suction of the impeding world away into nothingness. By convincing us to turn away from our own world, cyburbia throws us into an infinite regress capable of obliterating not only people but professions, architecture as much as urbanism. Trying to build common space, as well as private space, becomes pointless when people are pulled apart and cannot make it there. Unlike the "steering" we achieve in the material envelope of the car, in the new organizing movement, the world disappears behind us as we move through it. We cannot keep track of the world from whence we came, or indeed, the world to which we are going, which is to say, space and time vanish out from underneath us.

This destruction is far more effective than, but directly linked to, that achieved during the era of nuclear deterrence. One of the first uses of computers was to calculate the complex relationships of explosive charges necessary to create a nuclear chain reaction. Out of this, an extraordinary new power was built through calculation and its electronic extensions, allowing telecommunications to assert regulations and mobilize the ground for it, from multiple sites and variable distances, turning millions of messages into a network of microabsolutisms. We become, in this new world, more and more helpless against powers that operate from further and further away. In a vast system of billions of switches, a single phone can be turned on or off or monitored undetected, while a person's entire history can be tracked, down to even books purchased, through credit hits. Citizen or neighborhood control over such a system becomes unfathomable, and, more importantly, exhausting.

The information age's antiworldly and antidemocratic agenda is reflected in the re-engineering and downsizing of corporations, a savaging Los Angeles is hardly unique in experiencing. As companies turn internally to electronic communication and control over vast distances, the political power of the executive and senior manager grows exponentially while the power of the worker shrinks to zero. "Liberation" through such a space is often celebrated, yet many of the terms used to describe this liberation recall those of the "liberation" charted by Sigmund Freud, Edward Bernays (Freud's son-in-law and a public relations genius), and others via the unconscious. As with the unconscious, the issues of *what* and *whom* are liberated by cyberspace and its zone of free movement remains the central issue.

The consequence of cyberspace may be unfettered movement for some, but for everyone else the outcome is far less certain. The independence of communities and individuals, savaged with the rise of monopolies in the railroad, telegraph, and telephone eras, may slip completely away in the era of computers and telecommunications, as power becomes increasingly the switching of a great calculus, taking from one place and sending to another with ever-greater speed and capacity. When money operates "in" cyberspace, for example, through spreadsheet calculations, exchange rates, and telecommunications management of portfolios, entire communities and whole countries have been sucked out instantly like a horror-movie corpse, then robbed of any consciousness of why or how this happened. For instance at the end of 1994 American government officials and Wall Street executives experimented in currency and securities transfers out of Mexico. They could manipulate from a great distance, unseen, the precise number of millions of people to be plunged into poverty, plague, and death. Michael Camdessus,

Grief, 1994

The Language of Cities, 1995

head of the American-directed IMF, was hardly innocent when he called this "the first crisis of the twenty-first century."

When an architect/architectural critic recently tried to define public space, he noted that "the security of our freedom is dependent on the assembly of bodies."[8] This emaciated notion of the public dovetails well with the prevalent organizing fiction that the world can and must be shut out. Angelenos, typically, can exert unmatched control over how and with whom they interact. Unplanned contact is restricted to the immaterial realm of the phone or, if you are well off, fax and e-mail. This attempt to supersede face-to-face interaction alters even the nature of human friendship. Perhaps someone is not home. You do not just stop by. Perhaps they do not return calls. You do not hear from them for months. Where did they go? No matter. You do not need to see them. They do not even exist.

In cyburbia, conditions of contact that would prevail across continents or thousands of miles become common across thirty miles, ten miles, half a mile, and between rooms in a single home. Life, even in the best of circumstances, becomes the precursor of the computer bulletin board as animated conversation occurs between answering machines and digital signals, forever on the run, from Malibu to North Hollywood, Long Beach to Mount Wilson and beyond. Gatherings become an archaism, allowing us to avert the mess of sweaty, fractious, flawed, and uncomfortably differing humans that constitute the actual common world. In cyberspace, characteristically, we are seemingly unrestrained, able to say things we would never say face to face. It does not matter if the African-American female truck driver you are talking to is neither African-American, a woman, nor a truck driver. You will never see him or her. Does it make a difference? As in totalitarian fictions, the "who" of people ceases to carry any weight.

The glimpse of the void that arrives when fictions do burst, as they must, is terrifying. To think of entering the political realm from such a nonexistent foundation merely reiterates our weaknesses, so we leave everything outside our envelope for others to manage, turning holes of oblivion into zones of helplessness. Such a matrix of envelopes cannot be a city; it ceases even to be a society. People find themselves pulled apart by unseen movers and invisible hands steering from every direction, whether commerce, career, family, self-interest, or the vaguest convenience. "Go on, follow your dream," our confused imaginations urge us. We are left with an endless egotism of relationships without links, privacy without protection, place without neighborhood, identity without otherness, world without worldliness, and homes that make us feel exposed and fundamentally groundless.

The Metaphysics of Empire and Disappearance

Cyburbanites, even more than suburbanites, are unable to understand or combat arbitrary power; it is their fate to regard everything outside their controllable space—be it their home, office building, mall, car, or identity—through a screen. This screen is part haven and part defensive weapon, creating protection and magical sanctuary even as it gives unseen, effectively occult forces the platforms through which to propel their soft coding. The allure of this is that the few who make it inside can inhabit an environment the majority outside cannot understand, grasp, or challenge. Power becomes encrypted, action indexed by an electronic, blinking hieroglyph. You could trace the origin of this strange and fatal metaphysics to the screen—which before photography and cinema meant to hide and block things—being reconceived as a universal surface on which meaning could appear. Freud spoke early in this century of the "dream screen" and the "mystic writing pad," as if the screen were the site of imagination, apart from others, buried inside the body. While the notion of screening phone calls suggests the older meaning has not entirely vanished, this cinematic meaning of the screen allows us to interact and appear to imagine while turning away from the world and others. Whereas before we might go into a dark theater or sit with family and watch television, now, in more perfect form, we surround ourselves with the pseudo-meaning of a ravenous cybernetic envelope. We slide eagerly into its permanent, psychedelic refuge, a voyage without end.

This new refuge, unlike the old homogenized refuge of the suburban home, does not even need to materially exist. Inhabitants increasingly traverse a world falling apart yet are just as increasingly oblivious to it. The public nature of the built world is replaced with a great Hindu wheel of suffering. Once at the center, we can flame away in a riotous, soothing Godhead of pure signs; outside, all is war. While cyburbia beckons as the placid, motionless, secure center of this wheel, the new Brahmins cannot afford to arrest its spin. Instead, they turn to the ecstasy of worldlessness, the Rapture and Nirvana of withdrawal; the actual becomes a realm fit for losers, the defective, and expendable, or, as the cybernauts put it, "meat." In this way, the cyburbanite becomes the most devout proponent of simultaneous, total fictionality and utter barbarism.

African-American writer Henry Louis Gates, Jr. described this grim confluence of destruction and ignorance in a recount of Dexter King, the son of civil rights leader Martin Luther King, Jr., speaking of a new memorial to his murdered father. King suggested that interactive, virtual displays "could transport a person, say a kid who didn't know what it was like, to be in a civil rights march." He intoned enthusiastically, "We could actually take you into that experience."[9] The manufacture and virtualization of experience pulls people out of the world and politics entirely. It is enough to know "what it is like"—this way, there are no people clubbing us over the head, hauling us off to jail, or murdering us in cold blood. Indentured thinking reemerges through a neo-Hindu fatalism, the new veil, technology. Gates rightly asks, "When King's heirs devote themselves to building a virtual civil rights march, how long before we learn to content ourselves with virtual rights?"[10]

The answer is, we already have. Our problem is not merely "silicon snake oil," as Clifford Stoll has aptly called the hype around cyberspace, nor, as Theodore Roszak put it in 1986, the "cult of information." The problem is larger, as the political order, bureaucracies, and cartels have for some time been swarming into the realm of free electrons, making the world an increasingly hazardous and despotic realm, replacing the face-to-face with the facade-to-facade. In this new politics of appearance and disappearance, the majority are manacled steerage in ship after ship headed for the new world, their misery exceeded only by that of the rebellious, sick, and silenced who must be tossed overboard to get there.

The clearest indication of the politics of this new cyburban order can be seen in the fact that, since the beginning of the 1980s, public assemblies that do not fit the corporatist vision—those of pro-choice advocates, labor groups, and Gulf War protesters—have been systematically erased. In 1994, a public assembly, quite possibly the largest in Los Angeles's history, against city hall and the anti-immigrant Proposition 187, barely registered. Concern brought people into the streets but could not surmount the webs and waves blocking formation of public space. Framed as "threat," then subject to confusion and dispersal, marchers disappeared in scapegoating, recrimination, doubt, and uncertainty, the event over almost as soon as it had begun. The few demonstrators to actually "appear," to be allowed through the veil, were framed as anti-American, and so repressive legislation was accelerated. Proposition 187 passed "overwhelmingly."

What Constitutes a Polis or Two

Three recent events, each suggestive in a particular way, reveal possibility cannot be entirely squelched in the growing onslaught of the invisible empire.

The one group most consistently targeted by the mutating mechanism of disappearance and nullification revived briefly the tradition of the people's general strike. In the fall of 1995, African-American males marched on Washington, and in one of the largest gatherings in the capitol's history, called eloquently for their people to control their own communities. The media attempted to evaporate it, as everything else, as personality-based and spinnable, this time as a bigoted,

Run, 1995

A renaissance of architecture and enduring civic, political space offers the only brake on communities approaching a whirlpool towards which the United States is moving at growing speed.

anti-Semitic cult uprising. When professional African Americans joined the assembly in vast numbers from all over the country, it became increasingly difficult to disappear this unprecedented and real movement. But for whites, the event had vanished before it had even begun.

Another attack on cyburbia's frontier occurred around the same time in the fast-growing city of Ventura, along the coast west of the enormous San Fernando Valley. In this once-productive farmland, now an endless sprawl of decaying suburbs, voters approved a ballot initiative modeled on a state supreme-court sanctioned "antisprawl" measure passed in the Napa Valley. Up against a coalition of powerful agribusiness and development interests, locals blocked the rezoning of farmland around Ventura for development for thirty-five years, changeable henceforth only by a majority vote in city elections. Residents forced decision making back into the public realm by drawing a line that said "no further." This trend is spreading throughout California.

A fire of an even more serious kind popped up around the same time in the Midwest. In Wellston, Michigan residents who had been disputing a local issue in which they felt herded by local politicians declared every major decision affecting them subject to open vote in a town meeting. Framed by the *New York Times* and local party politicians as right-wing paramilitary fanatics, these quite postmodern locals reasserted the ancient right of the township to be formed anywhere, over any matter, the people in assembly constituting their own government, on the spot, as superior to states, just as states are superior to the federal government. This rediscovery of the principle of the elementary republic and power in place that New England pioneered—driving the American revolution, the structuring of the U.S. Constitution and Bill of Rights, as well as nineteenth-century abolitionist and anti-wage-slave movements—can also be regarded as a small miracle.

Where such interruptions will lead is anyone's guess; there undoubtedly have been and will be many more across the country, regardless of whether we ever find out about them. In a landscape dominated by bureaucracies, parties that cannot be seen, and proto-totalitarian cells disguised as grass-roots movements, it is all the more important to return to the forgotten principle of townships balancing townships, that miraculous device for protecting self-government Hannah Arendt identified in her historical work *On Revolution* as the "lost treasure" of our founding era.[11] The nets of cyburbia, like much in the twentieth century, seek to keep this treasure buried, for it is the one thing that can block untrammeled state and corporate power: not the irritating minority or malcontent easily dispatched, but all the people assembled in the world, differing, unmanageable, reaching their own decisions.

A renaissance of architecture and enduring civic, political space offers the only brake on communities approaching a whirlpool towards which the United States is moving at growing speed. Imagination must rediscover its existence in the world, for once in the tug of the new reality, we will not be able to extricate ourselves. The soldiers and politicians, the "perverts of the imagination [and] dotards of the differential calculus,"[12] will have prevailed against even themselves, rendering the people mere sound and fury, signifying everything yet mattering not at all.

Making our world a hospitable place, a place where the rights and capacities of self-government must grow and be enriched, needs to become the foremost concern of architecture and urbanism, for it is the political realm that will decide whether the world itself, as well as the private and public, can endure. Though magic beckons, an ancient and mighty domain offers franker solace and a more peaceable kingdom. We require a new birth of freedom in the world, and it is to the world that we must turn to discover the miracle of beginning anew.

Fear and Dreaming in the American City
From Open Space to Cyberspace

Udo Greinacher

Fear and dreaming have left an Ariadne's thread through America's urban history. They are the intangible and often irrational motives behind our actions that give form to the environments in which we live, from repeated visions of Arcadia (Thomas Jefferson's plan for the University of Virginia and Frederick Law Olmsted's design of Central Park) to segregated cities to gated suburban communities. Their impact on urbanization was not something I expected to find before I came to America from Germany. It was Lars Lerup at U. C. Berkeley who, through his Love/House, offered a beautiful glimpse of the power of such reverie. While waiting for a lover, his hero constructs "a house of shadows, a dream house never to be built, a place for the imagination."[1] Once introduced to such a compelling force for design, I began to explore the concept of fear with the same rigor. A study of the "Wall of Shame," Berlin's inhuman enclosure, provided many insights into the use of fear in urban planning. Investigating such a reprehensible strategy encouraged me to challenge the manifestations of fear in design.[2]

In this essay I explore the correlation between fear and dreaming in various contexts. The three scenarios described by J. B. Jackson in "The Westward-moving House"[3]—the initial settlement on American soil, the Midwestern homestead, and the rural farming community—serve as a point of departure. By including the nineteenth century city, the gated suburb, and the virtual community, I attempt to extend Jackson's discussion and bring it up to the present while speculating on the factors that provoke our fears, stimulate our dreams, and determine our actions.

From Permanence to Passing

Jackson's fictional account of "Three American Houses and the People who Lived in Them" goes far beyond a mere description of each habitat and its place in time to render a detailed picture of each house and its surroundings, the lives of its inhabitants, and the motives behind their actions. His first character, Nehemiah Tinkham, inhabits a heavy timber frame house situated in a small seventeenth-century New England village. More than a century later, Pliny Tinkham exchanges the constraints of the traditional house for the flexibility of balloon frame construction; his house and farm are largely independent from the neighboring community. In the 1950s, Jackson's last character, Ray Tinkham, occupies a house at the edge of town; he has access to community services that he can use for a fee.

To these scenarios, I add three others. The first, Elizabeth, Pliny's aunt, leaves a nineteenth-century village for a small company town before moving to the city, where she rents an apartment. The second, John, Ray's son, gives up his urban residence for a house in a gated community, which, like so many other houses built since the 1970s, consists of prefabricated elements assembled in a standardized plan. The third, Claire, John's daughter, is staking her claim upon the virtual world, much like early settlers such as Nehemiah did upon their arrival in the New World.

Nehemiah, the first of the Tinkhams to settle in America, had owned a small farm in the Old World. We can only speculate on the kind of hardships he endured while trying to make a living for his family. High taxation, an unrelenting landlord, political or religious persecution, or fields too barren to sustain a family might have made life barely possible. His fate, however, was shared by many in rural England. A new beginning, free of such hardships, must have been a strong incentive to entice a land-bound individual to pack a few belongings and subject his wife and six children to a journey of unpredictable outcome. Without this dream of a better life, Nehemiah would never have been able to overcome his fear of crossing the ocean, itself a world unknown to him, treacherous and full of dangers.

Upon his arrival in America in the mid-seventeenth century, he built himself a sturdy but inflexible house, much like the one in the Old World. Its heavy timber frame was built to last, but was unable to accommodate alteration or enlargement. Its spiritual center, the formal parlor with its Bible and hearth, was much like the simple hut of a hermit; here Nehemiah stood alone before God. The farmhouse faced a central meeting house that served as a kind of super parlor for the entire community, sheltering social, cultural, and religious functions. It reinforced the community's social order, based on the customs, traditions, and beliefs shared by its members, and doubled as an armory, supplying safety from Native Americans a little more than a gunshot away.[4]

In contrast to their roles in the Old World, fear and dreaming gave permanence to Nehemiah's existence. The New England community offered him the freedom to find his place in the vertical hierarchy between heaven and hell, and guaranteed him a place in the afterlife. At the same time, fear of a hostile wilderness inhabited by "savages" prevented him from wandering too far from the physical manifestations of his universe: the parlor and the meeting house.

Less than three generations later, however, Nehemiah's descendants perceived his lifestyle as confining, inflexible, and even despotic. As a result, they left New England's commons and meeting houses, searching for their dream of a more flexible and independent existence. In the 1860s, Jackson's second character, Pliny Tinkham, left the village and bought a homestead for his family. His rejection of the Old Testament way of life and his desire to succeed in a more nationalized economy influenced its layout. Everything was designed for self-sufficiency, expansion, and capital gain. The house stood amid the fields, no longer part of a communal context. Its balloon-frame construction allowed for expansion and modification as was needed. The variability of its structure led to a more flexible use of its many rooms. This permitted the house to incorporate social functions previously fulfilled by the church, meeting house, school, or tavern. In turn, the parlor no longer served as the spiritual center of the house.[5] Instead, the family worshiped God in the great out-of-doors.[6]

Unlike Nehemiah, who had to overcome his fears of a dangerous journey and was later held in check by what were perceived to be hostile people, Pliny sought land for commercial farming in an area that was already settled and emptied of its native inhabitants. His fears were of a different nature: survival depended on meeting the shifting demands of a national market. The satisfaction his ancestors had gained by living in a self-sufficient community gave way to a preference for individual freedom in a market society.

Although Pliny Tinkham viewed his farm as a speculative enterprise that could easily be sold, he nevertheless relied on it for his identity. Later generations, however, did not share this sentiment. Dissatisfied with an existence as independent landowners, Pliny's grandchildren sold the homestead and migrated throughout America. Their search for new homes was motivated by the promise of a stimulating and more comfortable way of life. In the 1950s, Ray Tinkham, Jackson's last fictional character, realized his dream of a more independent life by managing the family farm and building his home away from it at the edge of town. Although the dwelling was much better equipped than former Tinkham residences—it contained every available labor-saving device—it played only a small role in the daily life of its inhabitants. Built or acquired for convenience, the home no longer harbored many of the functions once considered vital to its identity. Work, education, and caring for the ill were not conducted here, and no one assumed that future generations would inhabit it. From a symbol of permanence the home had developed into a temporary retreat, a "place where certain experiences, certain external energies [were] collected and transformed for the benefit of a group."[7] Similarly, the relationship between house and community had shifted from a spiritual to a practical one. The community no longer stood for shared beliefs and social order; it was reduced to an assemblage of support structures: provider of water, gas, and sewage, as well as home to educational, commercial, and entertainment facilities.

Ray's desire to distance himself from his work, his refusal to let it define his identity, enabled him to dream of distant places and new occupations. The more varied economy of his time, his proximity to town, and better education gave him more possibilities in life than his ancestors had experienced. Whatever he might have gained in personal freedom, however, he lost by attaching little importance to the sense of self that comes through personal identification with community and vocation. Indeed, "it [was] easy for him to lose himself," to become a totally different person in varying situations. "He [saw] himself not as a child of God wishing to learn the parental command, not as a child of nature heeding the good impulse, but as an efficient and reliable instrument for transforming the invisible power within him into a power adapted to the world as he [knew] it."[8]

He Was a Man With Only One Story: He Had His Cellar in His Attic[9]

There were also Tinkhams who abandoned farming and migrated to towns and cities where they joined the industrial workforce. Pliny's aunt Elizabeth, for instance, worked as a spinster in a New England textile mill, where she received a decent wage for her work and an education at the company school. She was happy to escape the constraints of the village and preferred living in a well-run boarding house and participating in the many social events that took place on Sundays. The education she received introduced her to books other than the Bible and to worldly pleasures such as dance and theater, which in turn enticed her to move to the city in the early 1850s.

City life differed fundamentally from life in a farming community. Its constituency changed almost daily, as did opportunities for employment, entertainment, and place of residence. The population increased every year, and each influx of immigrants changed the character of entire neighborhoods. To make a place for oneself in such a transitory environment was a difficult undertaking. While memberships in literary circles, unions, political parties, and social or religious groups helped to induce a sense of belonging, participation in these organizations bore little resemblance to life in a tightly knit community such as Nehemiah's. Indeed, Stanley Milgram argues that "since urban dwellers come into contact with vast numbers of people each day, they conserve physical energy by becom-

Conventional houses, built with cellar and attic, supported a system of beliefs based on the opposition of heaven and hell, good and evil, past and future. Instead, the horizontal expanse of the city and the uniform layout of living quarters sustained a less specific perception of one's existence.

ing acquainted with a far smaller proportion of people than their rural counterparts do, and by maintaining more superficial relationships even with these acquaintances."[10]

In the city, few citizens enjoyed the privilege of a single-family residence. The majority lived in apartments that fostered anonymity by precluding any exterior manifestation of individuality. They did not provide much more than the raw space for temporary residence. Deprived of the sense of belonging inherent to the traditional house, these tenants were no longer surrounded by the memories, thoughts, or dreams of past generations, all of which had helped govern the relationship between individual and society in the village.[11] Deep-seated roots gave way to a more casual identification with a neighborhood, workplace, or social group. These, in turn, harbored a diverse amalgam of individuals with different languages, upbringings, religious beliefs, and customs.

As a result of the loss of traditional roots, fear and dreaming took different forms in the city than in the village. Conventional houses, built with cellar and attic, supported a system of beliefs based on the opposition of heaven and hell, good and evil, past and future. The attic, that point closest to the heavens, was a place of the imagination while the cellar, where darkness prevailed day and night, was a place where fears became exaggerated.[12] Urban tenements, however, lacked this polarity. Instead, the horizontal expanse of the city and the uniform layout of living quarters sustained a less specific perception of one's existence. Consequently, city dwellers defined themselves, their beliefs, customs, and circumstances more in relation to others than to an absolute. At the close of the nineteenth century, a vast underworld of labyrinthine character appeared in most cities. These underground passages and service tunnels, permanently removed from the purifying light, allowed fear that had previously been contained in the basement to spread horizontally underneath the city. In addition, a sense of danger permeated other places that daylight could not cleanse: dark alleys, gloomy taverns, run-down neighborhoods, and the night itself. Fear knew no boundaries, and became a constant companion to all urban residents.[13]

The rapidly changing character of the urban environment that exposed its citizenry to smells, colors, and sounds alien to them provided inspiration for their dreams as well as their fears. According to Walter Benjamin, "one of the most elementary and indispensable diversions of the citizen of a great metropolis, wedged, day in, day out, in the structure of his office and family amid an infinitely variegated social environment, [was] to plunge into another world, the more exotic the better."[14] Stimulated by the perception of a "city that never sleeps," these dreams provided the blueprint for escape from the drudgery of everyday life. As the novelty wore off, residents began to focus on the city's inherent dangers, and their fears altered the tenor of their dreams. Although still seeking an escape, they were now fleeing the dangers of the city rather than the tedium of daily life. Many sought better living conditions outside the city proper. The resulting sprawl challenged the livelihood of urban centers by transforming the ethnically and socio-economically diverse city into a series of discrete, discontinuous communities with little material contact among themselves.[15]

Following a century of urban flight, most American cities have deteriorated to a point where they no longer incite civic pride. A large number of people who have continued to live in the city are poor, and most of the more privileged who have chosen to remain or return have retreated into tightly knit, gentrified enclaves. During the 1970s and 80s, many downtown retailers abandoned the city's commercial core for suburban locations. The city then began to hold even less attraction for its suburban neighbors. White-collar workers abandoned the city in favor of suburban or edge-city office parks. The few remaining corporate headquarters have invested heavily in security in order to assure the safety of their employees. Their efforts have led to a self-imposed seclusion, and have minimized employee contact with both the good and bad sides of the city. With fewer opportunities to shop or work than twenty-five years ago, contemporary cities have lost much of what inspired residents' dreams.

Suburban Imagination: From "90210" to "911," "Baywatch" to "ER"
With John Tinkham we witness a return to an attitude that recalls the beginning of our family saga. John, Ray's son, moved to the city upon graduating from college in an attempt to complete his father's partial break from a farming life. Then, in the 1990s, he decided to move with his wife and children to a gated community in an outlying suburb in order to escape the city's pollution, danger, and vice.

For him, the gated community provided a protective and gratifying environment, just as the village or homestead had done for his ancestors. Composed of an ethnically homogeneous group of residents with shared values and similar social standing, this community seemed to offer the security that urban environs had failed to provide.

John's house closely resembles all of the others in the community. Constructed of prefabricated elements and following a standardized plan, it displays little personality towards the street or within its walls. Indeed the presence or absence of television sets defines the use of each room. The general lack of character not only allows for graphic TV shows to be viewed in an impersonal manner, but makes them a necessity. In such dull surroundings, John needs the extra stimulation to set his dreams and fears in motion.

The media has been happy to supply John and his fellow sleaze enthusiasts with an ocean of ugliness: repeated reruns of the beating of Rodney King, the L.A. riot, the Menendez brothers, the Bobbits, Susan Smith, and, of course, complete coverage of the O. J. Simpson trial. As the voyeuristic audience has become increasingly desensitized, the peepholes have grown larger and the images more graphic. In order to keep the flow of fear constant, should a lack of newsworthy murders occur, TV stations have programmed an array of fear stimulants throughout the day. Following the "nonstop lineup of misfits, weirdoes and psychopaths who spill their guts and their secrets, daily and nightly, on Oprah, or Geraldo, or Donahue, or Montel, or Ricki, or Maury, or Jerry, or Jenny, or Leeza,"[16] the stations provide viewers with sleazenews such as "A Current Affair," "Hard Copy," and "Inside Edition," or reality shows such as "Cops" and "911." Each of these programs depicts our surroundings as a lawless frontier, infested with thieves, rapists, child molesters, and murderers, the savages of today. And should our interest wane, we can still confront our biggest fear: our own mortality; "ER" and "Chicago Hope" do precisely that.

Television shows have also given John and other viewers ample opportunity to dream. The dreams do not take place in the suburbs, however, but on beaches ("Baywatch"), in urban hot spots ("Beverly Hills 90210"), and in remote and mythical locations ("Indiana Jones," "Startrek: The Next Generation"). These dreamscapes have much in common; they represent a paradise of beautiful people, lush vegetation, and unravaged lands, where, after initial conflict, law and order will prevail. Nevertheless, should John or his family try to capture their dreams and embark on a journey to their fantasy lands, they will be unable to experience the wonders they have seen on TV. On the contrary, their travel itinerary will consist of non-places that are already too familiar: drive-in bank machines, multilane freeways, concrete parking structures, duty-free shops, people movers, airport lounges, and shuttle buses, as well as international standard hotel rooms, chain restaurants, and nondescript, overpopulated beaches. Few of the spots encountered on their journey will possess a pervading spirit of place.[17]

The absence of meaningful spaces is equally manifest in John's work environs, which consist of an endless array of cubicles stacked together in an office tower. These cubicles are only distinguished by a haphazard attempt to express the hierarchy among employees. Office size, partition height, and proximity to a window or corner indicate the importance of its inhabitant.[18] With the exception of the executive offices on the top floor, vertical hierarchy is almost absent, and a trip on the elevator reveals nothing but the same layout on the floors above or below. Clearly, providing a work space that stimulates the imagination and caters to daydreams is not a priority for most employers. Employees thus have to resort to colorful newsletters and the occasional self-induced malfunction in order to overcome the boredom associated with many business routines and the sensory deprivation common to most workplaces.[19]

Outside of the office, John's life is one of convenience. Although he might occasionally long for something out of the ordinary, he is generally opposed to change and does everything in his power to maintain the status quo. He and his neighbors have thus undertaken all steps necessary to keep outsiders from settling in their community. They have taxed themselves heavily to pay for private streets, private sewers, private schools, and even a private police force for their subdivision. They have agreed on restrictions that they would not support for the entire nation: a ban on guns and satellite dishes and any other imaginable eyesore, as well as strict environmentalist practices. In short, they have taken every possible action to guarantee the well-being of their families by further dissociating themselves from the less fortunate, who might pose a threat to their lifestyle or safety.

Gated communities such as the one John lives in have advertised themselves as protected hamlets, "secluded from the world at large, yet close to all the finer things in life."[20] Nevertheless, despite all efforts to create a bucolic village atmosphere, free of crime, few of these communities have actually succeeded in their endeavors. Contrary to their pronouncements, they usually lie in an area sequestered from the outside world by miles of concrete freeways. Moreover, they rarely provide public gathering spaces that might host an event or invite unexpected encounters among its residents. Indeed, these gated enclaves tend to be nothing more than an assemblage of individuals lacking any communal spirit. While these communities provide residents with the comforting imagery of security—peripheral walls, checkpoints, and foot patrols—studies conducted by police departments have failed to indicate a decline in property crime due to such elaborate and expensive measures.[21] They only marginally protect the community from outside "hostiles"[22] and do not prevent crime that originates within their own walls.

See You in Cyberspace

Some residents, such as John's fifteen year old daughter Claire, have become disenchanted with the lack of conviviality and stimulation as well as the absence of real protection in their community. As a result, they have begun migrating to yet another new world, the world of cyberspace, the Internet. This new virtual environment, made possible by the fusion of current media technologies such as phone lines, cable networks, satellite links, and high-definition TV screens, is essentially a loose confederation of thousands of smaller, often locally run, computer networks. The popularity of this mode of communication has spawned a world-wide, time-zone spanning, digital community that challenges traditional communities everywhere. Cyberspace can meet the needs of people by providing employment, amusement, services, and forums for public gatherings. Users can attend to business from home terminals; download the daily newspaper or magazines from servers; browse home pages for travel information, home shopping, and product information; and teleconference with coworkers and clients rather than meeting them face-to-face. Cyberspace also enlarges the possibilities for home entertainment, enabling users to program their own animation sequences whenever and wherever they desire. Sites on the World Wide Web offer images and information, ranging from international politics to local community billboards, from world religions to alternative sex, and from corporate-sponsored discussions to the more or less private chat of virtual self-help groups.[23]

To some of its proponents, "cyberspace is a frontier region, populated by the few hardy technologists who can tolerate the austerity of its savage computer interfaces, incompatible communications protocols, proprietary barricades, cultural and legal ambiguities, and general lack of useful maps or metaphors."[24] By endowing the virtual world with the mystique of an unknown territory, these "cybernauts"[25] create an exciting mental image of an otherwise shapeless electronic environment comprised of bits, nodes, links, and codes. In their virtual frontier, they can dream of being conquerors, stake their claim by posting their own home page on the Net, acquire intellectual property by downloading software, erect software walls to protect their holdings, or attempt to overcome those erected by others. In short, cyberspace is to these twenty-first-century colonists what America was to the first settlers.

Claire, like many other users, approaches cyberspace as a mere consumer. Disappointed by the lack of stimulation in her daily life and accustomed to the ever-increasing sensationalism in the media, she longs for new distractions at the push of a button. Keyboard access to the Internet offers many more possibilities than the remote control of a television set. The Internet yields multiple points of view, multiple visions and stories, and presents the user with a steadily growing choice of links to visit. Indeed, cyberspace offers three significant pleasures that Claire finds increasingly lacking in the real world: immersion, rapture, and agency. Immersion takes place when she can inhabit a simulated environment by wearing a head-mounted stereo display.[26] Rapture comes about as she becomes fascinated with the three-dimensional representation of idealized, nearly flawless objects. Agency occurs as she takes an active role in the virtual world through contribution (adding links) or participation (chat groups).[27] By fulfilling these important needs, cyberspace offers virtual environs that compete with traditional communities for patronage.

According to William Mitchell, one of the virtual community's staunchest advocates, the experience of exploring cyberspace can be likened to "[Charles-Pierre] Baudelaire strolling through the buzzing complexity of nineteenth-century Paris."[28] Today, without leaving the comfort of her living room, Claire can leisurely wander about, listen in on conversations, participate in discussions, and meet like-minded people from all over the world. Indeed, on-line environments have come to resemble "traditional cities in their variety of distinct places, ... in their capacity to engage our senses, and in their social and cultural richness."[29] They have introduced millions of users to an exciting community with rapidly changing spaces to explore.

Consequently, a new breed of user has emerged: the virtual flaneur. Claire wanders through cyberspace, following various avenues according to her whims. Upon entry she can choose where to go, which site to enter, and what to see. Selecting any one of the options transports her to a new page filled with information that consists of text, images, and multiple links to related sites. Each path she chooses is lined with windows that she can glance at, enter, or ignore. As in the real world, one might encounter a dead end, an abandoned site, or an address no longer valid. She can either go forward—not necessarily in a linear progression, however—or turn back and start the journey anew. It is thus not surprising that many advocates of virtual communities refer to cyberspace as a truly democratic meeting ground with unlimited possibilities for chance encounters. In fact, they argue that the virtual community offers precisely what Claire has lost in the real world, the "sheer pleasure of communicating with ... newfound friends."[30]

Nevertheless, despite all efforts to create a virtual paradise that does not exclude, repress, deceive, or endanger its constituents, the electronic community has failed to become a utopia for everyone. Although recent findings contradict the myth that Internet users are predominantly male—men outnumber women only three to two rather than nine to one, as previously thought[31]—the number of African Americans and Latinos on the Net is rather low. While non-whites have embraced other high-tech paraphernalia, such as pagers and cellular phones, many still shy away from computers, modems, and e-mail accounts. Michael Marriott maintains that, to many people of color, "cyberspace is a predominantly white, male domain" and "computers...are the epitome of white nerdiness." Furthermore, he argues that their resentment of computers stems from "a deep-seated fear...that faceless functionaries might use them to spy, for instance, on household finances."[32]

The awareness that the virtual world might house potential dangers has become common knowledge. Virtual meeting grounds see the same kinds of crime that plague the real world, which had, ironically, caused some people to retreat into cyberspace in the first place. Bruce Sterling points out that "the slums of the urban city are already matched by the red-light districts of cyberspace, the porn boards, the kid porn boards, the sex chatlines."[33] Some users argue that it is precisely the smut that makes cyberspace less alien and more attractive. Many smaller bulletin boards have reportedly reinstalled "adult files" after an outcry from users. Bulletin board operators justify their actions by maintaining, "porn helps generate calls and...users insist on it."[34] As a result, John no longer dares leave Claire unattended in cyberspace for fear that she will come in contact with obscenity. Virtual crime, while arousing fear for the well-being of our children, also strikes at our worldly possessions: software pirates copy new programs and sell them illegally, thieves obtain social security numbers as well as credit and phone card numbers and their access codes, and white collar criminals cripple financial institutions through multimillion-dollar computer scams.[35]

Unfortunately, the measures proposed to fend off digital crime will make cyberspace less attractive in the long run. Attempts by governmental agencies to control and disinfect the virtual world will limit the free flow of information and reduce the diversity of the community. Server liability, FBI-wiretap-friendly formats, laws restricting the transmission of certain programs overseas, and parental lockout capabilities (such as that recently added on America Online), will eventually transform the global village into a digitally gated community. Sanitized and restricted, cyberspace will no longer provide the multifarious types of stimulation sought by most of its clientele. Its whimsical, at times chaotic, format will become

I see the value of cyberspace not in the replacement of our cities, but in its potential to rekindle our fondness for and fascination with urban environs.

more streamlined and commercial, "a place of fascinating images, places and information, but [with] little real contact with other people."[36]

Learning from NetCity

In spite of the threat of future restrictions, William Mitchell predicts that a world-wide, electronically served environment will eventually replace all but our residential communities.[37] He argues that in the future Net sites will supplant urban institutions such as libraries, museums, theaters, schools, and hospitals, and that the development of interfaces for these sites will supersede the design of their present-day counterparts.[38] Towns and cities will most likely be able to adapt to cyberspace, given their flexible response to technological change in the past.[39] They "will probably find opportunities to restructure themselves—to regroup housing, workplaces, and service facilities into reinvigorated small-scale neighborhoods (both urban and rural) that are effectively nourished by strong electronic links to a wider world, but simultaneously prize their differences from other places."[40] Residents of these neighborhoods, no longer forced to commute long distances for employment or services, will be free to participate in local affairs and establish relationships with their neighbors.[41] None of these projections, however, indicate how cyberspace itself might hold possible solutions for a more stimulating environment in the real world.

Those who casually stroll through the Net encounter a bustling environment similar to the San Francisco described by Dashiell Hammett in the 1920s.[42] His city was alive with street cars, stores, bars, hotel lobbies, and the many people who frequented them. This vibrancy, intrinsic to the charm of cities in earlier times, seems irrevocably lost in our contemporary downtowns. Today, abandoned and derelict buildings mark the periphery while a lifeless landscape of office towers dominates the city center. I see the value of cyberspace not in the replacement of our cities, but in its potential to rekindle our fondness for and fascination with urban environs. The attraction that it exerts on the millions that stroll through its maze of information might be used to reinvigorate our cities. Cyberflaneurs have become captivated with the Internet's ready supply of huge amounts of information that they can access at all times of day or night. New entries appear frequently and broaden the palette available to users.

We need to recognize the needs and desires of these virtual flaneurs and restructure our urban centers to accommodate them. More small, diverse businesses could join the huge department stores that now dominate the city core. Vacant lots could house market booths catering to a variety of small entrepreneurs. Their tenancy could change frequently, providing visitors with an ever-varied array of goods and services. More abandoned buildings could be transformed into spaces for offices, small businesses, or artist's studios. A balanced mix of retail, entertainment, white- and blue-collar professions, and large corporate businesses could very likely guarantee a vibrant street life that lasts far into the night. One can only hope that, if cities adapt to meet their needs, cyberflaneurs will once again venture into the city and explore its many attractions.

For over a century, fear has guided our actions and motivated our search for more ideal environs. Instead of being an obstacle that had to be overcome—as was the case with Nehemiah—fear developed into the driving force behind the flight from the city and, most recently, the escape into the virtual world. Meanwhile, dreaming has largely become disassociated from real life and relegated to idealized television portrayals. Unless we reclaim the city proper, fill its structures with new life, and provide it with dreams of a better future, we will be left with a derelict urban landscape that will haunt us and future generations. Attempts at revitalization do exist: the Third Street Promenade in Santa Monica, the reclaimed waterfront in San Francisco, and even Universal Studio's CityWalk, a simulation of an ideal downtown amid the suburban sprawl of Los Angeles. All three environments consist of a variety of small stores, restaurants, bars, cafes, bookstores, and entertainment facilities. They all provide public amenities such as squares, gardens, and benches, and cater to large crowds of flaneurs. Should we learn from the varied successes and shortcomings of these examples, we might provide visitors with experiences currently limited to cyberflaneurs: the unique gratification that is felt as one encounters a special locale, meets interesting people, or just finds an intimate place to rest and reflect.

The Pearly Gates of Cyberspace

Margaret Wertheim

The phenomenon known as "cyberspace" emerged literally as a response to fear. In the 1950s the United States military became concerned that its increasingly computerized defense systems were vulnerable to attack. Commanders discerned that a few strategically targeted missiles could wipe out the nucleus of control for the entire defense system, and in response to this weakness the idea emerged of a distributed computer network. Instead of locating all strategic computer power in a couple of central locations, it would be distributed across a network interconnected by high-speed data links. With a distributed system, even if some nodes were destroyed by enemy forces others would still be functional. A network would guarantee that military command could not be disabled.

Thus in the mid 1960s the Arpanet was born. Originally connecting only specialized military facilities, in the 1970s this network expanded to include scientific research institutes as well. But in the late 1970s, with the rise of computers in academe, a need was perceived for a broader network that would connect both scientific and general academic institutes, and so the National Science Foundation established the Internet.

Born out of military fear, cyberspace has in the last few years burst the boundaries of the ivory tower and exploded into public consciousness. With fifty million users already accessing the Internet, cyberspace is probably the fastest growing "territory" in world history. Once a domain only for the computer literate, with the user-friendly interface of the World Wide Web, cyberspace is rapidly turning into a truly public domain.

The mere availability of network technology, however, is not sufficient to explain why the public has rushed to embrace cyberspace with such enthusiasm. People do not adopt a technology simply because it is there. A need must be perceived. A latent desire must be there to be satisfied. The basis of fax technology, for instance, was patented in 1843—decades before the invention of the telephone—yet faxing did not take off as a public tool for more than one hundred years. What is the desire with which cyberspace resonates? What, in short, is the psychosocial vacuum that the Internet fills? If the military impetus was fear, what is the civilian impetus driving this mad dash into network-facilitated space? In this essay I suggest that, as a psychosocial phenomenon, the rush to cyberspace today can be seen as a modern parallel to the eruption of Christianity after the collapse of the Roman Empire. In particular, I want to draw an analogy between cyberspace and the Christian conception of heaven.

Just as early Christians envisaged heaven as an idealized realm beyond the chaos and decay of the material world—a disintegration all too palpable as the empire crumbled around them—so too, in this time of social and environmental disintegration, today's proselytizers of cyberspace proffer their domain as an ideal realm "above" and "beyond" the problems of the material world. While early Christians promulgated heaven as a realm in which the human soul would be freed from the frailties and failings of the flesh, so today's champions of cyberspace hail it as a place where the self will be freed from the limitations of physical embodiment. Like heaven, cyberspace supposedly washes us clean of the "sins" of the body. In short, cyberspace, like heaven, is billed as a transcendent domain—a metaphysical realm for the soul itself. "I have experienced soul-data through silicon," declared Kevin Kelly, the editor of *Wired*, in a 1995 forum in *Harper's* magazine. "You might be surprised at the amount of soul-data that we'll have in this new space."[1]

Furthermore, we are told, age, race, and gender will all dissolve in the embracing democracy of the digital domain. Just as heaven is open to all who follow the teachings of Christ, so too cyberspace is open to anyone who can afford a basic personal computer and a modest monthly fee. Along with the Kingdom of Christ, cyberspace extends its welcome to the entire human race. Such, at least, is the claim.

In his book *Travels in Hyperreality* Umberto Eco draws a parallel between the last years of the Roman Empire and America in the late twentieth century. The disintegration of a strong centralized government, the gradual dilution of ethnic homogeneity, and the collapse of the social polity leave both late antique Rome and late-twentieth-century America open to internal rupture and fragmentation. "The collapse of the Great Pax (at once military, civil, social, and cultural) initiates a period of economic crisis and power vacuum."[2] In this vacuum Eco locates the seeds of feudalism, where in lieu of central authority individuals emerge to lord it over disparate fiefs. The contemporary equivalent of the feudal lord, of course, is the international corporation.

As secular power disintegrates, people turn instead to mystical, magical, cultic, and religious forms to provide new grounding for their lives. Late antique Rome was a cauldron of mystico-religious fermentation—from the ascetic number-mysticism of Neoplatonism, to the hedonistic cult of Dionysus, to the Oriental cults of Mithra and Astarte. At the same time a great wave of religious fervor swept in from the Levant, among which were the followers of one Jesus of Nazareth.

Unlike the Jews, of whom they were a splinter group, these "Christians" opened their sect to anyone. One did not have to be *born* Christian, a simple baptism would suffice. Historians have noted that Christianity was a fundamentally democratic religion, and during its early years, was particularly welcoming to women. In Judaism, says historian Gerda Lerner, not only were women banished to a separate side of the synagogue and denied full education in the Torah, but the very covenant with God—the act of circumcision—was made only with males. Christianity posited no such gender-specific covenant.[3] Indeed religious scholar Elaine Pagels has shown that some early branches of Christianity even allowed women to be priests.[4] The great innovation of Christianity was its promise of salvation or redemption for *all*—regardless of gender, or race, or nationality. The kingdom of heaven was open to everyone—all one had to do was embrace the teachings of Jesus and, of course, adhere to them. By the end of the fourth century Christianity had become the official religion of Rome.

Sixteen hundred years later Eco reminds us that "it is a commonplace of present-day historiography that we are living through the crisis of the Pax Americana."[5] The rapid decline of central government and the fragmentation of "empire" are constant themes of the daily news. From the left, the homogeneity of the polity has been revealed as a dirty fiction—now that women, minorities, and gays are demanding to be heard—while from the right, anti-government sentiment has exploded into open violence and rebellion. "Barbarians," too, are pounding on our gates: the "Latin hordes" from the south whom, we are told, would sponge off our social security and health-care systems, and the "yellow hordes" of Asia who are supposedly stealing our jobs with their cheap labor and undermining our economy with their crafty electronics and mass-produced clothing. Proposition 187 is our Hadrian's Wall.

In response, Americans, like the Romans, are turning to religion for a new grounding for their lives. American society today vibrates with a palpable yearning for spirituality, whether it is the right-wing dogma of the Christian Coalition, California-style mysticism, or the pseudo-Native Americanism of an executive retreat to a sweat lodge. Cyberspace is not a religious construct—indeed many cybernauts probably eschew religion per se—nonetheless its appeal can be understood in essentially religious terms. I suggest that the role played by cyberspace in popular imagination today, while not being the product of a conscious theology, is not dissimilar to that played by heaven in early Christian imagination. Not

Androgynous, racially amorphous, and chronologically undefined, the cybernaut, like the angel, is an "ideal" being. Such, at least, is the dream.

being an *overtly* religious construct is, on the contrary, a crucial point in its favor—for the religious impulse is decidedly covert in many contemporary Americans. In this scientific age, overt expressions of religiosity make many people uncomfortable. The appeal of cyberspace therefore lies precisely in this paradox: It is a repackaging of the old idea of heaven, but in an avowedly secular and technologically sanctioned format. The "perfect" realm awaits us, we are told, not beyond the pearly gates, but beyond the network gateways—behind electronic doors labeled ".com," ".net," and ".edu."

That science itself has manifested a technological substitute for heaven should not perhaps surprise us, for, as English philosopher Mary Midgley has written,

> The idea that we can reach salvation through science is ancient and powerful.... Any system of thought playing the huge part that science now plays in our lives must also shape our guiding myths and color our imaginations profoundly. It is not just a useful tool. It is also a pattern that we follow at a deep level in trying to meet our imaginative needs.[6]

Belief in salvation through science and its technological byproducts is nowhere more deeply held than in America, where it is championed by a cast from across the political spectrum: from Newt Gingrich and Alvin Toffler to Al Gore and Kevin Kelly. In a society obsessed by technology, cyberspace almost *necessarily* becomes the contemporary vision of heaven—the metaphysical apotheosis of "the technological sublime."

Having sketched the outlines of my analogy, let me elaborate further on the parallels between cyberspace and heaven, for while some are immediately obvious, others, I think, are not. Clearly one of the first similarities is in the democratic promise of entry to all. Men and women, First World and Third, North and South, West and East—cyberspace is equally open to all. In principle anyway. Like heaven, cyberspace is unfractured by national boundaries, a space beyond "place," where men and women from *all* nations can mix together with mutual ease and equal access. Indeed, we are told, cyberspace dissolves the very barriers of gender, race, and nationality, reducing—or perhaps elevating—everyone equally to a disembodied digital stream. As with Christianity, there is something truly positive for women and minorities here. Many commentators have rightly noted that cyberspace potentially offers women a place free from the constant pressure of sexual harassment and gender-based judgment. A similar argument is made about race. Thus, we might agree with Laurie Anderson that the cybernaut becomes, in a sense, an angel—a being of the ether, unencumbered by the biasing baggage of a gendered and colored body. Androgynous, racially amorphous, and chronologically undefined, the cybernaut, like the angel, is an "ideal" being. Such, at least, is the dream.

Ironically, cybernauts use a profoundly physical, even muscular metaphor for their travels in hyperreality. "Surfing the Net" does not conjure up images of disembodied ethereality, but a vision of physical power—both for the human agent and for the space itself. Where the cybernaut is endowed with the grace and prowess of a surfer, the space is likened to the ocean. Here again, paradox comes to the fore. In a realm of disembodiment, we are promised the illusion of physical perfection. Angels, of course, were also perfectly formed. Graceful, gorgeous, and adorned with the ultimate elegant accessory—wings—they were the medieval "beautiful people." Like an angel, the cybernaut is freed from the aesthetic sins of the body. Bad breath, bad hair, acne, dandruff, limps, squints, fat, and wrinkles—all are left behind in the material world. Philosopher of cyberspace Allucquere Rosanne Stone has stressed that this aspect of cyberspace offers an especial appeal to teenage boys. With their bodies going through rapid and unnerving changes, teenage boys, she suggests, view cyberspace as a realm to escape from "the sense of loss of control that accompanies adolescent male embodiment."[7] Unable to constrain their metamorphosing flesh, they flee to a realm where they regain power and control. It is no coincidence that hackers and surfers alike are predominantly young men.

Cybernauts are not only freed from the sins of their own bodies, but also from those of others. In the age of AIDS, cyberspace offers a place to date in safety. In the seventies, Americans went to bars and discos in search of romance; in the eighties they went to gyms and clubs; but today such options carry heavy risks. Apart from catching a sexually transmitted disease, one could easily be raped or mugged on a night out in any major American city (to say nothing of the hangover one is likely to contract). It is so much safer to go on line, where romance can be found without ever leaving the living room. Tales of cyber-romance and even cyber-sex are legion. What could be safer, or purer, than utterly disembodied love? A Christian ideal, if ever there were one.

According to New York Web artist Adrianne Wortzel, cyberspace also frees us from psychological constraints. In America today, she suggests, many people do not feel they can express themselves freely in their real lives. She speaks of how more and more Americans living in a culture dominated by TV sitcoms feel compelled to put on a happy face and present a cartoonlike persona to the world. But such a distortion of the real self cannot be maintained for long without injury to the psyche, and Wortzel believes that cyberspace offers a therapeutic escape, a place where people feel able to let out "their true selves." And if you do not know what your true self is, cyberspace is a place in which you can simply make up a persona and try it on for size. Gender-bending is perhaps the most common experiment enacted by cybernauts, but it is by no means the only one. In MUD's (multiuser domains, cyberspace adventure games) players becomes witches, warlocks, princesses, and monsters. Indeed, says Wortzel, such realms are increasingly peopled with human-animal hybrids, as players experiment with the boundaries of their humanity. Even in ordinary "chat rooms," the cybernaut can "be" anything—as long as he or she can keep up a convincing front. The shy wimp can become the raging Lothario, the wall flower a sexual diva. On line, personality can be both exercised and played to the full. The realization and expression of the "true self" are of course also major religious themes, not least in Christianity.

A further aspect of the cyber-revolution that warrants attention in any analysis of parallels with early Christianity is the emphasis placed on images. Although at the moment most on-line communication and information is textual, that is rapidly changing. With the advent of the World Wide Web and new Web tools such as Java, images are proliferating, and many cyber-experts believe that the image is the future. Instead of sending each other textual messages, we will soon be able to send real-time videos, or animated "avatars" of ourselves to speak our words for us. Data itself will be rendered into graphical form, realizing William Gibson's prescient vision of a virtual landscape of information.[8] Meanwhile virtual classrooms and libraries will supposedly provide the inquiring mind with an infinite array of interactive visual extravaganzas designed to keep even the dullest student alert and interested.

To quote Dr. Diane Ravitch, former United States Assistant Secretary of Education,

> In this new world of pedagogical plenty, children and adults alike will be able to dial up a program on their home television to learn whatever they want to know, at their own convenience.... Young John may decide that he wants to learn the history of modern Japan, which he can do by dialing up the greatest authorities and teachers on the subject, who will not only use dazzling graphs and illustrations, but will narrate a historical video that excites his curiosity and imagination.[9]

The Internet will become an ocean of images, where anything and everything will be rendered into picture form for easy intellectual digestion and maximum entertainment value. Why read when you could watch?

An emphasis on image was also a feature of the Middle Ages, where churches became temples of art. Yet church art was not simply decorative; in an age of illiteracy it served to educate the populace about the Christian worldview. Paintings of biblical stories, of Christ, the Virgin, and the saints might have looked good, but they did much more than that. Much as PBS documentaries educate us today, religious art literally taught people about Christian cosmology. Not only cosmology, but also history, biology, agriculture, social science, ethics, and metaphysics were encompassed in religious art. The Christian era was nothing if not a visual one, and the church fathers understood well how to wield power graphically. Just as images played a major educative role in that time, so too, we are now being told, images will fill the educational vacuum in the age of cyberspace.

In another, final sense, cyberspace marks a return to our medieval past, for cyberspace, like heaven, is a metaphysical rather than a physical construct. In this respect it represents a dramatic reversal of the last five hundred years of Western history, which, since the Renaissance, and particularly since the seventeenth century, has been increasingly focused on the *physical* realm. The rebirth of man that characterized Renaissance culture was a reawakening to the body and to physical space. After the metaphysical obsessions of the Middle Ages, Renaissance artists turned their gaze outward to the material world—to the beauty of bodies, drapery, landscape, and physical form. The development of perspective representation was not just an artistic shift. It initiated a systematic examination of the nature of physical space, which prepared the Western mind for the revolution in physical science pioneered by Nicolaus Copernicus, Johannes Kepler, and Galileo Galilei. The primary outcome of that revolution was to wrest Europe out of the metaphysical cosmology of the medieval period and place mankind firmly in a material setting—the mathematized physical cosmology bequeathed to us by Isaac Newton.

Since the seventeenth century, Western science has been a process of gradually articulating in ever greater detail the physical world around us. Today scientists have mapped the physical arena at every conceivable scale—from the minuscule domain of the subatomic particle to the unimaginable magnitudes of the galactic superclusters. We have mapped every inch of our own planet (and a good deal of Venus and Mars as well). Like no other people before, we can pinpoint ourselves precisely, both geographically and astronomically, in our universe. Yet in the final analysis this obsessive scrutiny of physical space has become a hollow activity, for what we have discovered through this approach is ultimately a vast, cold, and apparently empty infinitude. Years of scanning the sky with radio telescopes have not resulted in a single confirmable message from the stars. Unlike our medieval forebears who lived in a cosmos thronged with other intelligent beings—angels, archangels, cherubim, seraphim, and the like—we find ourselves utterly alone. The very vastness of physical space, with its billions of light years of void and dust, makes this lonesomeness all the more unbearable and mocks our aspirations for cosmic friendship. The obsessive exploration of physical space and the concomitant materialist philosophy of nature that has been a defining principle of the "modern" Western era has rendered us a minute island of meaningless organic molecules awash in a sterile vacuum.

Our dream of outer space has long been accompanied by the belief that we would find friends among the stars. The failure of that hope—made all too palpable by visits of NASA probes to a lifeless Venus and Mars, and by the lack of any concrete response from the SETI project—has created a backlash against space exploration. People are tiring of the void. Not only do humans need companions, they need spiritual connection. Outer space provides us with neither. Stripping the cosmos not only of angels and gods, but also of spiritual content, physical cosmology has stranded us as psychic beings.

I suggest that a major appeal of cyberspace is that many people hope it might fill this vacuum in their lives. Kevin Kelly is not alone in believing he can experience "soul-data through silicon." Thus, in a very visceral way, cyberspace represents a return to profoundly medieval concerns because it refocuses attention from the physical to the metaphysical, from the soma to the psyche—not just for the individual, but for society at large. For cyberspace is above all a *communal* realm, teaming with potential friends—fifty million of them already, and growing every day. Like heaven, cyberspace is sold to us as a shared domain where legions of the faithful will commune together in a "paradise" of brotherly and sisterly love unimpeded by the tyrannies of distance and flesh. In this age of alienation and social disintegration—with rape and mugging rampant; and obesity, self-loathing, and sloth ever increasing problems—is it any wonder that we should feel drawn to such a vision? As with heaven, cyberspace is a place where we are promised the joys of freedom, power, connection, and even love—a realm where the failings of the body will supposedly melt away, where the soul will be free to express itself fully, where image and imagination will reign, and where, via the explosion of on-line databases, *all* can potentially be known. In such a space we would be not just angels, but gods—not mere slaves, but masters of our destiny.

Whether or not cyberspace can realize this vision is of course another matter.

Notes

NAN ELLIN
SHELTER FROM THE STORM

1. As Alberto Moravia contends, "With the Revolution of '89, the bourgeois world, a materialistic world firmly bound to duration, that is, to the passage of time, superseded the feudal world, a world completely alienated from and immovably situated outside of time." Alberto Moravia, "The Terrorist Aesthetic," *Harper's Magazine* (June 1987): 37.
2. Ibid., 37–38.
3. Jonas Frykman and Orvar Lofgren, *The Culture Builders*, trans. John Gills (New Brunswick, NJ: Rutgers University Press, 1987), 142.
4. Ibid., 270.
5. Ibid., 29 (citing Michel Foucault).
6. Ibid., 27.
7. Ibid., 24.
8. Ibid., 27.
9. Ibid.
10. Ibid., 125.
11. Ibid., 136.
12. Ibid., 109.
13. Ibid., 225.
14. Ibid., 94.
15. Ibid., 103.
16. Ibid., 105.
17. Ibid., 233.
18. Ibid., 238.
19. Ibid., 111.
20. Jeremy Bentham, cited in Anthony Vidler, "The Scenes of the Street," in *On Streets*, ed. Stanford Anderson, (Cambridge, MA: MIT Press, 1991), 54.
21. Vidler, "Scenes of Street,"58.
22. Ibid.
23. See John Friedmann, *Planning in the Public Domain: From Knowledge to Action* (Princeton, NJ: Princeton University Press, 1987).
24. Ibid.
25. Vidler, "Scenes of Street," 29.
26. Friedmann, *Planning in Public Domain*.
27. Baron Haussmann, cited in Robert Moses, "What Happened to Haussmann?" *Architectural Forum* (July 1942): 59.
28. Marshall Berman, *All That is Solid Melts Into Air* (Harmondsworth, UK: Penguin, 1982), 150.
29. Françoise Choay, *The Modern City: Planning in the 19th Century* (New York: George Braziller, 1969), 15.
30. Gary Wray McDonough, *Conflict in Catalonia* (Gainsville: University of Florida Press, 1986), 35.
31. César Daly, *Architecture privée sous Napoleon III* (Paris: Ducher et Cie, 1877).
32. Frykman and Lofgren, *Culture Builders*, 126.
33. Ibid.
34. Ibid., 140.
35. E. P. Thompson, "Time, Work-discipline, and Industrial Capitalism" *Past and Present* 38 (1967): 56–97.
36. David Harvey, *The Condition of Postmodernity* (Oxford: Blackwell, 1989), 11.
37. Charles Pierre Baudelaire, "The Painter of Modern Life" (1863), cited in ibid., 10.
38. Berman, *All That is Solid*, 15.
39. Paul Rabinow, *French Modern* (Chicago: University of Chicago Press, 1989), 77.
40. The roots of urban planning are sometimes located within Enlightenment thought or even earlier. I focus here, however, on its modern form as it crystallized around the last turn of the century along with—and in response to—the rise of the liberal state and industrial capitalism. Prior to this modern split between the container and its contents, nineteenth-century thinkers and designers (such as Claude-Nicolas Ledoux, Robert Owen, Charles Fourier, Etienne Cabet, Jean-Baptiste Godin, Karl Marx and Friedrich Engels, John Ruskin and William Morris, Baron Haussmann, Frederick Law Olmsted, and Ebenezer Howard) did not dissociate the physical landscape from the social one.
41. James Holston, *The Modernist City: An Anthropological Critique of Brasilia* (Chicago: University of Chicago Press, 1989), 52.
42. Ibid.
43. Jean Guiheux, *Europan* (Paris: Plan Construction, 1989), 18. Translated from the French by Nan Ellin.
44. Tom Schumacher, "Contextualism: Urban Ideals and Deformations," *Casabella* (1971): 81. Modernism diverged from both the romantic and classic traditions in its attitude toward public space. As Peter Calthorpe explains, "The romantic and classic traditions may appear contrary, but they share one basic trait: the public space— either street, square, or plaza—is the dominant form. The buildings are subservient. Though less true of the romantic, both traditions use urban buildings as the 'walls' of great outdoor 'rooms,'

with the facades ornamenting and unifying, and public art 'furnishing' these rooms. Garnier's plan expresses a totally new sense: the building becomes the object, not defining the public space, but situated in it.... The buildings become autonomous forms placed in a park-like setting." (Peter Calthorpe, "A Short History of Twentieth Century New Towns," in Sustainable Communities, ed. Sim Van der Ryn and Peter Calthorpe [San Francisco: Sierra Club Books, 1986], 203–04.) The proposals of both Le Corbusier and Frank Lloyd Wright were thus modern in their conception of form because they conceived of "the building as an autonomous object maintaining responsibility only to internal functions, rather than the old urban tradition in which the building defined the public space that it fronted." (Ibid., 206.)

45. Bernard Huet, "L'Architecture contre la Ville," AMC 14 (December 1986): 12. Translated from the French by Nan Ellin.

46. Holston, Modernist City, 52.

47. Vincent Scully, American Architecture and Urbanism (1969; revised edition, New York: Henry Holt, 1988).

48. Anthony Vidler, "The Third Typology," Rational Architecture, ed. Robert Delevoy (Brussels: Archives d'Architecture Moderne, 1978), 30.

49. Manfredo Tafuri, Architecture and Utopia: Design and Capitalist Development (1973; reprint, Cambridge, MA: MIT Press, 1976), 52.

50. Fredric Jameson, "Architecture and the Critique of Ideology," in Architecture, Criticism, Ideology, ed. Joan Ockman (Princeton, NJ: Princeton Architectural Press, 1985), 78.

51. Ibid., 80.

52. Gwendolyn Wright, "Inventions and Interventions: American Urban Design in the Twentieth Century," in Urban Revisions: Current Projects for the Public Realm, ed. Elizabeth A. T. Smith (Cambridge, MA: MIT Press, 1994), 27–37.

53. Edward T. Relph, The Modern Urban Landscape (Baltimore: Johns Hopkins University Press, 1987), 211.

54. See Nan Ellin, Postmodern Urbanism (Oxford: Blackwell, 1996), chapter 7, "Crisis in the Architectural Profession."

55. Ibid., chapter 4, "The Postmodern Reflex."

56. Prior to the nineteenth century, "one tended to find a more directly existential type of nostalgia, arising more 'naturally' from estrangement or alienation." By the latter part of that century, this combined with a more willful, synthetic, and politically driven nostalgia, which became "incorporated—for the most part capitalistically—into consumerist, image-conveyed nostalgia." This late-twentieth-century nostalgia both universalizes particulars and particularizes universals; it is "both collective on a global scale and directed at globality itself." Roland Robertson, "After Nostalgia? Willful Nostalgia and the Phases of Globalization," in Theories of Modernity and Postmodernity, ed. Bryan S. Turner (London: Sage Publications, 1990), 54–56.

57. Jameson writes, "The appetite for images of the past, in the form of what might be called simulacra, the increasing production of such images of all kinds, in particular in that peculiar postmodern genre, the nostalgic film, with its glossy evocation of the past as sheer consumerable fashion and image—all this seems to me something of a return of the repressed, an unconscious sense of the loss of the past, which this appetite for images seeks desperately to overcome." Fredric Jameson, cited in ibid., 54. See also Ellin, Postmodern Urbanism.

58. Advertisement for Good Housekeeping, New York Times, 9 October 1988.

59. Jon Pareles, "When Country Music Moves to the Suburbs," New York Times, 25 November 1990, sec. 2, page 1.

60. Suzanne Slesin, "Character Counts," New York Times Magazine, 4 April 1993.

61. Ibid.

62. Sharon Zukin, Loft Living: Culture and Capital in Urban Change (Baltimore: Johns Hopkins University Press, 1982), 68.

63. Benjamin Thompson, cited in Beverly Russell, Architecture and Design 1970–1990: New Ideas in America (New York: Harry N. Abrams, 1989), 115.

64. See Kevin Lynch, Image of the City (Cambridge, MA: MIT Press, 1960).

65. In 1961, in one of the earliest articulations, Jane Jacobs called for a return to the street. She claimed, "It is futile to try to evade the issue of unsafe city streets by attempting to make some other features of a locality, say interior courtyards, or sheltered play spaces, safe instead." (Jane Jacobs, The Death and Life of Great American Cities: The Failure of Town Planning [New York: Vintage, 1961], 35.) Jacobs's concern with the declining quality and quantity of public space was echoed by others such as Lewis Mumford (The City in History [New York: Harcourt Brace Jovanovich, 1961]), who also championed preindustrial cityscapes; Jurgen Habermas, whose discussion on "the structural transformation of the public sphere" appeared in 1962 (Habilitationsschrift, Strukturwandel der Öffentlichkeit [Darmstadt: Hermann Luchterhand Verlag, 1962]; published in French as L'Espace Public, [Paris: Payot, 1978]; published in English as The Structural Transformation of the Public Sphere: An Enquiry into a Category of Bourgeois Society, trans. Thomas

NAN ELLIN
SHELTER FROM THE STORM (contd.)

Burger [Cambridge, MA: MIT Press, 1989]); Serge
Chermayeff and Christopher Alexander (*Commu-
nity and Privacy: Toward a New Architecture of
Humanism* [New York: Doubleday, 1963]); and
Richard Sennett (*The Uses of Disorder: Personal
Identity and City Life* [New York: Random House,
1970], *The Fall of Public Man: On the Social
Psychology of Capitalism* [New York: Random
House, 1974], and *The Conscience of the Eye: The
Design and Social Life of Cities* [New York: Knopf,
1990]), who suggested that we combat the
decline of meaningful public space by juxtaposing
socially diverse neighborhoods (*Conscience of Eye*)
since plurality "is the condition sine qua non for
that space of appearance which is the public
realm" (*Uses of Disorder*, 11). A different perspec-
tive was offered by Oscar Newman, *Defensible
Space: People and Design in the Violent City* (New
York: Macmillan, 1972).
66. See Nan Ellin, *In Search of a Usable Past: Urban
Design in a French New Town* (Ph.D. diss.,
Columbia University, 1994) and Ellin, *Postmodern
Urbanism*.
67. See Peter Calthorpe, "Introduction" and
"Pedestrian Pockets: New Strategies for Suburban
Growth," in *The Pedestrian Pocket Book: A New
Suburban Design Strategy*, ed. Doug Kelbaugh
(New York: Princeton Architectural Press, 1989),
3–20 and Peter Calthorpe, *The Next American
Metropolis* (New York: Princeton Architectural
Press, 1993).
68. This discussion of interior design draws in part
from Paul Goldberger, "Four Walls and a Door,"
New York Times (14 October 1990): Home section,
40, 66–7.
69. "Hip Hotels Help Set Interior Design Trends,"
Cincinnati Enquirer, 22 June 1996.
70. Francis Fukuyama, "The End of History?" *The
National Interest* (Summer 1989) 3–18 and Francis
Fukuyama, *The End of History and the Last Man*
(New York: Free Press, 1992).
71. Martin Heidegger, cited in Harvey, *Condition of
Postmodernity*, 35.
72. Kathleen Stewart, "Nostalgia—A Polemic," in
Cultural Anthropology vol. 3 no. 3 (1988):
227–41.
73. Kenneth Galbraith, *The Affluent Society* (Boston:
Houghton Mifflin, 1960).
74. Sennett, *Fall of Public Man*, 5. More recent contributions to this discussion of the privatization of
public space include Roslyn Deutsche, "Question-
ing the Public Space," *Public* 6 (1992): 49–64,
Bruce Robbins, ed., *The Phantom Public Realm*
(Minneapolis: University of Minnesota Press,
1993), and Nancy Fraser, "Rethinking the Public

Sphere," in Robbins, *Phantom Public Realm*.
75. Jérome Bindé, "Le Pavillon des Aliénés ou le
Fantôme du Privé," in *Paysage Pavillonaire*, ed.
IFA (Paris: Institut Français d'Architecture, 1982),
37. Translated from the French by Nan Ellin.
76. This political rationality was linked to the rise of
the state, the expansion of capitalism, the primacy of scientific categories over juridical ones, and
the increased interest in the individual as an
object of political and scientific concern.
77. Phillip Corrigan and Derek Sayer, *The Great Arch:
State Formation as Cultural Revolution* (Oxford:
Blackwell, 1985).
78. Michel Foucault, *The History of Sexuality* vol. I
(New York: Vintage, 1980), 86. Paul Rabinow and
Hubert Dreyfuss elaborate, "In traditional forms of
power, like that of the sovereign, power itself is
made visible, brought out in the open, put constantly on display. The multitudes are kept in the
shadows, appearing only at the edges of power's
brilliant glow. Disciplinary power reverses these
relations. Now, it is power itself which seeks
invisibility and the objects of power—those on
whom it operates—are made the most visible. It
is this fact of surveillance, constant visibility,
which is the key to disciplinary technology." (Paul
Rabinow and Hubert Dreyfuss, *Michel Foucault:
Beyond Structuralism and Hermeneutics* [Chicago:
University of Chicago Press, 1983], 159).
"Whereas in monarchical regimes it was the sovereign who had the greatest visibility, under the
institutions of biopower it is those who are to be
disciplined, observed, and understood who are
made the most visible." (Ibid., 191.)
79. Moravia, "Terrorist Aesthetic."
80. See Mark Dery, *Escape Velocity: Cyberculture at the
End of the Century* (New York: Grove Press, 1996).
81. This discussion of virtual reality, RL, and MUDs
draws from Sherry Turkle, "Who Am We?" *Wired*
(January 1996): 149–51, 194–99.
82. Rachel Simon, community relations coordinator
for Barnes & Noble, Princeton, New Jersey.
83. Ralph Rugoff, "L.A.'s New Car-tography," *L.A.
Weekly* (6 October 1995): 35.
84. I am indebted to Ralph Rugoff for the discussion
apropos clothes and cars and to Mark Dery apropos body modification and its relation to cyberculture.
85. See Charles Jencks's essay in this volume.
86. Alexander Tzonis and Liane Lefaivre, "The
Narcissistic Phase in Architecture," *Harvard
Architectural Review* I (Spring1980): 24.
87. Ibid., 23.
88. Ada Louise Huxtable, "Is Modern Architecture
Dead?" *Architectural Record* 169 (October 1981):
104. According to Huxtable, "Style, as it is being
written about and embraced today, is no longer
style as we have previously defined and under-

stood it—as an attempt to give appropriate expression to a kind of life, or society, or collective need, or moment in cultural time." Instead, "Like so much else today, the emphasis is on self and the senses, with 'design' an increasingly hermetic and narcissistic process, serving as often to short circuit purpose and accessibility as to expand the horizons of constructive vision. Style is being dangerously confused with art." Huxtable believes that "This pursuit of style for its own sake is a logical consequence of the death of the twentieth-century belief in salvation through design and the architect's rejection of any social contract. If there is to be no brave new world, if scientific and technological progress are not to be the bearers of its art and joy, then modernism, with its very specific message of the perfectibility of the human condition through the quality of the built environment, can no longer be considered the only appropriate vehicle of expression for the conditions and spirit of this century." She maintains that "These factors, above all, have changed the rules, and the approach, to the practice of architecture today. There is no Zeitgeist demanding recognition and fealty, no unifying force or sentiment, no greater public good, no banner around which architects can rally. They can go in any direction and follow any muse. This is surely one of the most open, challenging, promising, and dangerous moments in the history of the building art."

89. Jean Baudrillard, "The Ecstasy of Communication" in The Anti-Aesthetic, ed. Hal Foster (Seattle: Bay Press, 1983), 2.

90. Steven Best and Douglas Kellner, Postmodern Theory: Critical Interrogations (New York: Guilford Press, 1991), 119.

91. Ibid.

92. Umberto Eco, Travels in Hyperreality (New York: Harcourt Brace Jovanovich, 1986), 7, 8, 30.

93. Harvey, Condition of Postmodernity, 300.

94. Daniel Solomon, "Fixing Suburbia" in The Pedestrian Pocket Book: A New Suburban Design Strategy, ed. Doug Kelbaugh (New York: Princeton Architectural Press, 1989), 96.

95. As Christine Boyer suggests, urban design that freely quotes from the past and mass imagery can engender a "blasé attitude," for it implies that the city is "after all just entertainment; we are only there to look and to buy. The city has become a place of escape, a wonderland that evades reality, for there is nothing more to think about in pure entertainment." With consumption replacing production as the primary economic role of our central cities, Boyer explains,

they become places of "pure play." M. Christine Boyer, "The Return of Aesthetics to City Planning," Philosophical Streets, ed. Dennis Crow (Washington D.C.: Maison Neuve, 1990), 97–98.

96. Harvey, Condition of Postmodernity, 97.

97. Charlene Spretnak, States of Grace: The Recovery of Meaning in the Postmodern Age (New York: Harper Collins, 1991), 223.

98. See Margaret Wertheim's essay in this volume.

99. Dery, Escape Velocity.

100. As Habermas explains, the post-1968 period has been witnessing an "exhaustion of utopian energies" (Jurgen Habermas, "The New Obscurity," trans. Phillip Jacobs, Philosophy and Social Criticism vol. 2 no. 2 [1986]: 3). As a communications zeitgeist replaces a labor zeitgeist (which prevailed from the French Revolution to 1968), he says, the specific utopian idea based on social labor is over. That idea arose out of a new perception of time such that hopes for paradise shifted to this world. With the advent of the communications zeitgeist two centuries later, Habermas observes, utopian expectations seem to be taking on a religious form once again.

101. This attention to the edge has nothing to do with the building of "edge cities" that create new barriers rather than breaking down old ones, and that are market-driven rather than the product of considered thought and action.

102. Liane Lefaivre, "Dirty Realism in European Architecture Today: Making the Stone Stony," Design Book Review 17 (Winter 1989): 17.

STEVEN FLUSTY
BUILDING PARANOIA

1. Herbert I. Schiller, Culture, Inc.: The Corporate Takeover of Public Expression (New York: Oxford University Press, 1989).

2. Promotional brochure for Metropolitan Structures West's California Plaza.

3. Gerald D. Suttles, The Social Construction of Communities (Chicago: University of Chicago Press, 1972).

RICHARD SENNETT
THE SEARCH FOR A PLACE IN THE WORLD

1. Michael Hammer and James Champy, Reengineering the Corporation (New York: Harper Business, 1993).

2. Friedrich Nietzsche, Thus Spake Zarathustra, trans. Marianne Cowan (Chicago: Gateway Editions, 1957).

3. Hammer and Champy, Reengineering the Corporation.

RICHARD SENNETT
THE SEARCH FOR A PLACE IN THE WORLD
(contd.)

4. Pico della Mirandola, *Oration on the Dignity of Man*, trans. Paul J. W. Miller (Indianapolis: Bobbs-Merrill, 1965).

JANE HARRISON
MULTIPLICATION + SUBDIVISION

I am grateful to Jonathan Wetherill and Craig Kim for their invaluable assistance.

EDWARD J. BLAKELY AND MARY GAIL SNYDER
DIVIDED WE FALL

1. Based on estimates of the total number of community associations, sample surveys of associations size, and our survey results that nineteen percent of all community associations are gated.
2. We conducted a survey of nearly 2000 community association boards throughout the United States through the auspices of the Community Association Institute in 1994, adding a separate set of questions for gated communities.
3. Peter Marcuse, this volume, 104. See also Peter Marcuse, "Of Walls and Immigrant Enclaves," in *Immigrant Absorption*, ed. Naomi Carmen (New York: Macmillan, 1996).
4. Jane Jacobs, *The Death and Life of Great American Cities* (New York: Vintage, 1961).
5. Oscar Newman, *Defensible Space* (New York: Macmillan, 1972).

PETER MARCUSE
WALLS OF FEAR AND WALLS OF SUPPORT

1. I have referred to the metaphorical understanding of walls in an earlier version of this paper, "Walls as Metaphor and Reality," in *Managing Divided Cities*, ed. Seamus Dunn (Staffordshire, England: Ryburn Publishing, 1994), 41–52.
2. W. H. Bau, "Fortifications," *Encyclopedia Brittanica*, vol. 9 (Chicago: William Benton, 1959), 538.
3. The Great Wall may also have been part of that history that led to the prominence of walls in Chinese city development. "Walls, walls, and yet again walls form the framework of every Chinese city. They surround it, they divide it into lots and compounds, they mark more than any other structures the basic features of the Chinese communities. There is no real city in China without a surrounding wall, a condition which indeed is

expressed by the fact that the Chinese used the same word "ch'eng" for a city and a city wall." (Ibid., 557.) I am not well enough informed on Chinese history to know if the linkage I am suggesting has substance.
4. There have in fact been military sieges of cities in very recent times: one thinks of Leningrad, Srebrenica, and the ghetto of Warsaw. But the defenses here were walls not ever calculated to hold back an attacking army, but whatever buildings, structures, and weapons were at hand. Stronger walls would not have helped. The most recent attempt to place confidence in physical walls as defense was probably the ill-fated underground bunkers built by Saddam Hussein against the invading forces of the United States and its allies in the Gulf War.
5. While the examples given here are confined to the United States, there is an international trend towards the creation of new and quite separate, bounded business districts, of which La Defense in Paris and Docklands in London are only the best-known examples. Such examples can be found in cities as different as Sao Paolo, Calcutta, and Johannesburg.
6. Nathan Glazer, "Divided Cities, Dual Cities: The Case of New York" in Dunn, *Managing Divided Cities*, 176–190. Glazer analogizes that distinction to one between the concept of "dual cities" and that of "divided cities," perhaps an analytically useful distinction but one too far removed from common use, it seems to me, to be viable. While I have expressed skepticism similar to Glazer's about the "dual cities" formulation (see Peter Marcuse, " 'Dual City': A Muddy Metaphor for a Quartered City," *International Journal of Urban and Regional Research* vol. 13, no. 4 [December 1989]: 697–708), I consider it useful, as he may not, to attempt to specify more carefully what the multiple divisions are and how they line up against each other.
7. I have discussed the concept of the "quartered city" in several other pieces. (See Marcuse, " 'Dual City,' " and Marcuse, "Housing Markets and Labour Markets in the Quartered City," in *Housing and Labour Markets: Building the Connections*, ed. John Allen and Chris Hamnett, [London: Unwin Hyman, 1991], 118–35.) "Quartered" is used both in the sense of "drawn and quartered" and of residential "quarters"; there are essentially four such quarters, the very wealthy not being bound by any specific spatial configuration as to where they live. See also John H. Mollenkopf and Manuel Castells, eds., *Dual City: Restructuring New York* (New York: Russell Sage Foundation, 1991), especially the introduction and conclusion, and Leonard Wallock, "Tales of Two Cities: Gentrification and Displacement in Contemporary New

PETER MARCUSE
WALLS OF FEAR AND WALLS OF SUPPORT
(contd.)

York," in *Begetting Images*, ed. Mary B. Campbell
and Mark Rollins (New York: Peter Lang, 1989).

8. For the concept of "home-less housing" and a dis-
cussion of its location, see Peter Marcuse and
Camilo Vergara, "Gimme Shelter (Home-lessness in
New York City)," *Artforum* (Spring 1992): 88–92.

9. "Citadel" was first used in the present context in
John Friedmann and Goetz Wolff, "World City
Formation: An Agenda for Research and Action,"
*International Journal of Urban and Regional
Research* vol. 6 no. 3 (1982): 309–44.

10. The conception of the architecture of the Knesset
shows an awareness of walls as symbols of power,
and attempts to achieve the exact opposite effect.

11. Neil Smith, "New City, New Frontier: The Lower
East Side as Wild Wild West," in *Variations on a
Theme Park: The New American City and the End of
Public Space*, ed. Michael Sorkin (New York, Hill
and Wang, 1992), 61–93.

KEVIN SITES
MIRRORS

1. "Mending Wall," *The Poetry of Robert Frost: The
Collected Poems, Complete and Unabridged*, ed.
Edward Connery Lathem (New York: Henry Holt,
1969), 33–34.

DORA EPSTEIN
ABJECT TERROR

1. Victor Burgin, "Fantasy," in *Feminism and Psychoanalysis: A Critical Dictionary*, ed. Elizabeth
Wright (Oxford: Blackwell, 1992) 87.

2. Jacques Lacan, "The Agency of the Letter in the
Unconscious or Reason Since Freud," in *Ecrits:
A Selection*, trans. Alan Sheridan (London:
Tavistock, 1977).

3. Nancy Chodorow, *Feminism and Psychoanalytic Theory* (New Haven: Yale University Press, 1989), 157.

4. Judith Butler, *Bodies That Matter: On the Discursive
Limits of "Sex"* (New York: Routledge, 1993), 3.

5. Victor Burgin, "Geometry and Abjection," in
Psychoanalysis and Cultural Theory: Thresholds, ed.
James Donald (New York: Macmillan, 1991), 11.

6. Elizabeth Wilson, "Psychoanalysis: Psychic Law
and Order?," in *British Feminist Thought: A Reader*,
ed. Terry Lovell (Oxford: Blackwell, 1990), 220.

7. Elizabeth Grosz, "The Body," in *Feminism and
Psychoanalysis: A Critical Dictionary*, ed. Elizabeth
Wright (Oxford: Basil Blackwell, 1992), 36.

8. Butler, *Bodies That Matter*, 2.

9. Elizabeth Grosz, "Bodies-Cities," in *Sexuality &
Space*, ed. Beatriz Colomina (New York: Princeton
Architectural Press, 1992), 250.

10. Mark Wigley, "Fear Not...," in *Mortal City*, ed.
Peter Lang (New York: Princeton Architectural
Press, 1995), 79.

11. Camilo José Vergara, "Bunkering the Poor: Our Fortified Ghettos," in *Mortal City*, ed. Peter Lang (New
York: Princeton Architectural Press, 1995), 27.

12. Mike Davis, "Fortress Los Angeles: The Militariza-
tion of Urban Space," in *Variations on a Theme
Park: The New American City and the End of Public
Space*, ed. Michael Sorkin (New York: Hill and
Wang, 1990).

13. Elizabeth Wilson, *The Sphinx in the City: Urban
Life, the Control of Disorder, and Women* (Berkeley:
University of California Press, 1991).

14. D. G. Shane, "Balkanization and the Postmodern
City," in *Mortal City*, ed. Peter Lang (New York:
Princeton Architectural Press, 1995), 67.

15. Robert Elias, *The Politics of Victimization: Victims,
Victimology, and Human Rights* (Oxford: Oxford
University Press, 1986), 120.

16. Ellie Ragland-Sullivan, "Hysteria," in *Feminism and
Psychoanalysis: A Critical Dictionary*, ed. Elizabeth
Wright (Oxford: Blackwell, 1992), 164.

17. Elias, *Politics of Victimization*.

ANNE TROUTMAN
INSIDE FEAR

1. C. S. Lewis, *Surprised by Joy* (New York: Harcourt,
Brace and World, 1955), 10.

2. Rainer Maria Rilke, *Les Cahiers de Malte Lauride
Brigge*, trans. Maurice Betz (Paris: Editions Emile-
Paul, 1935), 106.

3. D. W. Winnicott, *Playing and Reality* (New York:
Basic Books, 1971), 3–4.

4. "The capacity to create such an illusion [of transitional phenomena] defends the child against the
anxiety of being alone, without the mother."
Laurie Adams, *Art and Psychoanalysis* (New York:
Harper Collins, 1993), 178.

5. Shirley Jackson, *The Haunting of Hill House* (New
York: Popular Library, 1959), 40.

6. Gaston Bachelard, *The Poetics of Space*, trans.
Maria Jolas (Boston: Beacon Press, 1964), 222.

7. Jean-François de Bastide, cited by John
Whiteman, *The French Interior in the 18th Century*
(New York: Penguin Group, 1992), 76. Translated
from the French by Whiteman.

8. Walter Benjamin, *Illuminationen; Ausgewählte
Shriften* (Frankfurt: Suhrkamp Verlag, 1955), 415.

9. Roger Shattuck, *The Banquet Years* (New York:
Harcourt Brace, 1958).

10. Guillaume Apollinaire, *Il y a* (Paris: 1925); transla-
tion from Shattuck, *Banquet Years*, 213–14.

JOHN CHASE
MY URBAN HISTORY

Some of this material has appeared in "The Pet,
the Pirate Cave, and the Pagoda: A Hacienda for
Dog-Gone Everyday Life," *Offramp* vol. 1 no. 6,
ed. John Colter and Mark Skiles (Los Angeles:
Southern California Institute of Architecture,
1996), 16–29.

1. *The Teaching of Buddha* (Tokyo: Bukkyo Dendo
   Kyokai, 1993), 188.
2. Richard Sennett, *The Uses of Disorder* (New York:
   Vintage Books, 1970), 139.

MICHAEL DEAR AND JURGEN VON MAHS
HOUSING FOR THE HOMELESS, BY THE
HOMELESS, AND OF THE HOMELESS

This essay was written when Dear was a Fellow at
the Center for Advanced Study in the Behavioral
Sciences. Support from the Center and the
National Science Foundation is gratefully acknowledged.

1. Jennifer Wolch and Michael Dear, *Malign Neglect:
   Homelessness in an American City* (San Francisco:
   Jossey-Bass, 1993).
2. Hamilton, Rabinovitz, and Alschuler, Inc., *The
   Changing Face of Misery: Los Angeles' Skid Row
   Area in Transition* (Los Angeles: City of Los
   Angeles Community Redevelopment Agency,
   1987).
3. Robin Law, Marylyn Wright, and Jennifer Wolch,
   *The Employment and Residential Location of Low-
   Skill Workforce in Downtown Los Angeles*, Working
   Paper 18 (Los Angeles: Los Angeles Homelessness
   Project, University of Southern California, 1989).
4. Hamilton, Rabinovitz, and Alschuler, *Changing
   Face of Misery*.
5. Roger Farr, Paul Koegel, and M. Audrey Burnam, *A
   Study of Homelessness and Mental Illness in the Skid
   Row Area of Los Angeles* (Los Angeles: Los Angeles
   County Department of Mental Health, 1986).
6. Paul Koegel, M. Audrey Burnam, and Roger K.
   Farr, "Subsistence Adaptation Among Homeless
   Adults in the Inner City of Los Angeles," *Journal
   of Social Issues* 46 (1990): 83–107.
7. Farr, Koegel, and Burnam, *Study of Homelessness*,
   117.
8. Kay McChesney, "Families: The New Homeless-
   ness," *Family Professional* (1987): 1, 13–14.
9. Margaret J. Robertson, Richard Ropers, and Rachel
   Boyer, *The Homeless of Los Angeles County: An
   Empirical Evaluation*, Document 4 (Los Angeles:
   Basic Shelter Research Project, School of Public
   Health, University of California, 1985).
10. Koegel, Burnam, and Farr, "Subsistence
    Adaptation," 97.

11. Paul Koegel and M. Audrey Burnam, "Alcoholism
    Among Homeless Adults in the Inner City of Los
    Angeles," *Archives of General Psychiatry* 45
    (1988): 1011–18.
12. Ibid., 1013.
13. Lois Takahashi, Michael Dear, and Mike Neely,
    *Characteristics of the Homeless Population in Skid
    Row, Los Angeles, 1988–1989*, Working Paper 23
    (Los Angeles: Los Angeles Homelessness Project,
    University of Southern California, 1989).
14. Paul Koegel, M. Audrey Burnam, and Roger K.
    Farr, "The Prevalence of Specific Psychiatric
    Disorders Among Homeless Individuals in the
    Inner City of Los Angeles," *Archives of General
    Psychiatry* 45 (1988): 1087.
15. Michael Dear and Lois Takahashi, "Health and
    Homelessness," in *Community, Environment and
    Health: Geographic Perspectives*, ed. Michael V.
    Hayes, Leslie T. Foster, and Harold P. Foster
    (Victoria, B.C.: University of Victoria Press, 1992),
    185–212.
16. Farr, Koegel, and Burnam, *Study of Homelessness*,
    166–74.
17. Wolch and Dear, *Malign Neglect*.
18. Stacey Rowe and Jennifer Wolch, "Social
    Networks in Time and Space: Homeless Women in
    Skid Row, Los Angeles," *Annals, Association of
    American Geographers* (1990): 80, 184–205.
19. Madeleine Stoner, *The Civil Rights of Homeless
    People* (New York: Aldine de Gruyter, 1995).
20. Wolch/Dear Associates, *Downtown Strategic Plan:
    Homelessness and Social Services* (Santa Monica:
    Wolch/Dear Associates, 1992).
21. FJA, "Earthonauts, USA," *LA Architect* (September
    1993).
22. Michael Dear, Jurgen von Mahs, and Kaerensa
    Craft, *Genesis 1 Evaluation: Final Report*, Unpub-
    lished paper (Los Angeles: Department of Geo-
    graphy, University of Southern California, 1994).

LOIS TAKAHASHI
ADDRESSING FEAR THROUGH COMMUNITY
EMPOWERMENT

I am very grateful to the professional organizers
discussed in this chapter for their time and can-
dor. This research was supported in part by a
Faculty Research Grant from the School of Social
Ecology, University of California-Irvine. Research
assistance by Daniel Miyake was invaluable. I am
grateful to David G. White and Nan Ellin for comments on a previous draft. All errors and omis-
sions remain my responsibility.

1. The name of the organization, its staff, and
   involved individuals have been changed.
2. For this essay, I spoke with Bob and Tim using in-
   depth interviews. These interviews took place at

LOIS TAKAHASHI
ADDRESSING FEAR THROUGH COMMUNITY
EMPOWERMENT (contd.)

the CBOOC offices between late July and early
August 1995 and lasted between one and three
hours. The primary issues we discussed included
how the institutional structure and practices of
CBOOC influenced resident empowerment and
quality of life.

3. Allen J. Scott, *Metropolis: From the Division of
Labor to Urban Form* (Berkeley, CA: University of
California Press, 1988) and Rob Kling, Spencer
Olin, and Mark Poster, "The Emergence of
Postsuburbia: An Introduction," in *Postsuburban
California: The Transformation of Orange County
Since World War II*, ed. Rob Kling, Spencer Olin,
and Mark Poster (Berkeley: University of California
Press, 1991), 1–30.

4. Scott, *Metropolis* and Jennifer Wolch and Michael
Dear, *Malign Neglect: Homelessness in an American
City* (San Francisco: Jossey-Bass, 1993).

5. Kate Ascher, *The Politics of Privatisation:
Contracting Out Public Services* (London:
Macmillan, 1987); Neil Gilbert, *Capitalism and the
Welfare State: Dilemmas of Social Benevolence*
(New Haven, CT: Yale University Press, 1983); and
Julian Le Grand and Ray Robinson, eds.,
Privatisation and the Welfare State (London: George
Allen and Unwin, 1984).

6. Jennifer Wolch and Andrea Akita, "The Federal
Response to Homelessness and its Implications
for American Cities," *Urban Geography* 9 (1988):
62–85.

7. Wolch and Dear, *Malign Neglect*.

8. See Paul Davidoff, "Advocacy and Pluralism in
Planning," *Journal of the American Institute of
Planners* vol. 31 no. 4 (1965): 331–338; Lisa R.
Peattie, "Reflections on Advocacy Planning,"
Journal of the American Institute of Planners 34
(March 1965): 80–88; and Martin Rein, "Social
Planning: The Search for Legitimacy," *Journal of the
American Institute of Planners* (July 1969):
233–44. More recently, many scholars have
lamented the overuse of the term "empowerment" and the lack of specificity concerning its
definition. See Christopher Rissel, "Empowerment:
The Holy Grail of Health Promotion?" *Health
Promotion International* vol. 9 no. 1 (1994):
39–47. Empowerment has been described as individual change (e.g., increased positive self-image,
reduced helplessness, and improved coping skills),
group change (e.g., increased political participation and coalition building), and wider societal
and structural change (e.g., collaborative social
action and critical awareness of the influence of
structural forces). See Manuel Castells, *The City
and the Grassroots: A Cross-Cultural Theory of*

Urban Social Movements (Berkeley, CA: University
of California Press, 1983); Paul Florin and
Abraham Wandersman, "An Introduction to
Citizen Participation, Voluntary Organizations and
Community Development: Insights for
Empowerment through Research," *American
Journal of Community Psychology* vol. 18 no. 1
(1990): 41–54; Julian Rappaport, "Terms of
Empowerment/Exemplars of Prevention: Toward a
Theory for Community Psychology," *American
Journal of Community Psychology* vol. 15 no. 2
(1987): 122–44; Roberto E. Villarreal, Norma G.
Hernandez, and Howard D. Neighbor, eds., *Latino
Empowerment: Progress, Problems, and Prospects*
(New York: Greenwood Press, 1988); and M. A.
Zimmerman, "Taking Aim on Empowerment
Research: On the Distinction Between Individual
and Psychological Conceptions," *American Journal
of Community Psychology* vol. 18 no. 1 (1990):
169–77.

9. Robert McAfee Brown, *Liberation Theology: An
Introductory Guide* (Louisville, KY: Westminster/
John Knox Press, 1993).

10. Arthur F. McGovern, *Liberation Theology and Its
Critics: Toward an Assessment* (Maryknoll, NY:
Orbis Books, 1989). This is an extremely simplified
explanation of the complexity of scholarship on
liberation theology. For more in-depth discussions
see for example Michael R. Candelaria, *Popular
Religion and Liberation: The Dilemma of Liberation
Theology* (Albany, NY: State University of New York
Press, 1990); Richard L. Rubenstein and John K.
Roth, eds., *The Politics of Latin American Liberation
Theology: The Challenge to U.S. Public Policy*
(Washington, D.C.: Washington Institute Press,
1988); and Paul E. Sigmund, *Liberation Theology at
the Crossroads: Democracy or Revolution?* (New
York: Oxford University Press, 1990).

11. Multidenominational congregation-based organizations have grown in number and significance
across the United States. As a reflection of this
growth, financial support and recognition by
major religious and secular organizations has also
increased. As James H. Garland, the chairperson
of the U.S. Catholic Conference's Campaign for
Human Development (CHD), has suggested,
"When CHD awarded its first few grants in 1971,
it awarded only two to organizations that were
based in congregations, whereas, by 1992, 71 of
202 national grants went to congregation-based
organizations" (James H. Garland, "Congregation-
Based Organizations: A Church Model for the
90's," *America* [13 November 1993]: 15).
National networks of congregation-based organizations have also grown significantly during the
1980s and 1990s. For example, after changing
from neighborhood-based organizing to congregation-based organizing, the Pacific Institute for

LOIS TAKAHASHI
ADDRESSING FEAR THROUGH COMMUNITY
EMPOWERMENT (contd.)

Community Organizing (PICO) network grew from
four organizations in 1984 to eighteen organizations in forty-three cities in 1993 (ibid.).
12. Paul W. Speer, Joseph Hughey, Leah K.
Gensheimer, and Warren Adams-Leavitt,
"Organizing for Power: A Comparative Case
Study," Journal of Community Psychology vol. 23
no. 1 (1995): 57–73.
13. Much of this information is drawn from a CBOOC
publication celebrating their 1992 convention,
Congregation-Based Organization of Orange
County (CBOOC), Lighting the Way—Convention
1992 (Anaheim, CA: CBOOC, 1992).
14. Ibid.
15. This information was drawn from a newsletter
outlining an effort by NNO to establish a statewide
institutional framework for regional organizing
efforts. According to the newsletter, the objectives of the statewide organizing project are fourfold: increasing leadership capacity for regional
impact, timely and systematic research and information dissemination, training conferences at the
regional and statewide levels, and expansion of
organizing efforts to other areas in California.
16. Robert Jr. Bailey, Radicals in Urban Politics: The
Alinsky Approach (Chicago: University of Chicago
Press, 1974) and Sanford D. Horwitt, Let Them
Call Me Rebel: Saul Alinsky—His Life and Legacy
(New York: Alfred A. Knopf, 1989).
17. Paolo Freire, Pedagogy of the Oppressed (New York:
Seabury Press, 1970) and C. H. Keiffer, "Citizen
Empowerment: A Developmental Perspective,"
Prevention in Human Services vol. 3 no. 2/3 (1984):
9–36.

CHARLES JENCKS
HETERO-ARCHITECTURE FOR THE HETEROPOLIS

1. Oscar Newman, Defensible Space: Crime Prevention
through Urban Design (New York: Macmillan,
1972).
2. Mike Davis, "Frank Gehry as Dirty Harry," City of
Quartz: Excavating the Future in Los Angeles
(London: Verso, 1990), 236–40.
3. For a discussion of post-riot L.A. defensible architecture, see "A City Behind Walls," Newsweek (5
October 1992): 68–69.
4. Anthony Vidler, The Architectural Uncanny: Essays
in the Modern Unhomely (Cambridge, MA: MIT
Press, 1992).
5. See Michael Holquist, Dialogism: Bakhtin and his
World (London: Routledge, 1990) and Tzvetan
Todorov, Mikhail Bakhtin: The Dialogical Principle

(Manchester: Manchester University Press, 1985).
6. Linda Hutcheon, A Poetics of Postmodernism:
History, Theory, Fiction (New York: Routledge,
1988); my own writings on postmodern architecture since 1975 defined this fundamental agenda
of double coding.

DAVID TURNBULL
SOC. CULTURE; SINGAPORE:

1. Tay Keng Soon, quoted in Tyler Brule, "Singapore
Sting," Arena (UK Edition) (November 1995).
2. Tay Keng Soon, Mega-Cities in the Tropics
(Singapore: National University of Singapore,
Institute of South-East Asian Studies, 1989).
3. Simon Tay, "Drive," in Stand Alone (Singapore:
Landmark Books, 1991), 46.
4. The Official Guide (Singapore: Singapore Tourist
Promotion Board, 1995).
5. Yona Friedman, "The Ten Principles of Space Town
Planning" (1962), in Programs and Manifestos on
20th-century Architecture, ed. Ulrich Conrads
(Cambridge, MA, MIT Press, 1970), 183–84.
6. Constantinos A. Doxiadis, Architecture in
Transition (Oxford: Oxford University Press,
1963).
7. Kisho Kurokawa, "Metapolis—The Hishino Plan"
(1967), Metabolism and Architecture (London:
Studio Vista, 1977), 69.
8. Rem Koolhaas, "Singapore Songlines," lecture presented at the Architectural Association, London,
as part of Architecture and Complexity
Conference, 6 May 1994.
9. Urban Redevelopment Authority, Orchard Area
(Singapore: URA Publications, 1994).
10. Maggie O'Kane, "Inside Story: Eye of a Tiger,"
Guardian (UK), 20 May 1995.
11. Mary W. J. Tay, "Language as a Mirror of
Traditionalism and Modernization," in Asian
Traditions and Modernization: Perspectives from
Singapore, ed. Yong Mun Cheong (Singapore:
Center for Advanced Studies, National University
of Singapore, 1992).
12. Kwa Chong Guan, "Remembering Ourselves,"
paper presented at the Singapore Heritage Society
as part of the Substation Conference: Our Place in
Time, 18 September 1994.
13. S. Rajaratnan, quoted in Albert Lau, "The
National Past and the Writing of the History of
Singapore," in Imagining Singapore, ed. Ban Kah
Choon, Anne Pakir, and Tong Chee Kiong
(Singapore: Times, 1992), 50.
14. S. Dhanabalan, quoted in Lau, "National Past," 51.
15. B. G. Yeo, Straits Times, 8 December 1989.
16. Vogue (August 1995).
17. Ray Langenbach, "Looking Back at Brother
Cane: Performance Art and State Performance,"

DAVID TURNBULL
SOC. CULTURE; SINGAPORE: (contd.)

unpublished manuscript, 1995, National Institute of Education, Singapore.
18. Ibid.
19. Ministry of Information and the Arts and the Home Ministry, quoted in "Government Acts Against 5th Passage Over Performance Art," *Straits Times*, 22 January 1994.
20. B. G. Yeo, quoted in *Asiaweek*, 7 July, 1995:
21. Tay, "Drive."
22. Goh Chok Tong, quoted in *Straits Times*, 2 December 1988.

SHARON E. SUTTON
CREATING LANDSCAPES OF SAFETY

1. These stories are from a study of children's experiences of their neighborhood environments described in Sharon E. Sutton, *Weaving a Tapestry of Resistance: The Places, Power, and Poetry of a Sustainable Society* (Westport, CT: Bergin and Garvey, 1996), 172–73.
2. Robert Coles, *The Moral Life of Children* (Boston: Houghton Mifflin, 1986), 48.
3. James E. Crowfoot, "The Challenges of Sustainability: Changing Relationships and Organizations," unpublished paper presented at Power and Sustainablity: Rethinking Relationships, American Collegiate Schools of Architecture Administrators Conference, November 1994, 6, 8.
4. Robert N. Bellah, Richard Madsen, William M. Sullivan, Ann Swidler, and Steven M. Tipton, *Habits of the Heart: Individualism and Commitment in American Life* (New York: Harper and Row, 1985), 43.
5. Barbara Ehrenreich, *Fear of Falling: The Inner Life of the Middle Class* (New York: Pantheon, 1989), 80.
6. Andrew Hacker, "Who They Are," *New York Times Magazine* (19 November 1995): 70–71.
7. Bureau of the Census, *Money, Income, and Poverty Status in the United States 1989* (Washington, DC: U.S. Government Printing Office, 1989), table 21.
8. Deborah Prothrow-Stith and Michaele Weissman, *Deadly Consequences* (New York: Harper Perennial, 1991), 32.
9. Ehrenreich, *Fear of Falling*, 42–43.
10. Jerry Adler, "Bye-bye, Suburban Dream," *Newsweek* (15 May 1995): 44.
11. While lifestyle issues can be argued, suburban sprawl is clearly approaching the point of economic disutility. Some indisputable costs of low-density living include the following: the average suburban family spends eighteen percent of its income to maintain the fleet of cars that are needed to carry out daily survival activities; suburban households are major sources of pollution,

averaging ten automobile trips a day at a cost of forty to seventy cents per mile, much of it federally subsidized; urban infrastructure is not used to its designed capacity while country roads are burgeoning with traffic and new roads and sewers are being constructed on virgin land; the cost of building just two and one-half miles of an eight-lane highway is 100 million dollars, or the entire Empowerment Zone funding Detroit will receive over a ten-year period.
12. J. John Palen, *The Suburbs* (New York: McGraw-Hill, 1995), 101.
13. David M. Hummon, *Commonplaces: Community Ideology and Identity in American Culture* (Albany: State University of New York Press, 1990).
14. Ibid., 120.
15. Paul L. Wachtel, *The Poverty of Affluence: A Psychological Portrait of the American Way of Life* (Philadelphia: New Society Publishers), 49.
16. Jill Smolowe, "Danger in the Safety Zone," *Time* (23 August 1993): 32.
17. Samuel Bowles and Herbert Gintis, *Schooling in Capitalist America: Educational Reform and the Contradictions of Economic Life* (New York: Basic Books, 1976), 13.
18. FBI statistics cited by Smolowe, "Danger in Safety Zone," 32.
19. Prothrow-Stith and Weissman, *Deadly Consequences*, 18.
20. Smolowe, "Danger in Safety Zone," 32.
21. Daniel Kemmis, "The Last Best Place: How Hardship and Limits Build Community," in *Changing Community*, ed. Scott Walker (Saint Paul, MN: Graywolf Press, 1993), 277–87.
22. Ibid., 283.
23. Starhawk, *Truth or Dare: Encounters with Power, Authority, and Mystery* (San Francisco: Harper and Row, 1987), 327.

RICHARD INGERSOLL
LANDSCAPEGOAT

1. René Girard, *Things Hidden since the Foundation of the World* (Stanford, CA: Stanford University Press, 1987), 22. Girard sustains that the scapegoat "is a victim who is not only incapable of self-defense but is also unable to provoke any reaction of vengeance." The neologism "landscapegoat" and several of the themes of this essay were first presented in my editorial, "Landscapegoat," *Design Book Review* 31 (Winter 1994): 4.
2. Joel Barna, *The See-Through Years: Creation and Destruction in Texas Architecture, 1981–1991* (Houston: Rice University Press, 1992). The chief tenant of the Allied Bank Tower has changed twice since the savings-and-loans debacles of the mid-1980s.

RICHARD INGERSOLL
LANDSCAPEGOAT (contd.)

3. Richard Ingersoll, "In the Capital of White Noise,"
   Texas Architect 1–2 (1990): 36–41. The municipal
   government, critical of the sterile landscapes that
   Pei's office had already designed for several other
   projects in Dallas, including the City Hall Park,
   urged the developer to hire a different architect for
   the lower levels of the tower. Urban critic William
   Whyte was invited to Dallas in 1982 to explain
   why public places like City Hall Park were so antisocial. The developer of the Allied Bank Tower,
   Criswell Development, accepted the municipality's
   proposal to hire a second architect, Harry Weese,
   for the lower five stories and landscaping, but was
   dissatisfied with Weese's proposal and so took I.
   M. Pei's suggestion to hire Dan Kiley. Kiley was
   assisted in the elaborate fountain technology and
   design by WET Enterprises, the designers of the
   waterworks at Epcot Center, Florida.

4. John Brinckerhoff Jackson, *Discovering the
   Vernacular Landscape* (New Haven: Yale University
   Press, 1984), 3. The word "landscape" was originally used in reference to representations of the
   land and to gardens that were conceived as a
   series of pictures. Jackson has always been
   adamant in discovering the landscape outside of
   the conceptual frame.

5. "Dookie bottles" were first named and identified
   by Anwall MacDonald in his article "Dookie
   Bottles" in the Berkeley student publication
   Concrete vol. 4 no. 1 (1978): 4, 7. MacDonald
   interviewed several neighbors who said the bottles kept the dogs from "dookieing" on the lawn.
   Empirical evidence demonstrated that the bottles
   did not always work but that people believed they
   did.

6. Martha Rosler, "Tompkins Square Park," in *If You
   Lived Here: The City in Art, Theory and Social
   Activism*, ed. Martha Rosler and Brian Wallis
   (Seattle: Bay Press, 1991), 208–19. For an excellent
   description of the bidonvilles in the park see Don
   DeLillo, *Mao II* (New York: Penguin, 1991).

7. Eduard Bru, "Untested Territories," *Quadernos de
   Arquitectura* 193 (March–April 1992): 83.

8. See Maggie Gilchrist and James Lingwood, *Robert
   Smithson, El Paisaje Entropico, Una retrospectiva,
   1960–1973* (Valencia: IVAM Centre Julio Gonzalez,
   Generalitat Valenciana, 1993) and Robert
   Smithson, "Entropy and the New Monuments,"
   Art Forum (June 1966): 26–31.

9. Barbara C. Matilsky, *Fragile Ecologies: Contem-
   porary Artists' Interpretations and Solutions* (New
   York: Rizzoli, 1992), 80–85. Through research at
   the New York Public Library and the New York
   Botanical Gardens, Sonfist attempted to revive the
   Manhattan landscape of 300 years earlier.

He discovered some species that the Parks
Department did not include on its "approved"
trees planting list; their success in the Time
Landscape has forced a revision of the list.

FRED DEWEY
CYBURBANISM AS A WAY OF LIFE

1. Luce Irigaray, *An Ethics of Sexual Difference* (Ithaca,
   NY: Cornell University Press, 1993), 83.

2. Robert M. Fogelson, *The Fragmented Metropolis:
   Los Angeles, 1850–1930* (Berkeley: University of
   California Press, 1993), 276.

3. *New York Times*, 5 October 1995.

4. See Robert Fishman, *Bourgeois Utopias: The Rise
   and Fall of Suburbia* (New York: Basic Books,
   1987).

5. Ibid., 155–81.

6. The term "cyburbia" appears to have arisen
   around the same time in different places. It
   appears, though undeveloped, in Michael Sorkin's
   introduction to his anthology *Variations on a
   Theme Park: The New American City and the End of
   Public Space* (New York: Hill and Wang, 1992), xv,
   and may have even earlier uses. My use of it arose
   separately after reading a *Baltimore Sun* article
   describing video-game burnouts as "cyburbs." I
   turned this into "cyburbia" and used it to name a
   heavily virtualized Los Angeles in the year 2008 in
   "Floating World, Los Angeles," *The Wild Palms
   Reader*, ed. Roger Trilling and Stuart Swezey (New
   York: St. Martins, 1993), 56–59 (co-written with
   Ralph Rugoff); "cyburbia formed the subject of a 8
   October 1993 panel I organized and moderated at
   Beyond Baroque, in Venice, California, featuring
   Rugoff, Ed Soja, Anne Friedberg, and Ian Mitroff;
   see also my "Cyburbia: Los Angeles as the New
   Frontier, or Grave?," *Los Angeles Forum for
   Architecture and Urban Design* (May 1994): 6–7;
   and "Death in Cyburbia," *New Statesman* (16 July
   1994): 31–32, detailing Los Angeles's stew of
   race, caste, and power in the opening days of the
   O. J. Simpson matter. Interestingly, the term
   migrated via a friend to David Colker at the *Los
   Angeles Times*, who uses it still for his weekly
   review of software and digital media, evacuating
   the worldly and urban dimension. This is ironic,
   given the fact Los Angeles was shaped by the
   paper, its owners the Chandlers, and allied real-
   estate and development interests, literally developing the region through a merging of real estate
   and information. *The Nation* (3 July 1995) fea-
   tured an article on "Cyberbia," exchanging the "e"
   for the "u," thus neatly removing the (sub)urban
   reference to promote bulletin board systems and
   the Internet as a solution to the bleak world of
   the computer.

FRED DEWEY
CYBURBANISM AS A WAY OF LIFE (contd.)

7. For a discussion of "the new information enclosures," see James Brook and Iain A. Boal, eds.,
Resisting the Virtual Life (San Francisco: City
Lights, 1995). The book generally shies from
regarding the electronic in political terms, prefer-
ring to focus on economic, social, and technological forces in and of themselves rather than as
instruments of political disenfranchisement and
organization.

8. Michael Sorkin, lecture, Southern California
Institute of Architecture, 15 February 1996.

9. Dexter King, cited in Henry Louis Gates, Jr.,
"Heroes, Inc.," *New Yorker* (16 January 1995):
6–7.

10. Henry Louis Gates, Jr., "Heroes, Inc.," *New Yorker*
(16 January 1995): 6–7.

11. Hannah Arendt, *On Revolution* (Harmondsworth,
Eng.: Penguin Books, 1977), 151–52, 176,
253–54, 303–04.

12. After World War II, René Char, a leader of the
French resistance, in an epilogue to an extraordinary book of poetry, pondered the ancient question of the armature of freedom and what might
explain those who betray it: "Why this duplicity
whose symptoms disconcerted us? Because a
good many soldiers and politicians are perverts of
the imagination, dotards of differential calculus."
René Char, *Leaves of Hypnos*, (New York: Grossman
Publishers, 1973).

UDO GREINACHER
FEAR AND DREAMING IN THE AMERICAN CITY

1. Lars Lerup, *Planned Assaults* (Montreal: Canadian
Center for Architecture, 1987), 73.

2. See Udo Greinacher, "The New Reality: Media
Technology and Urban Fortress," *Journal of
Architectural Education* (February 1995): 176–84.

3. John B. Jackson, "The Westward-moving House:
Three American Houses and the People who Lived
in Them" (1953), in *Re-Reading Cultural
Geography*, ed. Kenneth E. Foote (Austin, TX:
University of Texas Press, 1994), 64–81.

4. Ibid., 68.

5. Gaston Baudelaire remarked that in a palace,
"there is no place for intimacy." Gaston Bachelard,
The Poetics of Space (Boston: Beacon Press, 1969),
29. In a similar manner, the multifunctional
nature of Pliny's homestead, although by no
means a palace, prevented any individual room
from playing a central role in the family's life and
offering a spiritual refuge from the world.

6. Jackson, "Westward-moving House," 73.

7. Ibid., 77.

8. Ibid., 80.

9. Joë Bousquet, quoted in Bachelard, *Poetics of
Space*, 26.

10. Stanley Milgram, "The Experience of Living in
Cities" (1970), in *Urbanman: The Psychology of
Urban Survival*, ed. John Helmer (New York: Free
Press, 1974), 3.

11. The importance of the house as a place for dreaming is extensively discussed in Bachelard, *Poetics
of Space*, chapter one, "The House. From Cellar to
Garret. The Significance of the Hut."

12. Ibid., 18ff.

13. Lee Rainwater summarizes the main kinds of danger in "Fear and the House-As-Haven in the Lower
Class," in *Urbanman: The Psychology of Urban
Survival*, ed. John Helmer (New York: Free Press,
1974). Although his study focuses on the lower
class, I believe his descriptions pertain to urban
residents in general.

14. Walter Benjamin, "A Berlin Chronicle," *Reflections*
(New York: Schocken Books, 1978), 23.

15. In "Cannibal City: Los Angeles and the
Destruction of Nature," Mike Davis refers to a
study that found a causal relationship between
landscape-destroying sprawl at the urban edge
and neighborhood decay at the center. In Russell
Ferguson, ed., *Urban Re-Visions* (Cambridge: MIT
Press, 1994), 49.

16. Larry Gelbart, "Peering Through the Tube
Darkly....," *New York Times*, 16 April 1995, Arts
and Leisure section, 33.

17. This description is drawn from the prologue to
Marc Augé, *Non-Places: Introduction to an
Anthropology of Supermodernity* (New York: Verso,
1995).

18. One of the few indicators of an employee's status
is the distance between his or her parking spot
and the entrance or elevator of the building.
According to Ann Black, a former employee at
Wendy's, the company awards some of these
spots as part of its "employee of the month"
competition.

19. Theodore Roszak, *The Cult of Information: The
Folklore of Computers and the True Art of Thinking*
(New York: Pantheon, 1986), 26. In his introduction, Roszak cites a study that estimated the loss
of time spent on in-house newsletters to be in
the tens of millions of dollars. In another study,
Richard Sennett observed a woman working on an
automated assembly line breaking the monotony
by pressing the "malfunction" button even though
no malfunction has occurred. Richard Sennett,
"Powers of the Eye," in Ferguson, *Urban Re-
Visions*, 64.

20. Timothy Egan, "Many Seek Security in Private
Communities," *New York Times*, 3 September
1995, section 1, 1 and 10.

21. Jim Carlton, "Walling Off the Neighborhood Is a

UDO GREINACHER
FEAR AND DREAMING IN THE AMERICAN CITY
(contd.)

Growing Trend," *Los Angeles Times*, 8 October 1989, sec. 1, 3.

22. The definition of "hostiles," which had originally meant Native Americans, broadened during the eighteenth and nineteenth century to include people of ethnic and cultural backgrounds other than Anglo-Saxon. More recently, the "other" has become everything we are unfamiliar with, including Californians who migrate to Washington or Arizona, or New Englanders who settle in Florida.

23. In his article "Some On-Line Discoveries Give Gay Youths a Path to Themselves," Trip Gabriel reports an incident where counseling over the Internet prevented a young man from committing suicide. *New York Times*, 2 July 1995, 1.

24. Mitch Kapor and John Perry Barlow, as quoted in William Mitchell, *City of Bits* (Cambridge: MIT Press, 1995), chapter 5.2. Retrieved from: http://www-mitpress.mit.edu/City_of_Bits/index.html.

25. Bruce Sterling, "The Virtual City," speech at the Rice Design Alliance, Houston, Texas, 2 March 1994. Available from http://riceinfo.rice.edu/projects/RDA/VirtualCity/Sterling/Sterling_VirtualCity.

26. Mitchell, *City of Bits*, chapter 2.6.

27. Janet Murray, director of the Laboratory for Advanced Technology in the Humanities at MIT, quoted in Charles Platt, "Interactive Entertainment," *Wired* vol. 3 no. 9 (September 1995): 149.

28. Mitchell, *City of Bits*, chapter 5.7.

29. Ibid.

30. Howard Rheingold, *A Slice of Life in My Virtual Community*, available through gopher://gopher.well.sf.ca.us/00/Community/virtual_communities 92, 1992.

31. Recent data compiled by Survey Working Group and published in "Number Game," *Newsweek* (31 July 1995): 8.

32. Michael Marriott, "CyberSoul Not Found," *Newsweek* (31 July 1995): 62.

33. Sterling, "Virtual City."

34. Katie Hafner, "Online on a Shoestring," *Newsweek* (6 March 1995): 76.

35. Roszak, "Cult of Information," xxix–xxx, cites the examples of computer fraud at the Continental Illinois Bank of Chicago in 1984, and at E. F. Hutton, a major brokerage house, in 1985. In addition, "Der Knack von Paris," *Der Spiegel* 35 (28 August 1995): 175–76 reported the theft of ten million dollars from Citibank, New York by Russian high-tech thieves.

36. Christopher Anderson, "The Accidental Superhighway," *The Economist* (1 July 1995): 15. Available through http://www.economist.com/ intro.htm.

37. Mitchell, *City of Bits*, chapter 7.4.

38. Ibid., chapter 4.2–4.7.

39. Ibid., chapter 7.4.

40. Ibid.

41. Ibid.

42. For one of the many examples of this environment see Dashiell Hammett, *The Maltese Falcon* (New York: Alfred A. Knopf, 1929; reprint, San Francisco: North Point Press, 1984).

MARGARET WERTHEIM
THE PEARLY GATES OF CYBERSPACE

1. Kevin Kelly, "What Are We Doing On-Line?," *Harper's* (August 1995): 39.

2. Umberto Eco, *Travels in Hyperreality* (San Diego: Harcourt Brace Jovanovich, 1986), 75.

3. Gerda Lerner, *The Creation of Patriarchy* (New York: Oxford University Press, 1986), 200–01.

4. Elaine Pagels, *The Gnostic Gospels* (New York: Vintage Books, 1981), 60–61.

5. Eco, *Travels in Hyperreality*, 75.

6. Mary Midgley, *Science as Salvation: A Modern Myth and Its Meaning* (London: Routledge, 1992), 1.

7. Allucquere Rosanne Stone, "Will the Real Body Please Stand Up?: Boundary Stories About Virtual Cultures," in *Cyberspace: First Steps, ed. Michael Benedikt* (Cambridge, MA: MIT Press, 1992), 107.

8. William Gibson, *Neuromancer* (New York: Ace Books, 1984).

9. Dr. Diane Ravitch, cited in Neil Postman, "Virtual Students, Digital Classroom," *The Nation* (9 October 1995): 377.

Author/Artist Biographies

Edward J. Blakely is dean and Lusk professor of planning and development at the School of Urban and Regional Planning at the University of Southern California, and was chair of the Department of City and Regional Planning at UC Berkeley. A Fulbright and Guggenheim Fellow, Blakely earned his doctorate in education and management from UCLA. He is the author of six books and more than 100 scholarly articles. His book *Separate Societies* (Temple University Press, 1992), written with William Goldsmith, was the recipient of the Davidoff Award and his book *Fortress America*, written with Mary Gail Snyder, is forthcoming.

John Chase is urban designer for the city of West Hollywood, California and a principal in the L.A. architectural firm of Chase & Burnett. Chase earned a B.A. in art history from the University of California at Santa Cruz and a M.Arch. from UCLA. He has taught architectural history and historic preservation at Art Center of Pasadena, SCI-Arc, and UCLA Extension. Chase is the author of *Exterior Decoration: Hollywood's Inside-Out Stage Set Houses* and *The Sidewalk Companion to Santa Cruz Architecture*. Chase's forthcoming books include *Las Vegas*, written with Frances Anderson, (Ellipsis, 1997) and *Are We Having Fun Yet?* (Verso, 1997).

Michael Dear is professor of geography and director of the Southern California Studies Center at the University of Southern California. He holds a Ph.D. in regional science from the University of Pennsylvania and is the author of *Malign Neglect: Homelessness in the American City*, written with Jennifer Wolch, and numerous articles. He is the co-editor of *Rethinking Los Angeles* with H. Eric Schockman and Greg Hise (forthcoming, Sage). In 1995–96, Dear was a Fellow at the Center for Advanced Study in the Behavioral Sciences at Stanford University.

Fred Dewey is a public space activist and writer on culture and politics whose criticism has appeared in London's *New Statesman, Los Angeles Times, L.A. Weekly, L.A. Reader, Details, Metropolis, Coagula, Framework, The Wild Palms Reader* (St. Martins Press, 1993), and *Jon Jost* (Flick Books, 1997, Holly Willis, ed.). Dewey has worked for director/producer Roger Corman and written a horror movie and the early draft of the remake of *Sabrina*. He has also taught at CalArts and Art Center in Pasadena and served as executive director of Beyond Baroque in Venice.

Cayewah Easley is an artist from New Mexico whose multimedia works incorporate elements of containment, compaction, and impression to explore cycles of memory and the body. She received a bachelor of science in environmental design from the University of California at Davis and a master of fine arts in Fiber from the Cranbrook Academy of Art. Easley is represented by the Hibberd McGrath Gallery in Breckinridge, Colorado.

Nan Ellin is assistant professor of urban design and planning in the College of Design, Architecture, Art, and Planning at the University of Cincinnati. She holds an M.A., M.Phil., and Ph.D. from Columbia University and a B.A. from Bryn Mawr College. She has previously taught at SCI-Arc, the University of Southern California, and New York University and was a Fulbright Scholar in France. She is the author of *Postmodern Urbanism* as well as several articles. Her current work includes a monograph on the architect/urban designer Deborah Berke and the design (with Muller Associates) for a community center in Covington, Kentucky.

Dora Epstein is a doctoral student in architecture at UCLA who turned to writing about cities and buildings when graffiti did not produce desired social change. Her publications include "Afraid/Not: Psychoanalytic Directions for the Tradition of Planning Historiography" in *Making the Invisible Visible: Insurgent Planning Histories* (ed. Leonie Sandercock, forthcoming), "Queerer Than Anyone Planned" in *Journal of Planning Education and Research*, and a photo essay in *Third Space* (Blackwell,1996, Ed Soja, ed.).

Steven Flusty received his M.Arch. at SCI-Arc and is currently a doctoral student in urban planning at the University of Southern California. He has served as co-director of the L.A. chapter of the International Network for Urban Research and Action and as consultant to the Community Redevelopment Agency of L.A. and to the Greenbelt Project Office of Frankfurt am Main. His articles have appeared in *L.A. Architect, Architecture California*, and *Zurich WochenZeitung*. His study *Building Paranoia: The Proliferation of Interdictory Space and the Erosion of Spatial Justice* was published by the Los Angeles Forum for Architecture and Urban Design.

Udo Greinacher is assistant professor of architecture in the College of Design, Architecture, Art, and Planning at the University of Cincinnati. Born and raised in Tübingen, Germany, he holds a first professional degree in Architecture from the Fachhochschule Stuttgart and a master's degree in architecture from the University of California at Berkeley. He has participated and placed in several design competitions in the United States and Germany and his articles appear in the *Journal of Architectural Education, Competitions, Center of Environmental Design Research,* and *Wettbewerb aktuell.*

Jane Harrison is a London-based architect and photographer. After receiving an M.Arch. from Rice University, she worked for Skidmore Owings & Merrill, David Chipperfield, and Sir Norman Foster and Partners. In 1991 she co-founded the architecture and urban design group a.topos with David Turnbull. With Turnbull, she produced a special issue of *A.D.* entitled "Games of Architecture" and is currently producing a book entitled *Fast Cities: The Accelerated Space of Advanced Capitalism.* She has taught at the Architectural Association in London since 1991 and is a member of the Academy Forum.

Richard Ingersoll is Associate Professor of Architecture at Rice University and is editor of *Design Book Review.* He received a Ph.D. in architectural history from the University of California at Berkeley. His publications include *Streets: Critical Perspectives on Public Space* (co-edited with Zeynep Celik and Diane Favro, UC Press, 1994), *Munio Gitai Weinraub, Bauhaus Architect in Eretz Israel* (Electa, 1994), and *Le Corbusier: A Marriage of Contours* (Princeton Architectural Press, 1989).

Charles Jencks is a professor of architecture at UCLA, a writer, and an architect. He is the author of *The Language of Post-Modern Architecture* (sixth edition 1991) *Architecture Today* (third edition 1994), and *The Architecture of the Jumping Universe* (second edition 1997), all from Academy Editions, as well as other highly acclaimed books on contemporary building and postmodern thought. His architecture, design, and furniture explore the ideas developed in his writing.

Peter Marcuse was in the practice of law for over twenty years before becoming a professor of urban planning, first at UCLA, then at Columbia University, where he currently teaches. He has written widely, most recently about the meaning and impact of globalization on urban social patterns and the interrelationship of race, class, and space. Marcuse's sabbatical in East Germany led to his book *Missing Marx: A Political and Personal Journal of a Year in East Germany* (Monthly Review Press, 1991). He is working on a history of the New York City Housing Authority.

Richard Sennett is university professor of the humanities at New York University. He is the author of numerous works of sociology, history, urban studies, and fiction. His most recent book is *Flesh and Stone: The Body and the City in Western*

Civilization. Sennett received his Ph.D. from Harvard University. He currently serves as chair of the Council on Civil Society and as a member of the Committee for New York. He is a Fellow of the American Academy of Arts and Sciences as well as the Royal Society of Literature.

Julius Shulman spent the first decade of his life in Connecticut before moving to Los Angeles. He attended UCLA and UC Berkeley for seven years without ever declaring a major or graduating. In 1936, he met Richard Neutra and began photographing his work, thus initiating Shulman's career as an architectural photographer. He has written two books on architectural photography and has co-authored several others. A biography on Shulman by Joseph Rosa appeared in 1994 (Rizzoli). Shulman is currently writing his autobiography and collaborating with David Gebhard on a book about Neutra, both forthcoming from Phaidon Press.

Kevin Sites is a television news producer. He is currently producing the "Law and Order" beat for NBC Nightly News. Prior to that, he was a producer for ABC programs including "This Week with David Brinkley" and "World News."

Mary Gail Snyder is a doctoral student in city and regional planning at the University of California at Berkeley where she received her master's degree in city planning in 1992. Both her academic work and professional work are in the fields of housing and community development. Her book *Fortress America*, written with Edward J. Blakely, is forthcoming.

Sharon E. Sutton is professor of architecture and urban planning at the University of Michigan. She holds a B.A. in music, an M.Arch. from Columbia University, and an M.S. and Ph.D. in psychology from the City University of New York. A Kellogg National Fellow, Sutton lectures and publishes on the topics of youth, culture, the environment, community service, professional leadership, and conflict management. She is the recipient of the American Planning Association's Education Award and is the author of several books, most recently *Weaving a Tapestry of Resistance: The Places, Power, and Poetry of a Sustainable Society* (Bergin and Garvey, 1996).

Lois Takahashi is assistant professor of urban and regional planning at the University of California at Irvine. Her articles on homelessness, attitudes toward human service facilities, and the promotion of community health appear in *Social Science and Medicine* and *Journal of the American Planning Association*. Takahashi holds an A.B. in architectural structures from the University of California at

Berkeley, an M.S. in public management and policy/architecture from Carnegie Mellon University, and a Ph.D. in urban planning from the University of Southern California.

Anne Troutman is chair of environmental design at Santa Monica College of Design, Art and Architecture. She also teaches at the Southern California Institute of Architecture and maintains her own architectural firm in Santa Monica. Troutman holds a B.A. in art history from Tufts University, an M.S. in arts administration from New York University, and an M.Arch. from SCI-Arc. A former journalist, she is currently writing a book entitled *Intimate Spaces and Erotic Places*.

David Turnbull is a London-based architect and writer. He received his professional degree in architecture at the University of Bath and worked for James Stirling and Michael Wilford and Partners before co-founding the architecture and urban design group a.topos with Jane Harrison in 1991. With Harrison, he produced a special issue of *A.D.* entitled "Games of Architecture" and is currently producing a book entitled *Fast Cities: The Accelerated Space of Advanced Capitalism*. He has taught at the Architectural Association in London since 1990 and is a member of the Academy Forum. He currently holds the Saarinen Chair at Yale University.

Jürgen von Mahs is a Fulbright scholar from Germany at the University of Southern California, where he is pursuing graduate studies in geography. His master's thesis focuses on siting strategies for controversial human service facilities.

Margaret Wertheim holds a bachelor of science in physics from the University of Queensland and a bachelor of arts in mathematics and computer science from the University of Sydney. She is the author of *Pythagoras' Trousers: God, Physics, and the Gender Wars* (Times Books, 1995) and of numerous articles on science, technology, and society. She wrote and directed the award-winning six-part television documentary series "Catalyst." She has also written eight other science documentaries for television and has written and produced three interactive video programs. Wertheim is currently writing a cultural history of space (Norton).

Jody Zellen is a Los Angeles artist whose work has been exhibited internationally. Recent solo exhibitions include installations at the Center for Contemporary Photography in Melbourne, SF Camerawork, Robert Berman Gallery in Santa Monica, and the Dorothy Goldeen Gallery in Santa Monica.